Playing Gay in the Golden Age of British TV

Playing Gay in the Golden Age of British TV

Stephen Bourne

Foreword by Mark Gatiss

The History Press

This book is dedicated to
Drew Griffiths (1947–84)

Cover illustration: A Luna Blue / Alamy Stock Photo

First published 2019

The History Press
97 St George's Place, Cheltenham,
Gloucestershire, GL50 3QB
www.thehistorypress.co.uk

British Library Cataloguing in Publication Data.
A catalogue record for this book is available from the British Library.

ISBN 978 0 7509 9013 4

Typesetting and origination by The History Press
Printed and bound in Great Britain by TJ International Ltd.

Contents

Foreword by Mark Gatiss

Peter Wyngarde popped my cherry. Not literally, of course, but it was the wildly popular *Jason King* actor's startling arrest in a Gloucester bus station in 1975 that set things off. It gave a name to the strange, fuzzy feeling I'd been having for years. The feeling I had when I saw Stuart Damon in *The Champions* and the lad in *Follyfoot*. Or the *Tomorrow People* episode in which the impossibly beautiful Jason Kemp appeared as a fey outsider, bullied by his schoolmates for being different, who was then revealed to be an all-powerful alien in eyeliner. I didn't know what this feeling was but somehow I knew it was secret and forbidden. I was gay.

When I was growing up, TV was my best friend. I can view the whole of my early life through its prism. A neon tapestry of memories and influences – standing stones and Ogrons and witchcraft and saggy old cloth cats and dystopian futures full of plague and societal breakdown. As I reached adolescence, something else began to make its presence felt. Just as the toy section of the Brian Mills catalogue began to hold less interest than the bit with men's underwear, certain less whimsical aspects of TV began to dominate my imagination. I'd comb the TV schedules for fragments of anything even remotely poofy. And fragments there were, a sort of 625-line version of real life – a stolen glance here, a delicate brush of the fingertips there – appearing in various plays for today, *Rock Follies*, foreign films on BBC2, *Penda's Fen* (the ultimate 1970s TV experience – folk horror crossed with homosexuality) and *Kids* with Jason Kemp (again!) as the 'tart with the golden heart' in the memorable episode 'Michael and Liam'.

And then, of course, there was *Jason King*. As the bestselling author-cum-ladykiller agent, Peter Wyngarde represented the height of early

1970s masculinity, though it's now hard to fathom with his dandified persona, handlebar 'tache and turned up shirt cuffs. Little did any of us know that Wyngarde was known in the profession as Petunia Winegum and had had a long and tempestuous relationship with fellow heartthrob Alan Bates. But as already stated, his status as housewives' favourite came crashing to earth in those bus station lavs. I have a vivid memory of this. The papers were full of scandalised headlines and I asked my mam what it was all about. With the deliberateness of speaking unfamiliar words, she said, 'He's been caught importuning for men, pet.' I'm not sure to this day if she really knew what that meant. What's clear from Stephen Bourne's terrific, fascinating and compulsively readable book is that Wyngarde had flirted with gay roles – almost hiding in plain sight – for years. He had appeared in Patrick Hamilton's *Rope* and then in the intriguing *South* in 1959, as the tormented Jan, his performance being much praised except by two old ladies who attacked him on a bus: 'Dirty perv. You should be ashamed of showing such filth on the telly!' This was followed by his performance as Roger Casement in *On Trial*, produced by Peter Wildeblood – who'd been imprisoned for his homosexuality and who famously chronicled his experiences in *Against the Law*.

What Bourne reveals is that these moments, these queer presences, have been with us pretty much since the beginning of TV. From Douglas Byng, the first drag act to appear on television ('I'm one of the queens of England!'), to live productions of *Rope* (adapted five times between 1939 and 1957). Inevitably, most of these appearances conformed to stereotype: unhappy, lonely men who often met tragic ends. Though as Bourne points out, performances such as Aubrey Morris's make-up man in 1962's *Afternoon of a Nymph* transcended the cliché. 'I'd like to be in your shoes,' he says to his actress friend. Literally or figuratively? Many of these early plays have been wiped, lost forever in the ether, but Stephen Bourne brings them vividly back to life, relating the compelling story of how these fragments of lives, personalities and politics eventually become a flood. Camp family favourites like Larry Grayson, John Inman and Melvyn Hayes (great care was taken to assure viewers that these men weren't actually homosexual, merely 'flamboyant') were joined by the more brazen presence of John Hurt in *The Naked Civil Servant*, the loving gay couple Rob and Michael in ITV's *Agony* and Nigel Havers in the well-remembered *Coming Out*. Bourne highlights lost gems too, such as the charmingly subversive *The Obelisk* and Drew Griffiths and Noel Greig's *Only Connect*.

Times were changing and we saw the presence of gay men filtering into soaps and other mainstream drama, culminating in *EastEnders'* gay couple Colin and Barry. Though criticised as more grey than gay, it's easy to forget the hostile climate in which these first, faltering steps were made.

The battles are not all won, but what *Playing Gay* demonstrates – in hugely entertaining and fascinating detail – is how far British broadcasting has come – and come out – into the sunlight.

Foreword by Russell T Davies

Playing Gay is a masterpiece, a meticulous, dazzling, witty and wise history of gay men on television. The range is astonishing – it covers everything from monoliths like *The Naked Civil Servant* down to every blackmailed husband or secret lover ever to appear on guest spots in *Z Cars* or *Upstairs, Downstairs*. And this is an immensely kind piece of work, resurrecting lost classics and forgotten heroes. The chapter on writer Drew Griffiths is achingly sad and compassionate, and restores his career to a much-deserved glory. And this isn't merely about drama; there's actual drama within the pages, as executives rage, audiences quiver and stars leap into the fray. Peter Wyngarde emerges as a true champion – and there's a hilarious meeting between Douglas Byng and Quentin Crisp which deserves to become a TV play in its own right.

Stephen Bourne is one of the soldiers, gatekeepers and champions of our community. I am in awe of his diligence and insight. It's an honour to see *Queer as Folk* in there alongside so many other titles, so many of them wrongly forgotten.

Acknowledgements

The late Terry Bolas
David Hankin
Keith Howes
Linda Hull
Molly Hull
Petra Markham
Simon Vaughan

Alexandra Palace Television Society
BBC Written Archives Centre
British Film Institute
British Library
Immediate Media

Author's Note

From the 1970s to the 1990s we referred to ourselves as the lesbian and gay community. It was not until 1998 that I first heard the term LGBT. Now we are known as the LGBTQI+ (Lesbian, Gay, Bisexual, Transgender, Queer or Questioning, Intersex) community but, for the purposes of this book, I will be referring to the gay community only, and focussing on how gay men were portrayed on British television in drama and comedy. There isn't space for actuality (documentary) programmes, though there is enough information in existence for a book to be written about the genre.

Playing Gay in the Golden Age of British TV is partly based on the thesis I submitted for the Master of Philosophy degree which was awarded to me in 2006. My thesis covered the early, formative years of British television from its beginnings in the 1930s to the 1970s. For *Playing Gay* I have added a section about the 1980s to make it possible to include the birth of Channel 4 in 1982. I also wanted to include the changes that occurred in gay representation throughout that decade until Channel 4 launched the first weekly lesbian and gay series, *Out on Tuesday*, in 1989. However, there are omissions. For more information I would highly recommend Keith Howes's *Broadcasting It: An Encyclopaedia of Homosexuality on Film, Radio and TV in the UK 1923–1993* (Cassell, 1993).

Though every care has been taken, if, through inadvertence or failure to trace the present owners, I have included any copyright material without acknowledgement or permission, I offer my apologies to all concerned.

The Golden Age of British Television

For the purposes of this book, the 'Golden Age' of British television refers to the 1950s through to the 1970s. The 1980s have been included for the advent of Channel 4. Anyone who is interested in the subject of British television history will have their own view of what the 'Golden Age' means and the period it covers. Here are some of those views by experts on the subject:

'Golden ages' are always partly illusory, seen through the nostalgic rose-tinted spectacle of hindsight. Yet they are often not without some degree of truth – otherwise the myth of a 'golden age' would not arise in the first place. As Irene Shubik remarked at a conference on television drama in 1998, the 1960s was a 'golden age' because of the autonomy given to writers, directors and producers, an autonomy which was eroded as television became increasingly 'cost-conscious' during the 1970s.

Lez Cooke, *British Television Drama: A History* (BFI Publishing, 2003)

I am not one who speaks of a golden age, as if there are no good programmes made today. I am well aware there are good programmes made in a quantity that was impossible before the present range of channels. But the 60s and 70s were certainly a golden age for producers who knew that, while there were only three channels, there was space for highly creative and challenging programmes. To give but one example: from 1964 the *Wednesday Play* rode high with a reputation for daring new ideas and styles. BBC1 screened more than 200 such plays in prime time. They caused trouble, brought protests, and had swearing. But they were made within a unique and shared concept of television that has gone.

Joan Bakewell, 'Enough excuses. The BBC must confront its moral crisis', *The Guardian* (20 November 2008)

The notion of a 'Golden Age' in any field is usually subjective and difficult to identify in such a sprawling cultural catch-all like television. You could make valid arguments for the 1950s and 1960s to be the 'Golden Age' of the television single drama, and equally could justify describing the 2000s as the 'Golden Age of Reality Television'. But UK TV as a whole? I would have to say the idea of the Golden Age of British Television should encompass a period when the BBC was no longer a monopoly and had to compete, before the multi-channel age diluted the viewing audience ... To that end I would elect the 1960s and 1970s – a time when the BBC learned to hit back against the powerful popularity of ITV, when the strength of the single play made television the true 'National Theatre' and when viewing figures for the biggest programmes were regularly around the 20 million mark resulting in 'shared experiences' for much of the population.

Dick Fiddy, BFI Archive Television Programmer
(by email, 21 January 2019)

My golden age of television began in 1952 when our walnut cabineted television set arrived and I watched a *Hopalong Cassidy* western ... I was almost literally glued to the box from that point forward ... It became my life and my love. I finally entered superficially sophisticated adulthood with *Monitor* featuring the early films of Ken Russell and John Schlesinger and the then shockingly irreverent political satire of *That Was the Week That Was*. The first 'golden age' ended with the arrival of *Doctor Who* in late 1963 ... The second 'golden age' began almost immediately in 1964 with the advent of BBC2 and the rich seam of single plays which enabled adult themes to be both aired on screen and then discussed at school and at work. Comedy, too, built on the wonderful 1950s legacy of *Hancock's Half Hour* which had successfully transferred from radio. The second gilded phase ended in 1969 when I left home finally, fell in love, and made a life beyond the screen until I returned to it to write some of its gay history in the late 1980s.

Keith Howes, author of *Broadcasting It: An Encyclopaedia of*
Homosexuality on Film, Radio and TV in the UK 1923–1993
(Cassell, 1993) (by email, 24 January 2019)

Preface

Television is more interesting than people. If it were not, we should have people standing in the corner of our rooms.

Alan Coren (1938–2007), humanist, writer and satirist

Television is for appearing on – not looking at.

Noël Coward (1899–1973), playwright

On 15 February 2000, I took part in one of Esther Rantzen's discussion programmes, screened on BBC2. The subject was soap operas and moral issues and I agreed to say something about the portrayal of gay men. As Esther charged at me with her microphone, and a camera zoomed in for my close-up, I composed myself and gasped, '*Queer as Folk* has revolutionised the way gay men are portrayed on British television. There's no going back to the days when poor Colin had to carry the burden of representation on his shoulders in *EastEnders*.' I meant what I said. Until *Queer as Folk* hit our screens on Channel 4 in 1999, a gay television drama as revealing and sexually explicit as this would not have been possible. For instance, when a gay couple was featured in an ITV play called *Friends* in 1967, an internal memo was circulated requesting that viewers should be warned about the homosexual theme. In *Queer as Folk* its openly gay creator and writer Russell T Davies revealed the diversity of gay men's lives in a stylish, energetic and provocative way. It also succeeded in 'crossing over' to a heterosexual audience.

Since *Queer as Folk*, numerous gay characters have been integrated into mainstream, popular television dramas. However, a few years earlier this wasn't possible in drama series like *The Bill*. In 1995, I wrote to an executive producer and asked him if a lesbian or gay police officer could be introduced. His response was not encouraging to say the least, implying that there was no interest in this facet of the officers' lives and that having gay men 'hanging around the place' wouldn't 'commend the programme usefully to the public'. Following this executive's departure from *The Bill* in 1998, an openly gay officer, Sergeant Craig Gilmore, played by Hywel Simons, was introduced on 10 April 2001.

Coronation Street, after forty-three years on the air, caught up in 2003. British television has definitely moved on from the days when a popular soap opera could only offer us *Crossroads*' prissy chef Mr Booth, who was forever mincing after motel owner Meg Richardson, and complaining about the price of fish. However, it would be wrong to assume that *Queer as Folk* is the *only* worthwhile gay British television drama from the past. There has been a gay presence on television since the BBC transmitted its pre-war service live from Alexandra Palace in the late 1930s, and some of the programmes have been groundbreaking.

When I was growing up and watching television in the 1960s and 1970s it seemed gay men only existed on television to be laughed at, and I cringed with embarrassment when everybody else laughed at the camp entertainer Larry Grayson and actor John Inman, who played the effeminate Mr Humphries in BBC1's popular situation-comedy series *Are You Being Served?* Then John Hurt gave us his acclaimed portrayal of Quentin Crisp in *The Naked Civil Servant* (1975), and at last I felt we were being taken seriously. However, from the standpoint of an isolated and closeted working-class teenager, which I was in the 1970s, gay men did not exist and I often felt I was the only one.

My mother introduced me to television when I was just 2 years old. She plopped me in front of Andy Pandy and she later told me that I was mesmerised. She had no fear of leaving me alone in the living room with Andy Pandy, Looby Loo and Teddy. An earthquake wouldn't have budged me. One of my earliest memories is witnessing the death of Martha Longhurst in *Coronation Street* in 1964. She had a heart attack in the Rovers Return and died clutching her glasses with one hand and a pint of milk stout with the other. I had never seen a dead person before so, naturally, I was upset. I was only 6 years old. I was 9 years old on 27 July 1967 when the Sexual Offences Act became law. I was too young to understand what this meant but I was fascinated by 'Auntie' Val Singleton making something interesting out of sticky-back plastic in *Blue Peter*. In 1967, I was a happy little boy growing up in a loving, caring, working-class family. In our home, a council flat on a housing estate on Peckham Road, my sister and I watched a lot of television. Years later, when I made friends with middle-class people, I discovered that their parents either restricted their television viewing or banned it in their homes altogether. So, my middle-class friends had no idea who Squiddly Diddly was, but my working-class friends did! In the 1960s my television viewing was broad and included almost everything from Ken Loach's hard-hitting *Cathy Come Home* (1966), about the pain and humiliation of homelessness, to the wonderful science fiction drama series *Doctor Who*, which traumatised one of my cousins – every time he saw a Dalek he hid, shaking with fear, behind the settee.

At my secondary modern school in the early 1970s, I was identified as a 'poof' and bullied for it. It was a horrible time, but television provided a way to escape the trauma of homophobic bullying. *Coronation Street* continued to be a favourite along with *Timeslip, A Family at War, Upstairs, Downstairs* and many others. In the 1970s Gay Liberation happened, but not in Peckham where I grew up. *Gay News* was on sale, but I never saw a copy. Though I was bullied at school for being a 'poof', I suffered in silence. There was no one to talk to. The victimisation I suffered couldn't be reported to the police, because I was terrified of them, and they were considered homophobic anyway. I did not find the courage to 'come out' (discuss my sexuality) until I was 22, but I escaped reality by watching lots of television, and I absorbed everything I could about gay images.

In 1985, when I went to the London College of Printing at the Elephant and Castle to study for a degree in film and television, I was very knowledgeable about television history. It proved to be of great use when my interest in researching how gay men had been portrayed in television expanded. In 1986, I visited the Hall Carpenter Archives to research a college essay on gay men in television. To my delight I discovered Keith Howes's superb and informative two-part survey of lesbians and gays in British television. Keith had put this together for the bi-weekly newspaper *Gay News* in 1977.

After I graduated in 1988, I was employed as a Research Officer by the British Film Institute (BFI) and the BBC on a project they funded jointly, which documented race and representation in British television from 1936 to 1989. Consequently, I discovered that the history of people of African and Caribbean descent on British television was vastly different from the one which had been previously understood and accepted. There were, it turned out, many more programmes featuring black people in the early years than we anticipated. With ongoing support from the BFI and the BBC we, the research team, pieced together the history. The range and depth of programmes we rediscovered – especially those made in the 1950s and 1960s – was surprising. Themes explored included decolonisation, the settlement of Africans and Caribbeans in post-war Britain, and mixed marriages. Racism was hardly absent. From 1958 to 1978 the progressive, cutting-edge programmes co-existed alongside the BBC's offensive *Black and White Minstrel Show*. However, I learned from this experience not to make assumptions about the historical portrayal of minority groups on the box, including gay men. There have always been positive exceptions to the rule.

In July 1992, my research into gays in television led to the launch of *Out of the Archives: Lesbians and Gays on TV* at the National Film Theatre (NFT; now known as BFI Southbank). This was a collection of lesbian- and gay-themed British television programmes. Working with Veronica Taylor in the BFI's Television and Projects Unit, I had already programmed the NFT's first black British television season, *Black and White in Colour*, in April 1992. Both seasons were curated under the umbrella of Television on the South Bank, a series of screenings which had been launched at the NFT in 1991.

Out of the Archives took place on four Tuesdays at the Museum of the Moving Image (now known as NFT3). They included the extraordinary Joe Orton play *Entertaining Mr Sloane* (1968), Howard Schuman's clever satire *The British Situation: A Comedy* (1978), *On Trial: Oscar Wilde* (1960), and *Blasphemy at the Old Bailey* (1977), the BBC drama documentary about the *Gay News* blasphemy trial. They were shown with two lesbian-themed dramas, *Country Matters: Breeze Anstey* (1972) and *Second City Firsts: Girl* (1974). *Girl* sold out in spite of a warning given to the audience that the only copy that we could find was technically imperfect. It didn't deter the audience, which included a number of older lesbians who fondly remembered seeing this landmark television play in 1974. It starred a young Alison Steadman as an army recruit who is seduced by a WRAC she-wolf! The season's other highlight was *Only Connect* (1979), a superb original drama written by two brilliant Gay Sweatshop writers, Drew Griffiths and Noel Greig.

Out of the Archives was so popular with audiences that I was invited to return the following year for a second season. Meanwhile, the BFI sent me on a UK tour of their regional cinemas with some of the programmes. The tour kicked off with a visit to Edinburgh on 22 February 1993, followed by Tyneside, Wolverhampton, Leicester, Hull, Manchester and Nottingham. I presented an illustrated talk followed by a screening of *Only Connect.*

This was groundbreaking work. Veronica gave me complete freedom to research the programmes and put them together. When the third *Out of the Archives* was showcased in July 1994, Keith Howes's indispensable *Broadcasting It: An Encyclopaedia of Homosexuality on Film, Radio and TV in the UK 1923–1993* had been published. It proved to be a magnificent 1,000-page reference book. When I interviewed Keith for *Capital Gay* (8 April 1994) he told me: 'Television and radio are as good as film, theatre, sculpture, painting and any of the other arts but they are totally neglected and derided in this country.' For Keith, *Broadcasting It* was a labour of love:

> Years ago, people never talked about television. It was disposable. It was irrelevant. And gays and lesbians always believed that we were invisible on the box or stereotyped and that is just not true. That's one of the reasons I did *Broadcasting It.* I grew tired of walking into gay bookshops and asking for books on television and being told, 'Yes, we have *The Celluloid Closet* by Vito Russo.' Also, I never sensed from gays and lesbians that they felt this was in any way an omission or a gap. I couldn't accept that. Now I find young people are passionately interested in the subject and can talk to me for hours about what they have seen.

I continued to programme *Out of the Archives* annually – every July – for ten seasons until the final event in 2001. When television producer Stephen Jeffery-Poulter hosted a tribute to the writer Howard Schuman during the fifth season in 1996, he explained to the audience their importance and relevance:

> I would just like to say a few words about these unique retrospective seasons. For the last five years *Out of the Archives* has showed a remarkable range of lesbian and gay programming exhumed for our edification and entertainment by cinema and television historian Stephen Bourne, whose efforts have been largely unsung.
>
> It is hard to underestimate the importance of this work. Lesbian and gay history and culture has, until very recently, been a hidden and secret one. Hardly surprisingly, as gay men were persecuted as criminals until

1967 and lesbians were almost literally invisible. Throughout history the individual contributions of lesbians and gay men to British society have been systematically denied, distorted or suppressed.

It's only in the last twenty-five years with the emergence of an identifiable lesbian and gay community that the daunting task of reclaiming our heritage has become possible. During that same period television has become the all-pervasive mass medium shaping the political, social and moral perspectives of this country's citizens.

By studying the way in which lesbians and gay men have been portrayed by television we can begin to understand the many subtle and not-so-subtle ways in which the great British public have been taught to perceive us – and how we have consciously and sub-consciously learned to define ourselves in relation to those images.

The screening of these archive programmes has exposed the negative and stereotypical images of lesbians and gays which, until very recently, were the predominant ones portrayed by television and which have fuelled the homophobia and discrimination which are still so rife in our society. However, the seasons have also celebrated the few precious occasions when, more or less accidently, certain honest representations of lesbian and gay lifestyles or individuals did make it to the small screen. They have also provided a rare opportunity for some of the creative talents of lesbians and gay men involved in television to talk about their unique contribution to the medium.

In this way *Out of the Archives* has been successfully unearthing, reclaiming and interpreting a lost heritage and thereby bequeathing it to future generations. We can now use this knowledge to challenge and encourage today's programmers to reflect more realistically the broad and growing sexual diversity of modern British society.

Throughout the 1990s, television plays with gay leading characters, or prominent gay themes, were rarely seen. Admittedly, during this period, the output of television drama had diminished – or in some people's view had been 'dumbed down'. The production of single plays on television was reduced but there were a handful that *were* produced and explored the diversity of gay life with three-dimensional characters and contemporary themes relevant to gay men in Britain. They included three by gay writers: Sean Mathias's *The Lost Language of Cranes* (BBC2, tx 9 February 1992), adapted from David Leavitt's novel; Howard Schuman's *Nervous Energy*

(BBC2, tx 2 December 1995); and Kevin Elyot's *My Night With Reg* (BBC2, tx 1 March 1997). Their work was a far cry from Patrick Hamilton's *Rope*, made by the BBC sixty years earlier.

Meanwhile, Keith Howes, Stephen Jeffery-Poulter and myself collaborated on a proposal for a television documentary about the history of gay men in British television. There had already been a two-part documentary about the history of black (African Caribbean) people in British television called *Black and White in Colour* (BBC2, tx 27 and 30 June 1992), on which I worked as a researcher. This was followed by *A Night in With the Girls* (BBC2, tx 15 and 16 March 1997), a two-part documentary celebrating the contribution made by women to the development of British television. It seemed only natural to have a similar archive and interview-based documentary about gays. Regrettably our proposal was rejected by everyone we took it to, including the BBC and Channel 4. I was disappointed, but in 1999 I began a Master's degree at De Montfort University. The subject of my thesis was the representation of gay men in British television drama from the 1930s to the 1980s. This enabled me to continue my exploration of the subject and to put it to good use. In 2006, I completed the thesis and was awarded a Master of Philosophy degree. Though I tried to get it published, it took twelve years to find a publisher. Thanks to The History Press, it has happened.

Out of the Archives

I am proud of *Out of the Archives*. I was thrilled that, in 2013, *Play of the Week: South* (1959) (see Chapter 6), the earliest known surviving gay television drama, was shown again at the BFI's 27th Lesbian and Gay Film Festival. Unfortunately, in their publicity for the screening, they claimed it was being shown for the first time since 1959. My rediscovery of the play in the 1990s and the inclusion of it in *Out of the Archives* in 1998 was completely overlooked. Four years later, in July 2017, *South* was shown again at BFI Southbank when the curator Simon McCallum included it in his season *Gross Indecency: Queer Lives Before and After the '67 Act*. On this occasion Peter Wyngarde, the star of *South*, participated in a Q&A after the screening. Other highlights from *Out of the Archives* which were included by Simon in this season were *On Trial: Oscar Wilde* (see Chapter 7), *Horror of Darkness* (see Chapter 10), *This Week: Homosexuals* (1964), *This Week: Lesbians* (1965), *Man Alive* (1967) and *Edward II* (1970) (see Chapter 15).

The following is a list of the all the programmes and special events I curated for the National Film Theatre for *Out of the Archives* from 1992 to 2001:

1992
On Trial: Oscar Wilde (Granada 1960); *Entertaining Mr Sloane* (Association Rediffusion 1968); *Country Matters* ('Breeze Anstey') (Granada 1972); *Second City Firsts* ('Girl') (BBC 1974); *Sex in Our Time: For Queer Read Gay* (Thames 1976); *Everyman: Blasphemy at the Old Bailey* (BBC 1977); *The London Weekend Show* ('Young Lesbians') (LWT 1977); *The British*

Situation: A Comedy (Thames 1978); *The Other Side* ('Only Connect') (BBC 1979) plus extracts from *Gays: Speaking Up* (Thames 1978); *Agony* (LWT 1979); and *Gay Life* (LWT 1981).

1993

The Wednesday Play ('Horror of Darkness') (BBC 1965); *Man Alive* (BBC 1967); *Within These Walls* ('One Step Forward, Two Steps Back') (LWT 1974); *Second City Firsts* ('Girl') (BBC 1974); *World in Action* ('Coming Out') (Granada 1975); *Play for Today* ('The Other Woman') (BBC 1976); *Play of the Month* ('The Picture of Dorian Gray') (BBC 1976); *Premiere* ('A Hymn from Jim') (BBC 1977); *Premiere* ('The Obelisk') (BBC 1977); and *Play for Today* ('Coming Out') (BBC 1979); plus a special event *At Home with Larry Grayson?* presented by Andy Medhurst including extracts from *Shut That Door!*, *The Generation Game* and *At Home with Larry Grayson*.

1994

Lord Arthur Savile's Crime (ABC 1960); *The Importance of Being Earnest* (ABC 1964); *This Week* ('Lesbians') (Associated Rediffusion 1965); *Within These Walls* ('For Life') (LWT 1975); *Crown Court* ('Lola') (Granada 1976); *Rebecca* (BBC 1979); *The House on the Hill* ('Something for the Boys') (Scottish TV 1981); *BBC Television Shakespeare* ('Coriolanus') (BBC 1984); plus extracts from *Z Cars* ('Friends'), *Dixon of Dock Green*, *Juke Box Jury* and *Rachel and the Roarettes* and a special event *Screened Out: Lesbians and Television* presented by Rose Collis.

1995

Monitor ('Benjamin Britten – Portrait of a Composer') (BBC 1958); *Steptoe and Son* ('Any Old Iron?') (BBC 1970); *Crown Court* ('Heart to Heart') (Granada 1979); *The Lost Language of Cranes* (BBC 1992); *Gays: Speaking Up* (Thames 1978); plus three special events: *Come Together* presented by Stephen Jeffery-Poulter with extracts from *Press Conference: Wolfenden* (BBC 1957, *This Week* ('Homosexuals') (Associated Rediffusion 1964), *Panorama* (BBC 1971), *Measure of Conscience* (BBC 1972); *A Tribute to Larry Grayson* with *At Home with Larry Grayson* (LWT 1983) and extracts from *Parkinson* (BBC 1978), and *The Good Old Days* (BBC 1983); and *An Englishman and a Heterosexual: A Look Back in Anger at John Osborne* presented by Keith Howes with *You're Not Watching Me, Mummy* (Yorkshire TV, 1980).

1996

Nureyev (BBC 1974); *Nijinsky 'God of the Dance'* (BBC 1975); *Crown Court* ('Lola') (Granada 1976); and *Grapevine* ('Gay Sweatshop') (BBC 1979) plus three special events: Jackie Forster interviewed by Rose Collis; Howard Schuman interviewed by Stephen Jeffery-Poulter; and *In the Life: Black Lesbians on British TV* with extracts from *Agony*, *EastEnders*, *Claire Rayner's Casebook*, *Framed Youth*, *Kilroy*, *Arena Cinema* and three programmes from Channel 4's *Out* series: *Double Trouble*, *Khush* and *BD Women*.

1997

On Trial: Sir Roger Casement (Granada 1960); *On Trial: Oscar Wilde* (Granada 1960); Nancy Spain presented by Rose Collis with *The Touch* (BBC 1956) and *Juke Box Jury* (BBC 1960); *Screen Two: Inappropriate Behaviour* (BBC 1987); *City Shorts: Came Out, It Rained, Went Back in Again* (BBC 1991); plus James Baldwin with screenings of *Bookstand* (BBC 1963), *Bookmark* (BBC 1984), *Frank Delaney* (BBC 1984), *Ebony* (BBC 1985) and *Mavis on 4* (C4 1987); and a special event *'60s Divas* with extracts from *Judy and Liza at the Palladium* (ATV 1964), *Show of the Week: Shirley Bassey* (BBC 1966), *Dusty* (BBC 1967), *Once More with (Julie) Felix* (BBC 1967) and *Sandie Shaw* (BBC 1968).

1998

Play of the Week ('South') (Granada 1959); *Total Eclipse* (BBC 1973); *Belles* (BBC 1983); *If They'd Asked for a Lion Tamer* (C4 1984); *Black Divas* (C4 1996); plus two special events: Mary Morris with screenings of *The Andromeda Breakthrough* (BBC 1962) and *The Spread of the Eagle* (BBC 1963) and *'70s Divas* with extracts including Roberta Flack, Joan Armatrading, Suzi Quatro, Bette Midler, Shirley Bassey, The Three Degrees, Amii Stewart, Gloria Gaynor, Diana Ross and Cilla Black.

1999

Me, I'm Afraid of Virginia Woolf (LWT 1978) and *An Englishman Abroad* (BBC 1983) plus three special events: *Black Divas* (C4 1996); *A Tribute to Jackie Forster* which included *Speak for Yourself* (LWT 1974), *The Day That Changed My Life* (BBC 1997) and *Gay Life* (LWT 1981); and *Lesbians: Vision On* which included *Out on Tuesday* ('Lust and Liberation') (C4 1989), *City Shorts: Came Out, It Rained, Went Back in Again* (BBC 1991), *The Late*

Show ('Dorothy Arzner') (BBC 1993), *A Woman Called Smith* (BBC 1997) and *Dusty at the BBC* (BBC 1999).

2000

Armchair Theatre: Afternoon of a Nymph (ABC 1962); *In Camera* (BBC 1964); *The Other Side* ('Connie') (BBC 1979); and *Wild Flowers* (C4 1990); plus Derek Jarman with screenings of *Books By My Bedside* (Thames 1989), *Derek Jarman – A Portrait* (BBC 1991), *Building Sites* (BBC 1991), and *Face to Face* (BBC 1993), as well as one special event *Not in Front of the Viewers*, an illustrated talk presented by Stephen Bourne with a screening of *Only Connect* (BBC 1979) introduced by W. Stephen Gilbert.

2001

Edward II (BBC 1970); *The Important Thing is Love* (ATV 1970); *Oranges Are Not the Only Fruit* (BBC 1990); plus one special event *Soap Queens* including Violet Carson in *Stars on Sunday* (Yorkshire TV 1972), Pat Phoenix in *Parkinson* (BBC 1975), an early episode of *Crossroads* (ATV 1968), and Noele Gordon on *Russell Harty* (BBC 1981).

Part 1

1930s to 1950s

1

Homosexuality, the Law and the Birth of Television

When the British Broadcasting Corporation (BBC) began broadcasting in 1922 (radio only; television followed in 1936) it did not consider homosexuality a subject that was fit for public discussion. In Britain, sexual relationships between men remained against the law until 1967. In that year, the Sexual Offences Act partially decriminalised homosexual acts. However, the ways such men are described is relatively new. Today, the term LGBTQI+ is considered inclusive and it is frequently used, but in the early part of the twentieth century the word 'homosexual' was still uncommon, and used mostly by academics or doctors. Admittedly it was a time of innocence about sex in general, but homosexuality was not discussed in families, or taught in schools. In 1992, James Gardiner explained some of the reasons for this 'silence' in his book *A Class Apart: The Private Pictures of Montague Glover*:

> In Great Britain before 1885, homosexual acts were not directly legislated against, but fell within the scope of the 1533 Act of King Henry VIII which made the 'detestable and abominable Vice of Buggery committed with mankind or beast' a criminal act punishable with 'death and losses and penalties of their goods chattels debts lands and tenements'.[1]

The 1533 Act remained in substance on the Statute Book until 1967. The last execution for 'homosexual buggery' took place in 1832, and the death penalty for the crime was not abolished until the 1861 Offences Against the Person Act. After 1861, men who were proved to have had sex with other men were imprisoned for life. With the passing of the notorious

Labouchere Amendment in 1885, *all* homosexual activity became a criminal offence and punishable by terms of up to two years' imprisonment with hard labour.

Gardiner added: 'in Victorian England homosexuality was considered a great evil by society at large, an unmentionable horror. The word homosexual was not even invented until 1869 and, together with its contemporary equivalent 'invert', was considered unprintable.'[2] Prosecutions were seldom reported in the press. Only the most sensational cases, involving members of the aristocracy or public figures, were highlighted, and even then with no real detail. The popular dramatist Oscar Wilde was the first 'celebrity' to become a victim of the 1885 Labouchere Amendment and, if his trials were widely reported, it was only to expose his 'consummate wickedness and show where the paths of such debauchery (particularly consorting socially with the working-classes) might lead.'[3] As far as the medical profession was concerned, homosexuality was considered at best a mental sickness, and one that could be 'treated' by aversion therapy. Men who were attracted to their own sex had little choice but to view themselves as sick and abnormal, social pariahs and perverts. For decades gay men referred to heterosexual men as 'normal', thus excluding themselves from any claim to normality.

Until the 1960s it was considered unthinkable for a gay man to be interviewed on television. That changed with two prominent actuality series: ITV's *This Week* (1964) and the BBC's *Man Alive* (1967). By the 1990s attitudes had changed, and in 1997 a range of lesbian and gay interviewees were seen on BBC television in the series *It's Not Unusual*, a history of lesbians and gays in Britain. They included Ray Bagley, who was born in Warwickshire. He explained what it was like to grow up gay in the 1930s, a time when television was in its infancy. He knew there was something different about himself when he was growing up, 'but you see no-one talked about this, it wasn't discussed, there was nothing on the television, in the papers, in books, or anything.'[4] Bagley's view is typical of most gay men of his generation; however, by the 1930s, there were gay sub-cultures beginning to emerge in cities up and down the country. Like-minded men began to reach out and meet each other in secret. However, because of the draconian law, which could lead them to imprisonment, discretion amongst gay men was still vital and information tended to be spread by word-of-mouth, much of it around London's West End in areas like Soho. Yet the experiences of individual gay men could vary. For example, in their autobiographies, the exhibitionist Quentin Crisp (see Chapter 19) and policeman Harry Daley gave contrasting accounts of their lives as homosexuals in London in the 1930s. Unlike most gay men of their generation, neither concealed their sexuality, and in doing so they both took enormous risks. Crisp was subjected to appalling homophobia, both verbal and physical. In *The Naked Civil Servant* (1968) he recalled:

> Blind with mascara and dumb with lipstick, I paraded the dim streets of Pimlico … As my appearance progressed from the effeminate to the bizarre, the reaction of strangers passed from startled contempt to outraged hatred. They began to take action. If I was compelled to stand still in the street in order to wait for a bus or on the platform of an Underground railway station, people would turn without a word and slap my face; if I was wearing sandals, passers-by took care to stamp on my toes.[5]

Harry Daley joined the Metropolitan Police in 1925 and completed his service in 1950. Stationed as a constable in Hammersmith, he did little or nothing to disguise his sexual preferences. In *This Small Cloud: A Personal Memoir* (1986), he wrote:

> My personal background to all this was one of great happiness. It was a period of making friends and enemies – the pleasure brought by the former easily outweighing the worry of the latter. My friendships outside the police were rather unconventional and seemed to be the cause of animosity towards me by certain policemen … The policemen hostile to me were mostly married men.[6]

In the early, formative years of British television, the lives of gay men remained invisible. In 1926, the BBC's Royal Charter barred the transmission of 'controversial material' but homosexuality was not mentioned specifically. The word 'homosexual' was not mentioned on British television until 1953, and the first factual programmes about homosexuality were not produced until 1957. In drama, only Patrick Hamilton's *Rope* – produced five times between 1939 and 1957 – presented gay characters, Granillo and Brandon, but they were not *explicitly* gay and, if any viewer *was* aware of their sexuality, the couple conformed to the popular image of gay men as immoral and unnatural.

When the BBC began its high-definition television service on 2 November 1936, there were only 300 receivers available to pick up their first transmissions, but the new medium soon began to catch on with the public and, according to John Caughie:

> Television drama was a central component of the early schedules, both pre-war, in the period up to September 1939 when the service was terminated for the duration of the war, and immediately post-war, when the service was reopened in June 1946. In the week beginning 25 December 1938, for instance, of the 22 hours 39 minutes transmitted, 14 hours 10 minutes were given over to drama (including some repeats) … In the immediate post-war period, drama usually occupied eight to ten hours of a very slightly expanded schedule.[7]

From 1936 to 1955, Britain had one television channel – the BBC – and all of its output was live. In the early years, television was transmitted three hours a day to a limited audience. This was predominantly affluent and middle-class because it was an expensive commodity – a television set cost the same as a new car. Between 1936 and 1949 it was only shown in the London area.

The early television dramas of the BBC were mostly photographed stage plays. For some, it was an exciting medium to work in. When the actress Pauline Henriques was interviewed about her television debut in 1946 in a production of Eugene O'Neill's *All God's Chillun Got Wings*, she recalled, 'I thought television was wonderful because theatre came into the sitting-rooms of viewers. We only had one television camera and it was static. It was fixed to the studio floor and didn't move and yet a sort of magic came out of this chaos.'[8]

From 1936 to 1957, virtually no retrievable examples of drama productions exist. Consequently, it is difficult to analyse the programmes in any depth, as John Caughie explained:

> While cinema historians have a continuous, though incomplete, history of films from the 1890s, television has a pre-history in which programmes themselves do not exist in recorded form. Transcription, or recording television on film, was not developed till 1947, and recording on tape was technologically possible first in the US in 1953, and was probably not readily available in Britain till around 1958. Neither was in routine use till the 1960s, and even when recording was possible there is a long chain of missing links which have been wiped from the record

either to reuse the tapes or to save storage space … This makes the recovery of the early history of television form and style an archaeological, rather than a strictly historical procedure.[9]

The BBC's adaptation of George Orwell's *Nineteen Eighty-Four* which, in 1954, was telerecorded (filmed on 35mm from a television monitor), is one of the few surviving television plays from the medium's early years. Sadly, none of the television plays mentioned in this book which were transmitted between 1939 and 1957 exist.

Television has always been looked upon as a poor relation to cinema and other art forms. When the television analyst and historian Keith Howes was interviewed in *Capital Gay* in 1994, he said: 'Television and radio are as good as film, theatre, sculpture, painting and any of the other arts but they are totally neglected and derided in this country.'[10] It took the British Film Institute (BFI) over half a century to consent to the National Film Archive (NFA) adding television to its title. The NFA began preserving film in 1933, just three years before the BBC launched its television service, but it was not until the late 1950s that it began to recognise the importance of preserving television. Though the NFA appointed its first Television Acquisitions Officer in 1959, it took until 1993 for the scale of this commitment to be recognised and the words 'and Television' were finally added to the title. Consequently, the NFA became the National Film and Television Archive.

Notes

1. James Gardiner, *A Class Apart: The Private Pictures of Montague Glover* (Serpent's Tail, 1992), p. 82.
2. *Ibid.*
3. *Ibid.*
4. Ray Bagley, 'The Age of Innocence (1920–1951)', *It's Not Unusual*, BBC2, tx 16 May 1997. See also Alkarim Jivani, *It's Not Unusual: A History of Lesbian and Gay Britain in the Twentieth Century* (Michael O'Mara, 1997), pp. 85–6.
5. Quentin Crisp, *The Naked Civil Servant* (Jonathan Cape, 1968), pp. 49–50.
6. Harry Daley, *This Small Cloud: A Personal Memoir* (Weidenfeld and Nicolson, 1986), p. 112.
7. John Caughie, 'Before the Golden Age – Early Television Drama', John Corner (ed.), *Popular Television in Britain: Studies in Cultural History* (British Film Institute, 1991), p. 25.
8. Pauline Henriques, interview with Stephen Bourne, Brighton, 4 August 1989.
9. Caughie, pp. 24–5.
10. Keith Howes, interview with Stephen Bourne, *Capital Gay*, 8 April 1994.

2

Douglas Byng and Auntie

Before Danny La Rue, Frankie Howerd, Kenneth Williams and a host of other closeted gay comedy performers appeared on British television, there was the pantomime dame and revue artist Douglas Byng. He was a television pioneer, dressed in women's clothes, in his own shows, before the war. All of Byng's shows were transmitted live from the BBC's north London studio at Alexandra Palace, or 'Ally Pally' as it became known. In the pre-war years of BBC television, from its launch in 1936 until the Second World War interrupted the service in 1939, the programme emphasis was on entertainment. In fact, the first programme on the opening afternoon (2 November 1936) was called simply *Variety*. Interviewed for *Here's Looking at You: The Story of British Television 1908–1939* (1984), the BBC producer, Cecil Madden, said:

> We had such frightfully good entertainment available to us. There were shows going on in all the London nightclubs and a great deal of money was being spent ... There was a cabaret, an artist or two in every place. Of very high class. The sort of people we really wanted and so we were able to draw on a great deal of ready-made entertainment.[1]

The BBC, nicknamed 'Auntie' in the 1930s because of its prim and prissy image, really wanted Douglas Byng. In the 1930s he was London's highest paid star of cabaret and a popular female impersonator. His gallery of female characters included Flora MacDonald, Naughty Nellie Gwynn and Nanna of the Manor. According to his biographer, Patrick Newley: 'Dougie paved the way for the likes of future stars such as Danny La Rue and comedians such as Kenneth Williams and Frankie Howerd both admitted their debt to him.[2] He often entertained royalty and the 'smart set' at such high-class venues as the Café de Paris, for £1,000 a week, a vast sum in those days. In his later years, Byng would look back with affection at the 1930s. Said Newley: 'he would recall with ease the glittering West End nightclubs, society parties and luminaries such as Noël Coward, Cecil Beaton, Lady Diana Cooper, Tallulah Bankhead and many more.'[3] As a gay man, Byng guarded his reputation, 'if not fiercely,' said Newley, 'then with care. He would never have dreamed of going cottaging or frequenting a private gay club.'[4]

So, 'Auntie' employed Byng for the new medium of television, even if he was a man in a frock who sang risqué songs with titles like 'Oriental Emma of the 'arem', 'Hot Handed Hetty (The Vamp of the Jetty)', 'I'm Millie, a Messy Old Mermaid', 'I'm a Mummy (An Old Egyptian Queen)' and 'I'm One of the Queens of England'. He has been credited as the first female impersonator to appear on television.

Though none of Byng's pre-war television appearances survive, because they were all transmitted live, his appearances in Pathé newsreels of the 1930s reveal an outrageously camp on-stage persona. These short films give us some idea of how he would have presented himself in his early televisions shows. For example, in a 1932 Pathé newsreel, filmed at the Monseigneur nightclub in London, Byng enters carrying a wig and a feather boa. He bows to the audience before he is helped into a dowager soprano costume by the bellboy. Byng then puts on the boa and wig and sings a funny song called 'Spring is in the Air', to yelps of laughter and applause from the audience.

Byng began making television appearances for the BBC in 1938 and these included two short series of his own: *Byng-Ho!* and *Queue for a Song*. One of Byng's many friends in the world of entertainment was the singer Elisabeth Welch, who was also a cabaret star at the Café de Paris. In 1992, when Elisabeth was interviewed about her pre-war television appearances, she described what it was like:

At Alexandra Palace, you had to climb over a whole sea of cables just to get to the camera, and when you got to the camera, which never moved, you just stood there in front of it. The cameras were like the old-fashioned still cameras used to take pictures – the cameraman wore a black hood over his head. But we had fun. It was wonderful.[5]

On 2 November 1938, he took part in an all-star cabaret for *The Television Festival Dinner* with Gracie Fields. This was televised live from the Dorchester Hotel in the presence of HRH the Duke of Kent.

The outbreak of war curtailed Byng's television career and he did not return to the small screen until 1947. When the comedian Bob Monkhouse was interviewed in *Radio Times* in 1986, he recalled seeing Byng on television in the late 1930s, 'singing something my mother said was much too rude for children to hear. For years afterwards, whenever my parents were whispering, I would ask, "Are you doing a Douglas Byng?"'[6]

In the early 1980s, Byng's biographer Patrick Newley became, for a brief period, Quentin Crisp's manager and press agent. Crisp, who was an effeminate and flamboyant homosexual, had paraded the streets of 1930s London wearing mascara and sandals. While Byng entertained the upper crust at the Café de Paris, Crisp was modelling nude for students on the art school circuit. Crisp was openly gay when it was a criminal offence and Byng kept his private life private. They were total opposites.

Crisp became an overnight sensation when John Hurt portrayed him in the acclaimed television drama *The Naked Civil Servant* in 1975 (see Chapter 19). By the time they met in 1983, Crisp was an international celebrity and more famous than Byng. Newley was helping Crisp tour the country in his popular one-man show. When he was booked to appear at Hove Town Hall, Newley decided to organise a visit to Byng's home in Brighton. Byng, then 90 (he died in 1987 at the age of 94), and Crisp, then 74, had never met, nor had anything in common other than being gay. Newley had no idea that he was about to witness a personality clash (or car crash) of two old queens: one who had been a television pioneer in the 1930s, the other whose life had been completely transformed by television in the 1970s.

When Newley and Crisp arrived on Dougie's doorstep, Crisp wore a black velvet suit and a fedora hat. He had blue rinsed hair and full make-up complete with mascara. Byng opened the door in a green velvet suit, mauve rinsed hair, rouged cheeks with traces of powder and a hint of mascara. 'He looked like Dame Gladys Cooper,' recalled Newley in his biography of Byng. He continued:

'How kind of you to make the effort to come,' said Dougie testily as he ushered us in. 'Oh, I think making any sort of effort in one's life is a mistake,' said Quentin in his best nasal tones as he glided through the doorway.

Dougie looked at me, tut tutted, and said, 'Peculiar, most peculiar.'

Tea was served with scones, cream and jam. Quentin tucked into them as if he hadn't eaten for a week. Dougie gave a violent twitch and a scone fell to the floor.

'This is very cosy,' said Quentin, looking round the room.

'Quentin's doing a one-man show at Hove Town Hall,' I said, trying to break the ice between them.

'Really?' said Dougie sharply. 'It's a terrible place. I wouldn't be seen dead playing there.'

'Oh, I go where I'm told,' said Quentin, lowering his eyes to the floor. 'I don't make decisions. They make them for me. I am an existentialist. You learn to swim with the tide – but faster.'

'Extraordinary,' said Dougie, turning to me. 'What on earth's he talking about?'

I realised, then and there, that the idea of these two men meeting together under the same roof was a gigantic mistake. I should have known. Both were dazzlingly egocentric, at times like haughty peacocks, and whilst Quentin was normally noted for his almost saint-like tolerance of other people, on this occasion his patience was sorely tested. Dougie, who wasn't working, was incensed that another person, who not only looked like himself, but was also more than a match in wit and style, should be appearing in a one-man show literally down the road. I racked my brains for a solution to the embarrassing situation but both of them solved it instantly. They decided to talk at the same time – and completely ignore each other. [7]

Notes

1. Bruce Norman, *Here's Looking at You: The Story of British Television 1908–1939* (BBC, 1984), p. 151.
2. Patrick Newley, *Bawdy But British!: The Life of Douglas Byng* (Third Age Press, 2009), p. 10.
3. *Ibid.* p. 19.
4. *Ibid.* p. 26.
5. Elisabeth Welch interviewed by Stephen Bourne, *Black and White in Colour: Black People in British Television since 1936*, Jim Pines (ed.), (British Film Institute, 1992), pp. 22–3.
6. *Radio Times*, 25–31 October 1986.
7. Newley, pp. 91–2.

3

Patrick Hamilton's *Rope*

In 1929, Patrick Hamilton's stage play *Rope* had a try-out performance by
the Repertory Players on 3 March, a Sunday night, followed eight weeks
later by a West End run at the Ambassadors Theatre. It was a psychological
thriller set in a fashionable Mayfair apartment where two Oxford
undergraduates, Granillo and Brandon, commit the murder of a fellow
student. After hiding his body in a trunk, they prepare for a cocktail party to
which the dead man's father and fiancée have been invited. Another guest
– the killers' mentor, Rupert Cadell – becomes suspicious, and returns to
challenge his hosts, who confess to their crime. Hamilton denied that he
based *Rope* on the real-life case of two homosexual lovers, Nathan Leopold
and Richard Loeb. In 1924, these American law students had attempted
to commit the 'perfect murder'. They killed a young boy, but escaped the
death penalty, though each received life imprisonment plus ninety-nine
years. However, Hamilton's biographer, Sean French, claimed that the
dramatist was not telling the truth: 'Books about famous trials were, with
trashy westerns, always his favourite leisure reading. His contention that
he was not influenced by the Leopold and Loeb case is simply not credible.
Certainly Bruce [Hamilton's brother], who probably never saw Hamilton's
denial, took it for granted as the inspiration.'[1]

It is generally accepted that Hamilton's play is about a homosexual couple.
For example, in 1978 the gay critic Jack Babuscio referred to them in *Gay News*
as 'a pair of young gays'.[2] In *Hitchcock* (1968), Francois Truffaut's brilliant
study of the films of the director Alfred Hitchcock, he described the couple in
the American film version as 'two young homosexuals'.[3] One of Hitchcock's
biographers, Donald Spoto, described them as 'homosexual lovers'.[4] For Sean
French, '*Rope* reads today as an intensely homosexual play (an aspect that is

brought out even more strongly in Alfred Hitchcock's film version).'[5] Then there is the celebrated French film director Jean Renoir, who once complained that Hitchcock's *Rope* conformed too closely to the American film industry's Production Code, a repressive form of censorship, which had been introduced in 1934. For many years the Code succeeded in eliminating homosexuality – which it referred to as 'sex perversion' and 'impure love' – from Hollywood films. Renoir complained: 'It's supposed to be about homosexuals and you don't even see the boys kiss each other. What's that?'[6]

Rope was popular with the BBC's television drama department, which adapted the play on four occasions from 1939 to 1953. The fact that five versions of *Rope* were made for television altogether (an ITV company, Granada, produced it again in 1957) demonstrates its importance to television producers. However, for some gay critics, this was a couple who conformed to the popular image of gay men as disordered outsiders, as Vito Russo explained in *The Celluloid Closet* (1981) in relation to Alfred Hitchcock's 1948 film:

> The lovers in *Rope* were warped individuals who murdered out of a belief in their own moral and intellectual superiority, which they believed placed them outside the law. By existing outside the culture, such gays were able to deny explicit homosexuality while at the same time reinforcing specific stereotypes.[7]

Alan Sinfield, in *Out on Stage* (1999), identified the following in the original text:

> Hamilton depicts a notable intimacy between the murderers; at one point Brandon puts his arm around Granillo as he shares a match for his cigarette. Also, their appearances correspond … to gender stereotyping. Brandon has the build of a boxer, whereas Granillo is slighter and 'rather ornately dressed', with an 'enormously courteous manner, something between a dancing-master and a stage villain'; at school Brandon was good at games, Granillo not.[8]

In the 1930s, Patrick Hamilton enjoyed success with both *Rope* and his second play, *Gaslight* (1938), but in his private life he was a troubled man. His shyness and alcoholism have been acknowledged in several biographies. He was married, but in the *Oxford Dictionary of National Biography* (2004), Nathalie Blondel observed:

Hamilton's attitude to women was based on an unhappy mixture of infatuation and misogyny. Intimate relationships were reserved for men … Hamilton never wrote love stories. Nor do his characters belong to families; rather they are lonely men and women who are sympathetically portrayed in their unhappy and somehow inevitable solitariness.[9]

For years *Rope* was a staple of repertory companies and radio, but when Hamilton adapted the thriller for the first of several BBC radio productions in 1932, listeners were warned in *Radio Times* about the play's likely effect upon those of a nervous and delicate disposition: 'All but macabre-fanciers are advised to switch off for this. Don't say afterwards that we didn't warn you!'[10] When *Rope* was broadcast at 9.40 p.m. on the evening of 18 January, *Radio Times* described it as 'a curious play, dealing with two neurotic young men who have a theory of murder as a fine art. They strangle a perfectly harmless friend, purely for the excitement of the thing … *Rope* is not everybody's play; it is strong meat.'[11] It was produced for radio by Val Gielgud, who later recalled:

> The British Empire Union … stated that 'a play of this description cannot but encourage in morbid and degenerate minds that morbid tendency which leads to the crimes depicted in this play.' The *Morning Post*, through an unnamed correspondent – who referred to the people who had seen the play acted as 'a section of the public which enjoys the degenerate' – protested against 'broadcasting stuff of this sort into millions of homes.'[12]

On radio in 1932, the role of Rupert Cadell was played by Ernest Milton. He recreated the role he had played in the 1929 West End production. Milton's most memorable film roles included two flamboyant characters: Archibald Raymond, the theatrical impresario in *It's Love Again* (1936), and Titus, the snooty clothes designer in *Fiddlers Three* (1944). Milton played Cadell once again when the BBC presented its first television adaptation of *Rope* on 8 March 1939. A second performance was transmitted on 13 March. It was billed as 'A TV Horror Play' and its producer was Dallas Bower. There was no distinction between drama producer and director in BBC television before 1955. Early drama producers 'directed' their productions. Once again, a warning was given to the audience, on this occasion by the popular on-screen announcer Jasmine Bligh. She told viewers that it was the BBC's duty to inform them that *Rope* may not be considered suitable for children or for those who were of a particularly nervous or sensitive disposition.[13]

BBC television's 1947 version was produced by Stephen Harrison (see Chapter 4) on 5 January, with a second performance on 7 January. His descriptions of the main characters, extracted from the stage directions by Patrick Hamilton, are revealing: 'Tall, finely and athletically built, and blond' Wyndham Brandon, played by Harrison's brother David Markham, conforms to what was then a popular image of a gay man, the vain and selfish aesthete who takes great pride in his appearance. Stephen Harrison and David Markham collaborated on several BBC television plays in the late 1940s and early 1950s, including Christopher Marlowe's *Edward II* and two versions of *Rope*. In the 1947 version of *Rope*, Charles Granillo was portrayed by Dirk Bogarde, and Granillo was a character described by Harrison as expensively and rather ornately dressed in a dark blue suit. He wears a diamond ring and can be described as something between a dancing-master and a stage villain.[14] According to Sheridan Morley, one of Bogarde's biographers: 'In his first starring role, Dirk was playing a complicated, tortured but highly sexually charged character and it was a forerunner of so many of his future roles.'[15] According to John Coldstream, another biographer of Bogarde: 'The neurotic killer was a plum part … For Dirk, travelling home on the train to Haywards Heath, it was the first time he had seen his new name in print [in *Radio Times*] and he noted in his scrapbook, he went pink in the face.'[16] Coldstream added that, in a BBC memo, producer Harrison commented that the young Bogarde 'has possibilities'. In a letter to a friend, Bogarde wrote: 'Stephen Harrison seemed pleased with what I did and has promised me more parts in the future, and altogether life has been grand fun for me!'[17]

Rope was important to Bogarde's career as it provided him with one of his first major roles, and such was his impact that he was immediately signed to a long-term film contract with the Rank Organisation. He then became one of Britain's most popular film stars. Yet, in spite of its importance to his career, Bogarde does not refer to *Rope* in *A Postillion Struck by Lightning* (1977), the first of his series of autobiographies, or in any of the subsequent six volumes. As far as Sheridan Morley was concerned, his appearance in *Rope* raised questions about Bogarde's sexuality:

As, later, did his work in such movies as *Victim, The Servant* and *Death in Venice* … he carefully denied the suggestion whenever possible. 'People can't understand how you can be unmarried, have an adoring family and simply wish to be on your own. I am not a homosexual, but if that's what people want to think, they'll think it' … he has never once commented on the suggestion that his interest in homosexuality was anything other than artistic and compassionate, except to characterize his forty-year life with Tony Forwood as asexual, often adding the intriguing piece of information that Forwood was anti-homosexual.[18]

Bogarde went to great lengths to conceal his homosexuality from the public, and this was later explained in BBC television's two-part *Arena* documentary *The Private Dirk Bogarde* (BBC2, tx 26 December 2001). The programme's author and narrator, Nicholas Shakespeare, told *Radio Times* (22 December 2001–4 January 2002), 'He made crucial omissions – notably, that he shared his life with Tony Forwood for almost half a century. It is an enviable friendship but he never talked about it with anybody. He certainly denied it to me and he denied that he was a homosexual.'

David Markham portrayed Brandon again in Stephen Harrison's 1950 production (tx 8 January with a second performance on 12 January) as part of the BBC's new *Sunday Night Theatre* series. Peter Wyngarde took the role of Granillo. Alan Wheatley portrayed Rupert Cadell, a role he recreated for Harrison's 1953 production of *Rope* (tx 8 December). In a letter to the author, Peter Wyngarde offered an insight into the 1950 version, and the personalities of Harrison and Markham:

> I can't tell you how thrilled I am to recall *Rope* which was my first television (Alexandra Palace and LIVE!). The climate at that time was obviously very anti-gay which is why I'm sure Stephen cast David, heterosexual in every way, and this allowed him to do the play for the BBC. As you know there is no reference [to homosexuality] as such in the play itself – but we were all aware of the source [the Leopold and Loeb case] which left no doubts. When it was written the sensation of rich boys committing such a horror had enough drama, without bringing in their sexual preferences. Of course, as it took place in America nice Jewish boys didn't do those things! I think it's a terrific play.[19]

In 1957, two years after the launch of independent, commercial television, Granada produced a fifth television version of the play (tx 2 October) with Alec McCowen, Ian Holm and Dennis Price, who had previously taken the supporting role of Kenneth Raglan in the BBC's 1939 production. Price was an English actor described by Keith Howes in *Broadcasting It* as 'practically the only "name" actor to play gay roles – at least five of them before it was "safe" to do so. Prancing along beside these were a whole raft of bachelors, dandies and aesthetes, including Lord Byron.'[20]

Notes

1. Sean French, *Patrick Hamilton: A Life* (Faber and Faber, 1993), p. 101.
2. Jack Babuscio, 'Psycho Gays – Homosexuality in the Films of Alfred Hitchcock', *Gay News* No. 181 (1978), p. 35.
3. Francois Truffaut, *Hitchcock* (Secker and Warburg, 1968), p. 216.
4. Donald Spoto, *The Dark Side of Genius: The Life of Alfred Hitchcock* (Plexus, 1983), p. 303.
5. French, p. 114.
6. Vito Russo, *The Celluloid Closet: Homosexuality in the Movies* (Harper and Row, 1981; revised edition 1987), p. 62.
7. Russo, pp. 94–5.
8. Alan Sinfield, *Out on Stage. Lesbian and Gay Theatre in the Twentieth Century* (Yale University Press, 1999), pp. 169–70.
9. Nathalie Blondel, 'Patrick Hamilton (1904–1962)', *Oxford Dictionary of National Biography* (Oxford University Press, 2004).
10. *Radio Times*, 15 January 1932.
11. *Ibid.*
12. Val Gielgud, *British Radio Drama 1922–1956: A Survey* (George G. Harrap, 1957), p. 166.
13. File T5/438, *Rope* 1939–54, BBC Written Archives Centre.
14. File T5/438. BBC Written Archives Centre.
15. Sheridan Morley, *Dirk Bogarde: Rank Outsider* (Bloomsbury, 1996), p. 30.
16. John Coldstream, *Dirk Bogarde: The Authorised Biography* (Weidenfeld and Nicolson, 2004), pp. 161–62.
17. *Ibid.*
18. Morley, p. 29.
19. Peter Wyngarde, letter to Stephen Bourne, 5 November 2001. Used with permission.
20. Keith Howes, *Broadcasting It: An Encyclopaedia of Homosexuality on Film, Radio and TV in the UK 1923–1993* (Cassell, 1993), p. 638.

4

Stephen Harrison
and *Edward II*

In 1947, the same year he produced *Rope*, Stephen Harrison produced Christopher Marlowe's sixteenth-century tragedy *Edward II* (tx 30 October). Both productions starred his brother David Markham who was married to Olive Dehn, the younger sister of the Oscar-winning screenwriter, film critic and poet Paul Dehn. Interviewed by the author in 2001 (she died in 2007), Olive recalled that her stepfather-in-law, Ernest Duveen, hated television and told his stepson, David, 'it will be the ruination of acting'.[1] This revealed something of the prejudice shown towards the television medium in the post-war years. However, it did not stop Stephen Harrison and his brother David from collaborating on several landmark productions.

Olive confirmed that her brother-in-law, Stephen, was homosexual:

> Though he was a very private man. Stephen was relaxed with his family and loved children. He always bought Christmas presents for our children, and took part in the festivities. He was a great gardener, wrote poetry and loved working in television. He was a good director. He was very fond of his partner, who died young, and Stephen found it difficult to cope without him.[2]

Olive and David's daughter, Petra Markham, revealed that she had two gay uncles, Stephen and Olive's brother Paul Dehn. However, because of the law, 'Uncle Ste, who was a shy man, would not come out. Paul was an extrovert and did not hide his sexuality. We knew he was in a relationship with the composer James Bernard.'[3]

Educated at Cheltenham College and New College Oxford, Stephen Harrison entered the film industry in 1929 and worked as an assistant director and film editor for Paramount in New York and Elstree. After joining Alexander Korda's London Films, he worked as the editor on such important productions as *The Private Life of Henry VIII* (1933) and *The Rise of Catherine the Great* (1934). When he joined the BBC in 1938, he worked as a junior television producer at Alexandra Palace. During World War Two he was a chief sub-editor for BBC radio's Home News Department. He resumed his television career as a drama producer on 13 May 1946.[4] He continued to work in the BBC's television drama department until he took premature retirement in 1963. He produced (and directed) over eighty television plays from 1946 to 1962, including thirty in the *Sunday Night Theatre* series. Most of these he brought to the medium from the theatre and they included three versions of Patrick Hamilton's *Rope* (1947, 1950 and 1953), Hamilton's *Gaslight* (1947), *The Happiest Days of Your Life* (1947), Ben Jonson's *Volpone* (1948), John Webster's *The Duchess of Malfi* (1949) and William Shakespeare's *Julius Caesar* (1951) and *The Merry Wives of Windsor* (1955). It is an impressive list, and yet his work is not known.

Regarding *Rope* and *Edward II*, could Harrison's sexuality have drawn him to producing these plays for television? In the Elizabethan era, homosexuality surfaced in much of the work of the English dramatist and poet Christopher Marlowe, including *Edward II*. The date of the play is uncertain but, in 1593, it may be the last that Marlowe wrote. It is practically the only dramatic work in the English language up until the twentieth century to depict same-sex passion. Edward II (1284–1327) was King of England (he reigned from 1307) and the first Prince of Wales. His love for Piers Gaveston, the son of a Gascon nobleman, angered many of his nobles but they lived together as a same-sex couple for fourteen years. Nobles resented Gaveston's closeness to Edward, and engineered his death in 1312. Edward II was murdered in 1327.

In Harrison's television adaptation, David Markham played King Edward II and Alan Wheatley was cast as Gaveston. It is impossible to know if the BBC censored an expression of gay love from Scene Two: 'He claps [slaps affectionately] his cheeks and hangs about his neck/Smiles in his face and whispers in his ears', spoken by Queen Isabella. It was very probably removed from early radio and television productions. By the 1980s, *Edward II* had become accepted as a 'gay classic' and in 1991 the gay director Derek Jarman made a memorable film version in which the homosexual relationship was made explicit. According to Robert Lindsey and Martin Wiggins, in their 1997 introduction to the New Mermaids edition of *Edward II*:

> So prominent has this aspect of the play become that rumours persist – they are inevitably hard to verify – that in some parts of Britain it was banned from school syllabuses during the late 1980s and early 1990s under the infamous anti-AIDS Clause 28 of the Conservative government's local government legislation, which prohibited public bodies from supporting works of art that condoned homosexual behaviour. 'In the Mercutio/Romeo relationship, and in *Coriolanus*, you can ignore the homosexual content if you so choose,' commented Gerard Murphy, director of the 1990 RSC production [of *Edward II*]; 'you *can't* in *Edward II*.'[5]

Petra Markham described her 'Uncle Ste' as a formidable but kind man who was also immaculate, scholarly but distant:

> Fastidious too. He would notice a flat A in my voice and tell me about it. He was nervous of children but, after I married, he loved to come to supper after his partner died. We do not know much about his partner, David, who was extremely shy. Uncle Ste did bring him occasionally to the family home in Ashdown Forest. My uncle loved collecting shells. That was his great thing. He had a spirit, he enjoyed travelling all over the world and, in 1966, he wrote an article in *The Saturday Book* on the ruined cities of Ceylon. But he was an introverted man and not confident. During the war, my father David was a pacifist and served time in jail. Politically the two brothers were distant. Socially they did not mix but, after the war, they became close and worked together. My father was a humanist and would have been completely understanding of his brother's homosexuality.[6]

Peter Wyngarde, who co-starred with David Markham in Harrison's 1950 BBC version of *Rope*, recalled in a letter to the author:

About David and Stephen. They were so completely unalike except for their natural charm and talent. Stephen was edgy and intellectual; David was a farmer, and totally un-lovie in every way. He was down to earth, forthright, gentle and in retrospect reminds me of a modern version of the bohemian set of the '30s. The climate at that time was obviously very anti-gay which is why I'm sure Stephen cast his brother in *Rope*. David was even more heterosexual than Ralph Richardson, in every way, which allowed him to do the play.[7]

When Stephen Harrison took premature retirement from the BBC in 1963, the television drama department was going through a major overhaul. A new Director-General of the BBC, Sir Hugh Carlton-Greene, had been appointed in 1960. He planned to shake up the organisation. The BBC documentary *Auntie: The Inside Story of the BBC* (tx 11 November 1997) included a 1982 interview with Carlton-Greene in which he stated that his main concern was the competition from ITV. The BBC share of the viewing audience had gone down in the late 1950s and, he said, 'something had to be done about it'. Consequently, in 1963, Carlton-Greene lured Sydney Newman from ITV and appointed him as the BBC's Head of Television Drama. Newman's job was to 'shake up' the drama department. In *Auntie: The Inside Story of the BBC*, in an interview from 1984, Newman explained what happened next: 'It was all rather stagey. The material used didn't cater for the mass British audience. BBC drama was still catering to a highly educated cultured class rather than the mass audience.' When *Z Cars*, a gritty new police drama series, was launched in 1962, it was an instant success and viewers started to return to the BBC.

In 1963, Stephen Harrison left the BBC at a time when their drama department was going through radical changes. Petra explained that, when he parted company with the BBC, his entitlement to a free BBC television licence ended. He never purchased his own licence or owned a television set again. He died in 1987 having lost his beloved partner, David, in 1978.

Notes

1. Olive Markham, interview with Stephen Bourne, 28 December 2001.
2. *Ibid.*
3. Petra Markham, interview with Stephen Bourne, 9 January 2019.
4. *The Television Annual for 1955* (Odhams Press, 1955), p. 151.

5. Christopher Marlowe, *Edward II*, Robert Lindsey and Martin Wiggins (eds.), (A & C Black, 1997), pp. xvii–xviii. See also Terence Michael Stephenson's interviews with actors Simon Russell Beale and Gerard Murphy, 'Sweet Lies', *Gay Times*, August 1990, pp. 34–6.
6. Petra Markham, *ibid.*
7. Peter Wyngarde, letter to Stephen Bourne, 5 November 2001. Used with permission.

5

Post-War Television and Law Reform

The 1953 Coronation of Elizabeth II boosted the popularity of television because it was televised live to the nation. The BBC used this event as a way of increasing the ownership of the medium. Consequently, television spread to over 50 per cent of the population. Technically, it became more sophisticated and widened the scope of the kinds of programmes which could be made. A second channel – ITV – began transmitting on 22 September 1955 and set out to be more popular and less high-brow than the BBC, which was forced to respond by becoming more populist in order to compete. For years the BBC had been producing what was essentially entertainment for middle-class viewers, and this was highlighted by the existence of two showcases for theatre-oriented works: *Sunday Night Theatre* (1950–59) and *Saturday Playhouse* (1958). In 1956, *Armchair Theatre* was launched by the independent broadcaster ABC with similar aims and the same audience in mind, producing a collection of single plays which became compulsive Sunday-night viewing. However, *Armchair Theatre* changed dramatically in 1958 when ABC headhunted the Canadian television executive Sydney Newman and encouraged him to come to Britain to make television more 'modern'.

Under Newman's guidance, *Armchair Theatre* quickly became independent television's most prestigious showcase for adult-themed drama and a flagship for quality in the late 1950s and early 1960s. He assembled a progressive young team, including Peter Luke, Irene Shubik, Ted Kotcheff and Philip Saville, and effectively reinvented what the television play was supposed to be. Writers such as Alun Owen, Harold Pinter and Ted Willis took the 'working class' themes of late 1950s British cinema, theatre and novels, and turned them into a form that became dubbed by the press as 'the kitchen sink drama'. Occasionally gay characters surfaced, but not that many. Regrettably a number of the early productions have not survived, and these include John Bethune's acclaimed adaptation of Oscar Wilde's *The Picture of Dorian Gray* (tx 22 January 1961) starring Dennis Price and Jeremy Brett.

An unidentified journalist, previewing *The Picture of Dorian Gray* in the *Coventry Evening Telegraph* (21 January 1961), reminded readers that 'The Victorians lived in that feudal Trollopian world where the rich were very rich and the poor were very poor – and nobody knew or cared very much about it. But Wilde made them care. With Dorian Gray he made them realise that the society they admired was rotten and riddled with vice and moral decay.' The critic for the *Liverpool Echo* (23 January 1961) was impressed by the two lead actors: 'Jeremy Brett made a fine Dorian and Dennis Price as the evil Lord Henry Wootton seemed the personification of the devil. And the portrait was excellently contrived – the loose-lipped, lascivious leer of Dorian's degenerate youth superbly captured.' The reviewer for *The Stage* (26 January 1961) singled out Price: 'there could not be a better actor than Dennis Price to extract the correct note of distinguished depravity from his part. Price fits as correctly in Oscar's rarefied world as he does into an elegant glove.'

The Picture of Dorian Gray may have vanished, but two early *Armchair Theatre* productions that *do* exist and feature gay supporting characters are Alun Owen's *The Rose Affair* (tx 8 October 1961) and Robert Muller's *Afternoon of a Nymph* (tx 30 September 1962), both written for television. Owen's *The Rose Affair* updated the story of Beauty and the Beast and featured Harold Lang as Johnston, manservant to Betumain (Anthony Quayle), a lonely, disfigured millionaire. Throughout the play the chameleonic Johnston projects a fey demeanour. His frequent changes of costume and persona are camp. The critic for the *Belfast Telegraph* (9 October 1961) informed readers: 'I got most pleasure out of the antics of Harold Lang as the manservant who took a ghoulish delight in looking after his strange master.'

In Muller's *Afternoon of a Nymph*, Aubrey Morris was cast as Joe, make-up man to the young, ambitious actress Elaine (Janet Munro). In *Anatomy of a Television Play* he is described by Muller as 'Affectionate. Not too overtly effeminate. Might have started off as an actor. Simply not ambitious enough.'[1] Joe's appearances are brief and, on paper, he has all the hallmarks of a gay stereotype. He's theatrical, camp, over-attentive and repeatedly uses words like 'love' and 'dear'. He says to Elaine: 'It must be really nice being a pretty girl like you,' but Aubrey Morris manages to portray the effeminate character as a decent, kind human being, and a professional when he is in charge of the make-up. Admittedly he has led an incomplete life: 'I'd like being in your shoes,' he confesses to Elaine, and he makes his final appearance in close-up, holding one of Elaine's dresses tightly to his chest. The critic for *The Stage* (4 October 1962) noted 'the play was touching especially the pathetic make-up man (Aubrey Morris) who so desperately wanted to be liked.'

It was John Osborne's controversial stage play *Look Back in Anger* that introduced the character of the 'angry young man', a popular figure in British drama of the late 1950s and early 1960s. Osborne's play changed British theatre by giving a voice to a new generation who were desperate to be heard on stage and screen. Opening at London's Royal Court Theatre on 8 May 1956 and directed by Tony Richardson, it was acclaimed by theatre critics, who saw it as a breakthrough. However, not everyone understood it, or liked it. Noël Coward, a theatrical giant popularly known as 'The Master', found the gritty working-class attitude being expressed in drama both self-satisfied and displeasing. He wrote in his diary (February 1957):

> I wish I knew why the hero [of *Look Back in Anger*] is so dreadfully cross and about what? I expect my bewilderment is because I am very old indeed and cannot understand why the younger generation, instead of knocking at the door, should bash the fuck out of it.[2]

Another theatrical giant, the celebrated actor Laurence Olivier, wasn't impressed, either: 'It stinks, a travesty on England, a lot of bitter rattling on', but his contemporary John Gielgud had a different reaction to Osborne's bitter attack on middle-class complacency. His was more mellow and thoughtful:

> I remember going and not expecting to enjoy it, and enjoying it hugely, and thinking, Oh I see now, this is a whole new lot of people … Now I know how a new sort of class has evolved, politically and socially … and it's very well shown in this play.[3]

Look Back in Anger was first produced for television by the BBC on 16 October 1956, but it was a 25-minute excerpt, a 'special performance' before an invited audience from the Royal Court Theatre. Just over a month later, Granada television screened a full-length version on 28 November 1956. The role of Osborne's 'angry young man', Jimmy Porter, was played by Kenneth Haigh in both the stage and television productions but, according to Alan Sinfield in *Out on Stage*:

There was something excessive about Osborne's concern with gayness. Jimmy Porter in *Look Back in Anger* goes out of his way to talk about Webster. He is the only one of Alison's friends (i.e. upper-class and feminine) that he likes, and offers the exception to Jimmy's famous complaint that there are no good brave causes any more – 'old Gide and the Greek Chorus boys' … And what about that *ménage à trois* – Jimmy, Alison/Helena, Cliff? The homosocial relationship between Jimmy and Cliff is interesting and sometimes moving in its understatement. 'You've been loyal, generous and a good friend. But I'm quite prepared to see you wander off, find a new home,' Jimmy says when Cliff decides to leave … The initial critics maintained a discreet distance from such thoughts but, Osborne records, [the homosexual television personality] Gilbert Harding 'grabbed my knee in almost fatherly affection and demanded, in front of the company of floppy bow-tied waiters, I admit that Jimmy and Cliff were in love with each other.'[4]

Discussions of homosexuality on television in the 1950s were practically non-existent, and it was the Conservative MP, Sir Robert Boothby, who made the historic first mention of the word 'homosexual' on television on 27 November 1953 in the BBC series *In the News*. This happened shortly after the celebrated stage actor John Gielgud was arrested for 'persistently importuning'. The arrest was part of the post-war rise in police activity that targeted homosexuals and led to a 'witch hunt' in the 1950s. Gielgud's arrest highlighted the absurdity of the law as it stood at the time, and gave the media an opportunity to debate the subject of law reform.[5] For the BBC, homosexuality was still a taboo subject. For instance, in 1953 an attempt was made to put together a 'dummy' radio programme about the subject. However, according to a memo that has survived in the BBC's Written Archives, dated 23 October, just two days after Gielgud's arrest, strong opposition to the proposal was expressed.[6]

On 3 December 1953, homosexual law reform was raised openly for the first time in the House of Commons by Boothby and Labour's Desmond Donnelly.[7] Then, in March 1954, the journalist Peter Wildeblood was sent to prison for eighteen months for 'homosexual offences' (conspiring to incite acts of gross indecency). He had been charged under the draconian law which had long been known as the 'blackmailer's charter'. Wildeblood later became a campaigner for homosexual law reform and wrote movingly about his experiences of his conviction and prison sentence in his book *Against the Law* (1955). According to Philip Hoare in his obituary of Wildeblood in *The Independent* (25 November 1999):

> If the Montagu case of 1954 was the highest-profile gay trial since Oscar Wilde's, then Peter Wildeblood's *Against the Law*, the published account of one of its protagonists, is its *De Profundis*. And, like Wilde's text, Wildeblood's book appeared both apologetic – perhaps for the very existence of homosexuals; and at the same time combative – for their human rights.

Against the Law was partly responsible for important gay law reform because it forced the Conservative government of the day to review the laws on homosexuality. In the book, Wildeblood made three main points: that sexual acts between consenting adult men should be decriminalised; that the imprisonment of men convicted of gay sex actually encouraged homosexuality rather than cured it; and that the penal system was in need of some drastic reform. The Conservatives set up the Wolfenden Committee in 1954 to review the law on homosexuals. Published in 1957, the Wolfenden Report (The Report of the Departmental Committee on Homosexual Offences and Prostitution) recommended that 'homosexual practices' in private between consenting males over the age of 21 should not be considered a criminal offence. This was the first radical break in the chain of prohibition from Henry VIII's 1533 Act. By 1957, gay men were being subjected to the most vicious forms of blackmail. In fact, around 90 per cent of blackmail cases involved gay men. But in spite of the Report's recommendations, the law was not changed until 1967.

The Report debunked many of the myths about homosexuality (disease, threat to the stability of the nation, the seduction theory, etc.) but it continued to view homosexuality as immoral and likely to lead to antisocial behaviour, hence its statement that legal reforms should not be seen as an approval of homosexuality. It also recommended that the male homosexual age of consent should be 21 on the grounds that a lower age would lay young men open to 'attentions and pressures of an undesirable type', although elsewhere the Committee implied that an age of 16 was appropriate since men should surely be able to withstand such pressures as well as young women.

It was in this climate that one of the new independent broadcasters, Granada (based in Manchester), *not* the BBC, produced one of the first factual programmes for television about homosexuality. Called *Homosexuality and the Law*, the programme was screened on 5 September 1957, the day after the publication of the Wolfenden Report. The programme no longer exists, but in Granada's television archive, a seven-page document has survived which outlines some legal, medical and historical aspects relating to homosexuality, and a synopsis of the programme. The introduction to the programme reflects the attitudes of the time, and a willingness to start debating the subject on television:

> This is a programme about a source of human unhappiness which until recently, was considered quite unfit for public discussion. As usual, in such matters, the taboo made the problem insoluble. It was one of the few remaining social questions that still seemed so embarrassing and difficult that the easiest course was to pretend they didn't exist, except in the darkest corners of criminal law. The homosexual individual came into the light of publicity, from time to time, as a person charged with 'a certain offence': and there were people, quite a large number of people, who didn't even know what was meant. There still are. There are people tonight who will switch off this programme because that is the state of mind they prefer.[8]

However, Sidney Bernstein, the founder of Granada television, was apprehensive about transmitting the programme. He was not convinced that viewers were going to understand what the programme was about: '"What?" said [producer] Denis Forman, disbelievingly, "Well," said Sidney, "how many people really know what buggery is?" "Good Lord," said Forman, "*everybody* knows what buggery is."'[9] Not to be outdone, the BBC followed with their first actuality programme about the subject in their *Lifeline* series. Transmitted at 10.20 p.m. on 26 November 1957 between the evening news and a programme of music for violin and harp, *The Problem of the Homosexual* was introduced by 'A consultant psychiatrist', 'A doctor' and 'A Queen's Counsel' but no further information is available. The programme, which lasted 25 minutes, was transmitted live. No recording exists.

On 22 October 1964, Associated Rediffusion, an ITV channel, made the first television documentary about homosexuality. 'Homosexuals' was included in *This Week*, an important current affairs series which had begun in 1956. It followed other 'taboo' subjects, such as abortion, suicide, drug addiction and sex. It was produced by Jeremy Isaacs, and focussed on the 'problems' encountered by gay men in Britain. It made comparisons with Holland, where homosexuality was not against the law, and it was the first time on television homosexuality was dealt with in a non-judgemental way. 'Homosexuals' also included several revealing interviews with gay men, who were extremely brave in facing the camera, considering the legal implications, though some interviewees appeared in silhouette so they couldn't be identified. Homosexuality was still a criminal offence. While researching the programme, the presenter, Bryan Magee, interviewed over 200 men and many of the experiences he documented found their way into a book called *One in Twenty* (1966). It was translated into eight languages and continued to sell into the 1970s.

Notes

1. John Russell Taylor, *Anatomy of a Television Play* (Weidenfeld and Nicolson, 1962), p. 32.
2. Barry Day (ed.), *The Letters of Noël Coward* (Methuen, 2007), p. 232.
3. Jonathan Croall, *Gielgud: A Life* (Methuen, 2001), p. 397.
4. Alan Sinfield, *Out on Stage: Lesbian and Gay Theatre in the Twentieth Century* (Yale University Press, 1999), p. 260.
5. Stephen Jeffery-Poulter, *Peers, Queers and Commons: The Struggle for Gay Law Reform from 1950 to the Present* (Routledge, 1991), pp. 13–16. *A Bill Called William*, produced by Stephen Jeffery-Poulter for Channel Four (tx 3 July 1997) was a television documentary about the controversial and historic attempt to legalise homosexual acts which resulted in the 1967 Sexual Offences Act.
6. Memo from D.F. Boyd, Chief Assistant, BBC Talks Department to Isa Benzie, Producer, BBC Talks Department, 23 October 1953. File R34/872/1. Policy – Sexual Offences, File I, 1953-54. BBC Written Archives Centre.
7. Jeffery-Poulter, *ibid*.
8. Synopsis for Granada television's *Homosexuality and the Law*. Courtesy of Granada Media.
9. Caroline Moorehead, *Sidney Bernstein: A Biography* (Jonathan Cape, 1984), p. 251.

6

Peter Wyngarde and *South*

In the 1920s and 1930s, gay characters in stage plays were usually depicted as either corrupt or morally pitiful (cf. Noël Coward's *The Vortex*). Homosexuals existed in almost total isolation outside a predominantly conservative heterosexual society. In post-war Britain, especially during the Cold War, under the influence of McCarthyism, homosexuality was perceived as morally reprehensible, and also politically dangerous. In Britain, until 1958, direct discussion or the depiction of homosexuality was banned from the stage. However, attempts were made to overcome this, resulting in the staging of a number of 'banned' plays, including Julien Green's *South*. According to Nicholas de Jongh:

> In view of the Lord Chamberlain's renewed anxiety about homosexuality, producers played their cards furtively when attempting to win licences for gay-related plays. 'A wall of secrecy has been built around [*Cat on a Hot Tin Roof*'s] possible production,' Robert Muller, the *Daily Mail* theatre critic wrote on 14 April 1956. 'No one admits to having obtained the British rights or having submitted it to the censor. Already *Tea and Sympathy*, *The Children's Hour*, *The Maids* (by Jean Genet) and *South* have been refused licences.' Binkie Beaumont and Donald Albery, supported by Stephen Arlen and Ian Hunter, decided to challenge the Lord Chamberlain's edict upon the licensing of plays that dealt directly with the subject.[1]

South, set on a plantation in America's South Carolina in 1861, just before the outbreak of the Civil War, focusses on Jan Wicziewsky (pronounced

Veechefsky). He is a proud and disciplined American army officer of Polish extraction. He falls hopelessly in love with Eric MacClure, a young plantation owner. Julien Green's drama explores Jan's inner conflicts as he finds himself sexually attracted to MacClure. Green was born in Paris to American parents (from Savannah, a city in the southern state of Georgia) of Scottish-Irish ancestry. In his obituary of Green in the *Savannah Morning News* (19 August 1998), Doug Wyatt described Green as a novelist who wrote in French about Catholicism, sexuality and the American South: 'His best known works include [the play] *Sud* (*South*) … he filled many of his novels with a dark mix of murder and madness, sex and suicide.' Wyatt noted that Green's novel *Moira*, published in 1950, was set in the University of Virginia and centred around a student's discovery of his homosexuality. Wyatt added that, in 1997, Green's work was the focus of an international symposium in Savannah, drawing scholars from France and Ireland. Jean-Pierre Piriou, a professor of French at the University of Georgia who organised the event, described Green as 'one of the major 20th-century French writers'.

Green's homosexuality was highlighted by David Parris in *Who's Who in Contemporary Gay and Lesbian History: From World War II to the Present Day* (2001). He described him as:

The first and so far only foreign member of the Academie Francaise, remarkable for his extraordinary longevity and his ability to reinvent himself … In advanced years … he reinvented himself yet again, revealing that even as he was penning the novels that earned him a place in the Academie, he was having a turbulent gay sex-life … He saw homosexuality as an insoluble problem, adding, 'All you can say is why?' Green kept a diary and wrote voluminous autobiographies, and it is perhaps these personal writings that may come to be seen as the most interesting part of his work, especially for gay readers who may well be put off by the constrained, provincial Catholic atmosphere of the novels that made his early reputation.[2]

South premiered in Paris in 1953, but almost didn't transfer to the British stage because of the censorship difficulties. It was given its British premiere at London's Arts Theatre Club on 30 March 1955 with Denholm Elliott as Jan. Elliott was later revealed to be bisexual. A few years later, Elliott recreated the role in a revival of the play at the Lyric,

Hammersmith which opened on 7 April 1961. Alan Sinfield described Wicziewsky as a man who is unable to accept the love of any of the women in the play:

> And heavily meaningful remarks suggest that he is tragically doomed to an unrequited passion. Finally, as each is about to leave for the army, Wicziewsky achieves an enigmatic conversation with another young man, MacClure, who is evidently the person he loves. MacClure almost understands that he is being wooed; he responds by recalling 'a sudden affection for a classmate'. But he is in love with the young woman of the house – though not, Wicziewsky accuses, with a passion such as he himself feels. Wicziewsky abruptly provokes a duel with MacClure, in which he gets himself killed.[3]

After portraying Granillo in BBC television's 1950 version of *Rope* (see Chapter 3), Peter Wyngarde readily accepted a more complex, overtly gay role in Granada television's adaptation of *South*. The *TV Times* revealed this was a role Wyngarde 'has long coveted'.[4] Wyngarde was suited to the role, for he was an actor who was attracted to exciting and challenging characters. Keith Howes has described Wyngarde as:

> An incomparable player of dashing, juicy rakehells, men on the edge, pagan creatures. A star in the grand style, with the ability to lengthen his vowels and pierce with his eyes, never afraid to add touches of the absurd and the surreal. Remembered now not for his extraordinary range and charisma during the 1950s, but for his campy thriller-writer sleuth Jason King in the early 1970s (*Department S; Jason King*).[5]

South was showcased in Granada's *Play of the Week* series on 24 November 1959. It was adapted for television by Gerald Savory and directed by the Canadian Mario Prizek. This was described by Tina Bate as:

> A play to baffle, bewilder, and yes, annoy nearly everyone of the ordinary ITV public who set eyes on it. Yet – whatever the mixed motives in presenting this banned play – Independent Television should have been congratulated for screening *South*, one of the most adult, tragic and penetrating dramas of our time. In the role of Jan, a man who could not talk about his love like other men, Peter [Wyngarde] tackled a difficult and

unusual role, giving a stunningly and immensely powerful performance, which was controlled and brilliantly pitched.[6]

Throughout the play, words such as 'monster', 'fiend' and 'disturbed' are used to describe Jan. He is prone to violent outbursts, but one or two scenes reveal his predicament as a closeted homosexual experiencing the pain of unrequited love. For example, he asks for the hand in marriage of Edward Broderick's daughter. However, Broderick knows the real reason for Jan's request to marry: he wants to pretend to the world that he is heterosexual. This is not made *explicit* – for example, the word 'homosexual' is never mentioned – but Broderick refuses Jan's request. He says, not unsympathetically, 'You won't save yourself by marrying my daughter.' The audience is left to decide what Jan is saving himself from. Enlightened viewers would have known, but others remained in ignorance. Broderick then asks a very direct question: 'Shall I tell you who you are in love with?' but Jan refuses to listen to the answer. The play only goes so far in revealing the true nature of Jan's 'problem', but his predicament is handled sensitively.

In another memorable scene, Jan reveals his 'secret' to the young boy Jimmy. He is in love, he explains, 'as no human being was ever in love before', but the person he loves cannot love him. 'A single glance was enough to foresee years of useless suffering,' says Jan. 'It's better not to know what men are thinking. It's either sad or shameful … I'm not ashamed but I am alone.' Later, it is made clear, for those who wished to see it, that Jan is homosexual. Angelina's question to Regina, 'Who is he in love with?' is followed by a close-up of Jan's face which then dissolves into a close-up of Eric MacClure's face. This is Oscar Wilde's love that dare not speak its name being spoken. In the 1950s it may not have been possible for a man to *explicitly* express his love for another man, but Julien Green (and the television version of his play) offered plenty of clues.

Peter Wyngarde loved the play and he expressed as much in a letter he sent to the author, dated 5 November 2001:

South is brilliant. It is an allegory of what was known as Greek love between a man and a man, and a poetic inditement against war. The final scene when Jan forces Eric onto his sword must be the most symbolic and poetic gesture of love between a man and a man, who are enemies. Of different creeds, different beliefs different religions even …

The director (shamefully, I have forgotten his name) was extremely successful – a top director of television at the time and a great feather in Granada's cap. It was his choice to do the play. I am grateful to him for allowing me to play Jan.

The young Canadian actor who played Eric was very very naïve and had just got married and totally unaware of the main plot and was quite happy to play the subplot … He really was oblivious to begin with … The difficulty was in the swordfight. As far as he was concerned, he wins the fight. Our problem was to get him (and the fight arranger) to accommodate the symbolic gesture in what must be an exciting duel. Each time we rehearsed he'd just thrust the blade into me. The only explanation we could come up with (at that time) was that having lost the girl to him, Eric, Jan commits suicide. He bought this.

The critical response was, with a few exceptions, vitriolic. One of the exceptions was the television critic for *The Stage* (26 November 1959) who stated that Jan was homosexual and that his love for Eric was profound, adding that 'Green's dialogue was so full of compassion, understanding and tenderness that his subject didn't seem distasteful … needless to say Peter Wyngarde as Jan, the man who couldn't talk of his love like other men, gave a stunningly brilliant performance, controlled and delicately pitched.' Other critics were not so enthusiastic and some were downright nasty. According to Peter Marshall in the *Daily Sketch* (25 November 1959): 'I do NOT see anything attractive in the agonies and ecstasies of a pervert, especially in close-up in my sitting-room. This is not prudishness. There are some indecencies in life, like the street women we used to see, that are best left covered up.' Phil Diack, in the *Daily Herald* (25 November 1959), was also upset. *South* made his flesh creep: 'I found the dialogue that revealed the homosexuality of the hero immensely, powerfully and thoroughly distasteful. It made me sweat. It made my flesh creep. But it moved me to pity, too – and nearly to tears.'

Peter Wyngarde, who died in 2018, may have been brave, adventurous and reckless to take on the role of Jan in *South*, but he relished every minute of it, even if it resulted in him being physically assaulted on a number 22 bus:

After the transmission I was the next day travelling on a 22 bus to rehearsal for my next job. Two old chars were sitting behind me and one kept nudging the other and saying 'it's him innit?' The other had a good peep – actors have a built-in antenna for any compliment – and I'd already started preening myself and was about to turn around and ask them if they'd enjoyed the transmission last night – when the second woman shouted 'It is! It is!' and before I could react both women smashed their handbags on my head shouting 'Dirty perv. You should be ashamed of showing such filth on the telly' and other revolting expletives. I've never made such a hasty retreat from a double decker bus as I did that morning.[7]

It is important to acknowledge that the screening of *South* predated several landmark British films that dealt with homosexual themes. After decades of censorship and stereotyping, these films have been credited as breakthroughs in the sympathetic treatment of homosexuality and gay characters in cinema. Needless to say, the television adaptation of *South* is the *real* groundbreaker in terms of screen depictions. Two films about Oscar Wilde were released in 1960: *Oscar Wilde* starring Robert Morley and *The Trials of Oscar Wilde* starring Peter Finch. Then in 1961 came *Victim* starring Dirk Bogarde, and *A Taste of Honey* featuring Murray Melvin. These are acknowledged as British cinema's first serious depictions of homosexuals, but *South* should be recognised for its bold attempt to confront television viewers with the subject. However, it could be argued that Jan conforms to a familiar stereotype: the troubled, closeted gay man who commits suicide. When the actor Kenneth Williams saw the original stage production at the Arts Theatre Club, he complained in his diary:

> It's about a young homosexual in love with a normal young man; of course he commits suicide. Really, this is the kind of thing that seems inevitable in all the homosexual writing. They're always killing themselves. Totally misleading & distorted picture of life, for there are a great number of happy homosexuals – at least as happy as heterosexuals. I'm sick of this 'persecuted queer' stuff.[8]

Notes
1. Nicholas de Jongh, *Politics, Prudery and Perversions: The Censoring of the English Stage 1901–1968* (Methuen, 2000), pp. 111–12.
2. David Parris, 'Julien Green', Robert Aldrich and Garry Wotherspoon (eds.), *Who's Who in Contemporary Gay and Lesbian History: From World War II to the Present Day*, (Routledge, 2001), p. 169.

3. Alan Sinfield, *Out on Stage: Lesbian and Gay Theatre in the Twentieth Century* (Yale University Press, 1999), p. 179.
4. Sarah Snow, 'Play Bill', *TV Times*, 21 November 1959, p. 11.
5. Keith Howes, *Broadcasting It: An Encyclopaedia of Homosexuality on Film, Radio and TV in the UK 1923–1993* (Cassell, 1993), p. 950.
6. Tina Bate, *The Official Peter Wyngarde Website*.
7. Peter Wyngarde, letter to Stephen Bourne, 5 November 2001. Used with permission.
8. *The Kenneth Williams Diaries*, Russell Davies (ed.), (HarperCollins, 1994), p. 112.

Part 2

1960s

7

On Trial

On 8 July 1960, in the year following his appearance as the troubled Jan in *South* (see Chapter 6), Peter Wyngarde returned to Granada's television studio for an episode of *On Trial*. He took the lead in a realistic and skilfully edited reconstruction of the trial for high treason of the Irish patriot Sir Roger Casement. The case itself was an interesting and notorious one, although much more for its aftermath than for the matter for which Casement actually stood trial. On Good Friday 1916, when the First World War was at its height, Casement was arrested after landing from a German U-boat on the Irish coast. His trial for treason, overshadowed by the existence of his notorious private 'Black Diaries' which revealed his homosexual 'practices', was one of the most sensational in British history. In the conclusion to *On Trial*, Brian Inglis, who later published a biography of Casement, explained that the diaries, thought to be forgeries by his Irish supporters, were used to 'blacken' his name and led to the collapse of the campaign to reprieve him. Casement was executed and, in the words of the playwright George Bernard Shaw, became a martyr to the Irish cause.

Casement's trial was one of the last of the great state trials at bar, and it is still of enduring interest to lawyers. However, since his counsel, Sergeant Alexander Sullivan, declined to put him into the witness box, the four-day trial in the court of the Lord Chief Justice in June 1916 lacked the cut and thrust which marked Sir Edward Carson's cross-examination of Oscar Wilde. *On Trial* concentrated on the moments of high drama: the collapse of Sullivan from illness at the end of the third day, Casement's two speeches from the dock, the solemnity of the three judges, each wearing a black cap, passing the death sentence. As for Wyngarde, though most of his on-screen time was spent silently observing the proceedings, he gave a remarkable performance in the title role. His portrayal of Casement, sitting scribbling furiously or quizzically listening from the dock, dominated the proceedings, and his final, emotionally charged speech was powerful and moving.

Following the screening of the Roger Casement drama, on 5 August 1960, the flamboyant gay actor Micheal MacLiammoir gave a charismatic performance as the poet, dramatist and critic Oscar Wilde in the *On Trial* series. Produced by Peter Wildeblood (see Chapter 5) and directed by Silvio Narizzano, this sympathetic dramatisation of the 1895 trials used the original transcripts. Wilde is seen in the dock at the Old Bailey with flashbacks to the previous case when the Marquis of Queensberry was the defendant.

Wilde had been having a relationship with Lord Alfred Douglas, known as 'Bosie', and Bosie's father, the unstable Marquis of Queensberry, left a card at Wilde's club accusing him of 'posing as a somdomite' [*sic*]. He meant 'sodomite'. Encouraged by Bosie, Wilde issued a writ against Queensberry, alleging libel. The case came to trial on 3 April 1895 but the defence, led by Edward Carson, exposed Wilde's association with a string of young men, mostly prostitutes from the working classes. The civil case against Queensberry was lost and Wilde was arrested. His trial on charges of gross indecency opened on 26 April 1895 but Wilde staged a magnificent defence of the 'love that dare not speak its name'. However, he was found guilty and received the maximum sentence of two years' hard labour, the judge describing the case as the worst he had ever tried. Wilde died in 1900.

This was one of three on-screen portrayals of Oscar Wilde in 1960. The other two, *Oscar Wilde*, starring Robert Morley, and *The Trials of Oscar Wilde*, starring Peter Finch, were made for the cinema. According to Keith Howes in *Broadcasting It* (1993), Granada's 'hypnotic' *On Trial* 'lit' by MacLiammoir as the no longer brazen Wilde, 'was the first to present male prostitutes or "good time" boys on the screen. Neither of the Wilde cinema films emphasised the sexual partners, save for Bosie, in any way.'[1]

When *On Trial: Oscar Wilde* was rediscovered in Granada's archive in the early 1990s, it was screened by the curator Stephen Bourne in the first of his annual *Out of the Archives* lesbian and gay television retrospectives at the National Film Theatre in London. When its director, Silvio Narizzano, who had by then come out as gay, introduced the screening on 21 July 1992, he told the audience:

We pretended the *On Trial* series was all about famous trials, rather than just the Wilde. I was very straight; married at the time. I wondered why they gave me this one to direct. I'd like to say there was a kind of liberal thing from Granada, but there really wasn't.

Notes

1. Keith Howes, *Broadcasting It: An Encyclopaedia of Homosexuality on Film, Radio and TV in the UK 1923–1993* (Cassell, 1993), p. 575.

8

Ena Sharples' Father

Behind the scenes, the treatment of gay men working in television who were known to be homosexual, or suspected of it, could be appalling. At Granada's television studio in Manchester, an openly gay writer called Tony Warren confronted homophobia shortly after creating and writing the first batch of scripts for a new drama serial called *Coronation Street*. From the start, this was one of the most successful programmes ever produced for television and, almost sixty years later, it is still popular. Salford-born Warren anticipated a short run for the series. He scripted the first thirteen episodes. He was conscious of himself as someone who was 'theatrical' and, in his autobiography, *I Was Ena Sharples Father* (1969), he described how, while waiting anxiously for the screening of the first episode of *Coronation Street*, he went to a church in Manchester and lit a candle: 'I am neither Roman Catholic nor given to formal religion,' he said, 'but I had been brought up on Ivor Novello musicals, so it seemed the right thing to do.'[1]

Warren was forced out shortly after the programme was launched on 9 December 1960. He blamed this on the anti-gay attitudes of some of his colleagues at script conferences. Warren revealed this to Melvyn Bragg during an interview for London Weekend Television's *The South Bank Show* (5 November 1995):

The blokes took over. They came in and most of them had never seen anything like me in their lives before. And here was I, and I had invented it. It got very unpleasant because I was openly gay at a time when it was not considered sensible to be openly gay but somebody had to stand up and say 'Yes, I'm gay.' But they ganged up, they really did gang up, and I don't think they even knew they'd done it until there was a terrible morning when there was a story conference and I sat there and I listened and then I got to my feet – nobody got to their feet to address story conferences – and I said: 'Gentlemen, I have sat here and listened to two poof jokes, to an actor who is referred to as a poof, to a line dismissed because it is poofy, and I would remind you that without a poof none of you would be in work this morning.' One of them said, 'But Tony, we didn't mean you'. I said, 'You call my brothers, you call me.' Nothing was quite the same after that.

In 2007, at Manchester's Cornerhouse cinema, Warren took part in a debate on whether Corrie had become the 'queerest soap of them all'. Other guests included Corrie writers Jonathan Harvey and Damon Rochefort, as well as the soap's Antony Cotton, who had been playing the street's openly gay knicker stitcher Sean Tully since 2003. Warren reminded the audience that, when he created the series in 1960, homosexuality was a criminal offence. 'I never went past Strangeways jail without thinking, "Is that where I'm going to end up?"', he revealed. 'Although I was out to other gay people at Granada, it was almost unwise to let people know.' He informed the audience that, after his confrontation with his colleagues at Granada, he didn't know he felt so strongly about being gay until that moment, 'and from then on I never pretended to another soul that I was anything other than what I am'.

At the event, Warren was asked if Corrie was the queerest soap on British television. He replied: 'Maybe now, yes. We lagged disgracefully behind for a long time but, now, we're hopefully queer enough.' When he created the series in 1960, it would have been impossible to have a gay character. Instead, Warren cleverly used the language of fellow homosexuals he met and sometimes befriended in Manchester's gay village in the speech of strong, feisty female characters like Elsie Tanner, who also had a big heart. 'The gay village is not new,' said Warren. 'I'd known all these queens in the village. Some of them were sensational. I remember giving Elsie lines they would say. When you think of some of the things she came out with, how many straight women have you heard say that?'[2]

The fame and royalties from creating the series earned Warren sufficient 'clout' to enable him to become involved in projects on his terms, but personal problems and alcoholism plagued his life. Warren failed to repeat his success. Miraculously, he survived. He continued to write scripts for

Coronation Street on an occasional basis until 1968 and his name continued to appear on the credits of the programme. For Ken Irwin in *The Real Coronation Street* (1970):

> The truth about Tony Warren was that he was a Little Boy Lost as far as television was concerned, and he was slowly beginning to realise it. Everything had happened far too quickly. He was young and a complete innocent when he turned out that first script for The Street. After that, I suspect he was incapable of controlling the success the show brought in its wake.[3]

When Warren was interviewed by Jack Tinker for *Coronation Street*, published in 1985 to commemorate the programme's 25th anniversary, he reflected:

> Everyone wants to top their last creative achievement. But for me, at twenty-three, that was impossible. I had built an insurmountably high wall and I could never leap over it. So instead I banged my head against it. Now I have learned to walk round it ... Twenty-five years on I would be a fool to regard the Street as a monster that gobbled me up. If I ever thought of it as an albatross round my neck I now wear it as a glittering albatross in my lapel. Something for people to see. I regard it as having done something worthwhile with my life and I say that because the people who see it tell me so.[4]

Tony Warren died in 2016 and *Coronation Street* continues. In December 2020, the series will celebrate its 60th birthday.

Notes
1. Tony Warren, *I Was Ena Sharples Father* (Duckworth, 1969), pp. 66–7.
2. Dianne Bourne, 'Corrie creator's jail fear', *Manchester Evening News*, 11 May 2007.
3. Ken Irwin, *The Real Coronation Street* (Corgi Books, 1970), p. 54.
4. Jack Tinker, *Coronation Street* (Octopus Books, 1985), p. 15.

9

John Hopkins and *Z Cars* ('Somebody ... Help')

In the 1960s, gay characters were conspicuous by their absence from popular, long-running drama series like Granada's *Coronation Street* and BBC1's *Doctor Who*, but this did not deter gay viewers from enjoying them. Some of them had fun watching the larger-than-life women who inhabited *Coronation Street*. In the 1960s, these included the blousy battler Elsie Tanner and the hair-netted harridan Ena Sharples.[1] The time traveller Doctor Who also had a special appeal to young lads who were growing up gay in the 1960s. In a letter to *The Pink Paper* (19 August 1994), Jack Parker reflected:

> The character was deeply attractive to boys, like me, growing up gay at a time when suitable role models were pretty thin on the ground. Doctor Who was an outsider who always won respect. He was eccentric and outlandish in appearance but seemed oblivious to the fact that people thought him strange.

However, from time to time, some intriguing gay characters or themes surfaced in popular television, including a 1964 episode, written by John Hopkins, for BBC1's groundbreaking police drama series *Z Cars*.

When the BBC launched *Z Cars* in 1962 it brought to television a gritty realism that was missing from the corporation's *Dixon of Dock Green*, a police drama series that had been running successfully since 1955. There was room for both of them, but *Z Cars* was much more hard-hitting than *Dixon*. It provided opportunities and, in some cases, a launching pad for a new generation of writers and directors who were breaking into television drama. They created something new and challenging for viewers. David Thomson observed that:

> In time, it became a personality show for [actor] Stratford Johns, maybe. But it was extraordinary in its time, because it stripped away the flim-flam gentility of *Dixon* and said, look, this is what our country is like. This is how wicked and disturbed some people are, and why it's so hard to be a cop.[2]

Z Cars, created by Troy Kennedy Martin, was set in the fictional Newtown, based on Liverpool. It was launched in the same year as other groundbreaking BBC programmes such as *That Was the Week That Was* and *Steptoe and Son*. For television historian Anthony Hayward, *Z Cars* 'captured the public's imagination and ran until 1978 and provided a launching pad for John Hopkins, as well as other great writers, including Allan Prior and Alan Plater'.[3]

Z Cars challenged viewers, and between September 1962 and December 1964, John Hopkins wrote fifty-seven episodes. One of his most watched episodes, 'Centre of Disturbance', was about an unexpected but brutal shooting incident in a shop full of people who are left traumatised. It was screened on 13 May 1964, less than a month before Hopkins included a homosexual blackmail victim in an episode called 'Somebody … Help' (tx 3 June 1964). Hopkins later explained that his objective with all the episodes that he wrote was to set an event, or the circumstances surrounding an event, in motion:

> But I always thought in terms of it developing as a controlled improvisation. I would have an event, I would know where it was going, but I would follow the characters as they reacted to and took part in the events that were happening around them. It is an uncomfortable situation because at no point … does anybody take a stand or give us answers to the questions being posed. They leave the questions to you, the audience, and that makes it difficult because maybe they're showing you things that you don't want to think about … there is a kind of writing which is very easy – and we see it all the time – where the writer presents all the questions and all the answers. But there is another kind of writing, which presents some of the questions and none of the answers. It is not my place, as a writer, to give you my answers.[4]

Regrettably, 'Somebody ... Help' no longer exists. No recording has survived. For reasons which have not come to light, the script for this episode has vanished from the BBC's collection of microfilmed scripts of the entire *Z Cars* output at their Written Archives Centre. However, some information about 'Somebody ... Help' has survived. A synopsis which was released to the press explained the plot:

> A middle-aged man Frank Wood tells the police that he is being blackmailed. He is upset, unsure of his actions, and tries to withdraw the complaint. Then he gathers up his courage and makes a charge. He confesses that he is a homosexual and is being blackmailed by his former lover.[5]

In *Radio Times* ('A Man Outside the Law', 28 May 1964), Hopkins summarised the predicament faced by Frank Wood:

> A man attempts to blackmail him. Wood has only to go to the police, tell them, and they will make every possible effort to catch the man. Given normal circumstances Wood's course of action is plain but Wood is a homosexual, a man outside the law, unable to go to the police without incriminating himself. If he reveals the attempt to blackmail him he will also reveal why he is being blackmailed. Then he faces trial, possible conviction, prison, probation anyway, the certainty of local scandal, even the end of his business career. The man who preys on anyone like Wood can count on his reluctance to go to the police, in nine cases out of ten, 'screw' money out of him until there is no money left and then pass on to the next victim. In nine cases out of ten he can practise safely, secretly, until the tenth man stands up and says 'No.'

Without the existence of the episode, or the script, it is impossible to assess how the gay characters were portrayed. Attempts to interview surviving actors in the cast failed to produce any information because the leading actors, including John Paul who played the blackmail victim Frank Wood, and Stratford Johns, who played Detective Chief Inspector Barlow, were deceased. However, it is clear from the content of Hopkins's *Radio Times* synopsis that he was sympathetic towards the plight of the homosexual who existed outside the law in Britain. John Paul played a succession of authority roles during the 1950s and 1960s, mainly on television. He was a quietly spoken, solidly built, quite handsome, thoughtful character actor who was probably best known for *Doomwatch* in the early 1970s, but at the time of *Z Cars* he was familiar to viewers for playing the lead in the series *Probation Officer* (1959–61). So, the representation of the gay man in 'Somebody ... Help' would have been sympathetic, substantial and 'straight-acting'.

Hopkins was one of the most socially aware writers working in television at that time. After graduating in English from St Catherine's College, Cambridge, he joined the BBC in 1957. One of his first assignments was assistant producer on the popular daytime radio soap *Mrs Dale's Diary*. He began contributing to *Z Cars* in 1962. For Hopkins: 'Everything for me, as a writer, began with *Z Cars*.'[6] His exploration of racism in *Z Cars*: 'A Place of Safety' (1964) is both challenging and disturbing. Hopkins described it as 'the best or the most completely realised episode of *Z Cars* that I wrote'.[7] Hopkins's *Fable*, screened in *The Wednesday Play* series in 1965, was a controversial drama exploring interracial relations in a Britain seen as an imaginary apartheid state in which the black-white relations were reversed. So, it isn't surprising that Hopkins focussed on a homosexual blackmail victim in 'Somebody ... Help'. He later explained what motivated him:

> When I was about sixteen I saw a news trailer in the cinema of the first images coming out of Belsen. When I saw those images I felt as if I had walked into the concentration camp. I felt destroyed by those images. I didn't understand it at the time. I was far too young. But it was the beginning of my concern for people who are victimised and violated, and that concern has gone on all through the rest of my life.[8]

Hopkins's most ambitious television drama, *Talking to a Stranger* (1966), was a quartet of plays in BBC2's *Theatre 625* series. Starring Judi Dench, it looked at the break-up of a family as seen in turn by the various members.

For 'Somebody ... Help', Hopkins could have been influenced by the British film drama *Victim*. When *Victim* was released in 1961 it had an enormous impact on the lives of gay men who, for the first time, saw credible representations of themselves and their situations in a commercial British film. One audience member recalled:

> I saw *Victim* in Blackpool which was then, and even more so now, the gay 'capital' of north-west England. I viewed the film alone, and did not

tell anyone that I was going to see this particular film. On entering the cinema everyone was given a close scrutiny by two men who I assumed were plain clothes police. During the film, several members of the public walked out of the cinema complaining. The response to the film from homosexuals at the time was predominantly sympathetic, although some older homosexuals objected to any exposure of the subject. I only discussed the film in homosexual bars and in the workplace, with fellow homosexuals. Discussion of the film in any other circumstances would have been unthinkable in 1961.[9]

Perhaps Hopkins had seen the film, and was aware of the 1957 publication of the Report of the Wolfenden Committee on Homosexual Offences and Prostitution. This suggested that 'homosexual practices' in private between consenting males over 21 should not be considered a criminal offence. At that time homosexuals were open to the most vicious forms of blackmail. *Victim* (in 1961) and *Z Cars*: 'Somebody ... Help' (in 1964) focussed on the vulnerability to blackmail of anyone suspected of being homosexual. Janet Green and John McCormick's script for *Victim* highlighted the fact that around 90 per cent of blackmail cases involved homosexuals. *Z Cars*: 'Somebody ... Help' may have influenced public opinion and led to the 1967 Sexual Offences Act which partially decriminalised homosexuality, but unlike *Victim* this episode has not been mentioned in any book about homosexual law reform. This is another example of how an innovative British television programme has been marginalised or made invisible in social and political histories of Britain.

David Brunt, who has researched the history of *Z Cars*, explained that 'Somebody ... Help' was one of only four episodes from that season's *Z Cars* that did not get a repeat screening. He added that, when the series was screened in Australia, 'Somebody ... Help' was given an 'AO' (Adults Only) rating that required 'a post-watershed time slot. As they were reluctant to screen the programme outside their regular 7.30–8.20 slot, this effectively meant a straightforward ban.'[10]

Hopkins was immensely proud of the contribution he made to *Z Cars*:

My hope in *Z Cars* was always that I could make the situation stay with you after it had finished, so that you would never be able to say 'Thank God' and then go away. It was a miracle how we commanded fifteen million viewers every week and how years later people are still watching it. We laid pain out there.[11]

Hopkins has always been held in high regard, and when he died in 1998 David Thomson commented in the *Independent on Sunday*:

> His [*Z Cars*] work had a novel philosophy that cops and crooks were tethered together in a shared bondage; that cops might break down in their work. Very little else in TV then allowed for such insoluble problems, or for such inner violence beneath the smooth flow of life. As such, Hopkins was a pioneer figure for a kind of urgent, confessional TV – personal but social and political, too – that was carried on by Ken Loach and Tony Garnett (Loach had directed on *Z Cars*), Mike Leigh, Stephen Frears, Alan Bennett, Alan Plater (a *Z Cars* writer), David Hare, David Leland, many others. And Alan Clarke.[12]

In May 2006, the National Film Theatre in London paid tribute to John Hopkins with a retrospective of his work. Screenings included two episodes of *Z Cars* and *Horror of Darkness* (see Chapter 10). His friend, Alan Plater, described him in *The Guardian* (1 May 2006) as 'A kind, gentle, intense and driven man' who took his work very seriously: 'We would talk long into the night about writing, but then he would go off at unpredictable tangents, enthusing one moment about the great Italian director Ermanno Olmi, the next about a group called the Honeycombs who had a number one hit in 1964'. But he was never forgotten. In 1989, BBC2 celebrated its 25th anniversary. The then controller telephoned Alan Bleasdale to say they planned to repeat *Boys from the Blackstuff* because it was the most important piece of drama ever seen on the channel. 'No, it wasn't,' Bleasdale replied. '*Talking to a Stranger* was.' In the event, the BBC repeated both, the Hopkins quartet preceded by a short introduction from Bleasdale, in which he confessed these were the plays that inspired him to come out of the closet with his typewriter.

Notes

1. Vicky Powell interview with Stephen Bourne, 'Soap Gets in Your Eyes', *Gay Times*, July 2001, pp. 21–2.
2. David Thomson, 'Made in Britain, and bleak as hell', *Independent on Sunday* (23 August 1998).
3. Anthony Hayward, 'Obituary: John Hopkins', *The Independent* (1 August 1998).

4. Jim Pines (ed.), *Black and White in Colour: Black People in British Television Since 1936* (British Film Institute, 1992), pp. 92–3.
5. Thanks to *Z Cars* expert David Brunt for providing this information.
6. 'One man let you meet these people ... his name is John Hopkins', *Radio Times* (4 September 1969), pp. 52–5.
7. Pines, p. 92.
8. *Ibid.*, p. 97.
9. Stephen Bourne, *Brief Encounters: Lesbians and Gays in British Cinema 1930–1971* (Cassell, 1996), pp. 242–3.
10. David Brunt, letter to Stephen Bourne (28 August 2003). Censor's report from the ABC TV Archive in Australia, 25 February 1965.
11. Pines, p. 94.
12. Thomson, *ibid.*

10

The Wednesday Play

The writer John Hopkins had consideration for people he believed were 'victimised and violated' (see Chapter 9). In the 1960s, he created one of the earliest original television dramas in which a homosexual character was one of the leads. It was called *Horror of Darkness*. Recorded on 2/3 March 1964, it was more than a year before viewers were made aware of its existence in various press reports. They were given a chance to see it on 10 March 1965 when BBC1 screened it in its flagship drama anthology series *The Wednesday Play*. According to Tise Vahimagi in *British Television: An Illustrated Guide* (1994), the series 'set out to stimulate its audience with seasons of dramas in which the writers had the opportunity both to produce original work and to exercise themselves in dramatising the original ideas of others'.[1]

The Wednesday Play was launched on 28 October 1964 after the BBC had appointed Sydney Newman as its Head of Television Drama (see Chapter 5). From 1964 to 1970, this highly acclaimed but controversial series became a byword for challenging, left-of-centre drama. The producer James MacTaggart was determined to assist Newman in his ambition to bring 'gutsy, spontaneous and contemporary' drama to BBC television. The results were spectacular. MacTaggart's year as producer saw the first four Dennis Potter plays, writer Nell Dunn's *Up the Junction*, which was directed by the *Z Cars* 'graduate' Ken Loach, and *Three Clear Sundays*, writer James O'Connor's remarkable exposé of death row, also directed by Loach.

According to James Green in the *Liverpool Echo and Evening Express* (3 February 1965), the BBC held back the transmission of *Horror of Darkness* because 'At the time it was recorded the BBC were under critical fire for presenting too many grim and kitchen-sink dramas. Having made *Horror of Darkness* they had second thoughts.' In the same article, Hopkins described his play as 'emotionally violent … A rather grim play about human relationships.'

In *Horror of Darkness* Nicol Williamson played Robin Fletcher, a sad, tortured soul. After a two-year absence from the life of his friend Peter Young (Alfred Lynch), he unexpectedly arrives at his London flat where he lives with his partner Cathy (Glenda Jackson). At first, Peter and Cathy embrace him. They welcome him into their home and agree to let him stay, but almost immediately Robin becomes a disruptive influence. Eager to take over Cathy's role, it becomes apparent that the attention-seeking Robin is in love with Peter, but his love is unrequited. After Peter rejects him, Robin commits suicide. Michael Beale in the *Newcastle Evening Chronicle* (11 March 1965) praised Hopkins for being 'one of our best writers for television' and informed his readers that he gave 'an original interpretation of the eternal triangle in which a happy-go-lucky companionship in a London flat was suddenly blasted into tragedy by the realisation of the truth of the emotions of three young people … the intelligent use of the camera often gave the scenes a stark and disturbing reality.' However, as Clifford Davis commented in the *Daily Mirror* (11 March 1965), it was 'crammed with hidden tensions, involved meanings, and the unwholesome frustration that unnatural sex can presumably bring'.

In 1965, Hopkins put the gay man at the centre of a television drama. In an emotionally charged scene, brilliantly written and acted, Robin declares his love for Peter. It could be the first open expression of the love of one man for another on British television. It is as powerful as Dirk Bogarde's admission of sexual desire for another man when he admits 'I wanted him!' to his wife in the film *Victim* (1961). Also outstanding is the scene towards the end of the play when Robin's friend and possibly ex-lover, Philip Moss (Wallas Eaton), visits Peter and Cathy. Wallas Eaton is superb as a man who is trying to control his emotions. Clearly Philip loved Robin and, devastated by the loss of his friend, in desperation he asks the couple to explain what had happened to him because 'I didn't know his parents. Obviously,' he explains. In one of the play's few tender moments, Philip wipes a tear from his cheek when Peter tells him how Robin killed himself. However, not everyone was convinced by the tragic suicide of Robin. According to Keith Howes in *Broadcasting It* (1993):

The style was edgy, dialogue terse, the subject complex and compelling, with Nicol Williamson gripping as the unwanted, unlovable guest. Ground-breaking for the BBC, but very much following the path of least resistance: killing off the queer rather than seeing him resolve the situation and realise that the colourless Peter has nothing to offer him.[2]

Television critics praised it, including Gerald Larner who commented in *The Guardian* (11 March 1965) that 'it was a most powerful and impressive play'. Stewart Lane in the *Daily Worker* (13 March 1965) was impressed with Nicol Williamson's portrayal of Robin: 'A superbly restrained and balanced piece of work.' In *The Observer* (14 March 1965), Philip Purser praised Hopkins as a writer who has 'sought hard to overcome the traditional limitations of TV drama … He's the man who takes the showy techniques invented (or re-invented) by other hands and quietly puts them to useful work.'

Mixed reactions were recorded in BBC1's Duty Office Log for 10 March 1965. Viewers' feelings about the play on the evening of the transmission ranged from the confused – 'There are six of us watching this play. What is it all about? Perhaps you will ring back and tell me' – to the outraged – 'Disgusting stuff. Never in my life have I thought that the BBC would sink so low.' Finally, 'What has come over the BBC? You are always showing us plays about perverts. First we have lesbians thrown under our noses – now this.' Other reactions were favourable and enthusiastic: 'First class. Excellent'; 'Brilliant. The tense relationship between the players was brought out marvellously … Terrific'; 'One of the best plays I have seen on TV. Excellently acted, marvellously written and beautifully done in every way.' But *The Wednesday Play* series had its critics, and one of the most vocal was the campaigning housewife Mary Whitehouse.

In 1964, Mary Whitehouse helped launch the Clean Up Television campaign which soon afterwards became known as the National Viewers' and Listeners' Association (NVALA). In her 1967 book *Cleaning Up TV*, she made the following attack on *Horror of Darkness*:

> It is surely more than coincidence that plays dealing with homosexuality and abortion were shown on the BBC at the time when these issues were to be debated in the House of Commons and the Press. Take, for instance, *Horror of Darkness*, a play based on homosexual love in which the central character commits suicide. This was a most powerful play, it is true, but what was the likely effect on the thousands of homosexuals

who must have seen it? What does it do for them to present their problem as totally unanswerable and to leave them with the idea that suicide
is the only way out? Was it at least part of the idea behind this play to
move people to compassion so that they hastened to change the law and
legalise sodomy? We need to understand the human tragedy of situations
like these. But when the emphasis is on one aspect only it becomes sus-
pect. There are thousands of men with homosexual tendencies who have
found creative outlet for their sexual energies and understand what self-
discipline and faith can do for them. Why should these not become the
theme of a Wednesday play?[3]

Mary Whitehouse's attack on *The Wednesday Play* and *Horror of Darkness*
in particular did not deter BBC1 from showcasing several other plays in the
series which included gay or sexually ambiguous themes or characters. For
example, when Barry Foster played the title role in *The Interior Decorator*
(tx 14 April 1965), written by Jack Russell, his character expressed
menacing sexual ambiguity as he weaved his spell over his wealthy (female)
client. As Marjorie Norris commented in *The Stage* (22 April 1965):
'I enjoyed the concept of a *chi-chi* interior decorator succumbing at last to
a desire to vent his underlying contempt of wealthy and tasteless patrons
by persuading the silly woman to accept his monstrous vulgarities as *avant
garde*.' In *The Connoisseur* (tx 4 May 1966), written by Hugo Charteris,
Derek Francis played Stoupe, a cynical public school housemaster who is
a connoisseur of antiques and young men. To keep one of his favourite
pupils happy (Viscount Ballantyne, played by Ian Ogilvy), Stoupe turns a
blind eye to some rather sinister fun and games in the dorm. It is a younger
pupil (Christopher, played by Richard O'Sullivan), who 'spills the beans' by
writing an article for a tabloid newspaper. The article exposes Ballantyne,
who has been running a brothel in the school and making sexual advances
towards another pupil. It was *The Connoiseur* that prompted Milton
Shulman to acknowledge the work of *The Wednesday Play* team in his
'Inside TV' column in the *Evening Standard* (17 May 1966):

The single play is the most maligned, and conversely the most important
aspect of TV drama. It is the cradle for new ideas, the nursery for fresh
playwrights and the laboratory for TV of the future ... many of these
plays are groping in new directions, trying to find original techniques
and unfamiliar themes, they irritate the cosy and the orthodox and

offend those pressure groups that insist that morality exists only in the *status quo* ... *The Connoisseur* took a devastating look at the master-and-pupil relationship in public schools. Not only did it deal intelligently with the question of homosexuality in such a cloistered environment, but it caught with pointed relevance the inherent snobbery and ambitious motives that influenced the actions of both teachers and boys.

James Broom Lynne adapted *Wanted: Single Gentleman* ... (tx 18 October 1967) from his 1963 stage play *The Trigon*. The critic who reviewed the stage play in *Theatre World* (July 1964) described the lead characters, Arthur and Basil (two bachelors in their 30s), as 'inexplicably bound together emotionally'. According to Alan Sinfield: 'There is no indication of sexual passion as such between Arthur and Basil, but there are gross hints.'[4] *Radio Times* (12 October 1967) described its leading characters in the television version as sharing a 'tumultuous existence in which Basil (Alan Rowe), caught up in the fantasies of war and sex, is always threatening violence. Fat, good-natured Arthur (John Stratton) meanwhile dreams of Boy Scout days.' Keith Howes commented in *Broadcasting It* (1993), 'No one mentions the word "queer", but it is apt for every aspect of the production.'[5]

On 1 October 1969, Peter Terson's *The Last Train Through the Harecastle Tunnel* opened the final season of *The Wednesday Play*. This enjoyable play took the form of a 'Pilgrim's Progress' in which Fowler (Richard O'Callaghan), a naïve but wise young trainspotter, takes the historic trip on the last train through Harecastle Tunnel. On his journey he encounters a variety of characters, including Adam Coulson (Joe Gladwin), the landlord of a boarding house who once worked on the railways, and his gay son Jackie (Griffith Davis), who hates the railways. Adam persuades Jackie to accompany Fowler on the final trip through the tunnel, but Jackie has other plans.

On the station platform, Jackie explains to young Fowler that he has not lived up to his father's expectations. He describes his father as someone who is only interested in steam engines and brasses: 'He was only happy when he was driving the gentry in his red choo-choo.' Adam is disappointed with his son's lack of interest in trains. 'I can remember,' Jackie tells Fowler, 'when I was about five he found I liked playing with dolls. He compromised by dressing them up in railway uniforms.' However, just before the last train arrives at the station, Jackie unceremoniously dumps

Fowler. First he enters the gentlemen's public lavatory, to 'pay a call', then reappears on the arm of a tall, handsome, blond stud. 'Excuse me,' he says to Fowler, 'I've met a friend.' In the script of the play, held in the BBC's Written Archives Centre, there is a pencilled note in the margin: 'Jackie and Queer move out of shot behind Fowler. He watches them then looks back to train.' This brief sequence is significant, for it is one of the first in a British television drama to acknowledge a same-sex encounter in a public place, known in the gay world as 'cottaging'.

Some viewers objected to the presence of Jackie. The Audience Research Report (25 November 1969) revealed that the main objection of a considerable group concerned the:

> Oddity and general 'unsavouriness' of some of the train-spotter's railway companions, comment running on the lines of 'Could we have a few plays with normal subjects and people – everyone is sick to death of all this kinky stuff'; 'in the end it was, as so often, a series of situations contrived so as to include homosexuality.'

Notes

1. Tise Vahimagi, *British Television: An Illustrated Guide* (Oxford University Press, 1994), p. 133.
2. Keith Howes, *Broadcasting It: An Encyclopaedia of Homosexuality on Film, Radio and TV in the UK 1923–1993* (Cassell, 1993), p. 362.
3. Mary Whitehouse, *Cleaning-Up TV: From Protest to Participation* (Blandford Press, 1967), p. 167.
4. Alan Sinfield, *Out on Stage: Lesbian and Gay Theatre in the Twentieth Century* (Yale University Press, 1999), p. 182.
5. Howes, p. 900.

11

The *Wednesday Play* That Got Away

The Wednesday Play continued to challenge viewers until it ended in 1970, but not all of them have survived in the archives. One of the many losses is *Spoiled* (tx 28 August 1968), in which the writer Simon Gray and director Waris Hussein tackled a difficult subject in true *Wednesday Play* spirit. After a schoolmaster has a brief encounter with one of his male pupils, he completely severs their relationship. According to the television critic for the *Birmingham Daily Post* (31 August 1968), the result was 'an absorbing play, frightening, not because of its subject, but because of the way the characters reacted to what happened'. The same critic added that the pupil was 'not all innocence. He had a sly look in his beautiful eyes.' Even Mary Whitehouse, a vocal opponent of the 'permissive society', approved. Following his review in *The Guardian* (21 March 1968), in which Stanley Reynolds warned readers that the homosexuality in the play would raise her hackles, Mrs Whitehouse responded in a letter to *The Guardian* (27 March 1968): 'Contrary to his [Stanley Reynolds] expectations I, too, found *Spoiled* a first-class play … this production had a quality of genuine "reality" which was both moving and challenging.' However, she added that homosexuality in *Spoiled* 'without wallowing in it, or normalising it, or justifying it … was shown as the tragedy it is.'

In *Spoiled*, the pupil, Donald, played by Simon Ward, is a 19-year-old school-leaver who falls in love with Howarth (Michael Craig), his (married) tutor, while retaking a mathematics O-level exam. Donald is an inhibited, neurotic young man, dominated by his possessive, widowed mother. This 'fatal attraction' leads to a tense and complicated relationship, including a sexual encounter which is discovered by the tutor's (pregnant) wife.

Howarth is stricken with guilt over what he has done and cannot face either Donald or his wife. Rejected, Donald fails to sit his exam and haunts Howarth's home. It is Howarth's wife who finally turns Donald away and viewers are left with the impression that Donald is now 'spoiled' and will drift into the more established life of homosexuals, which has been seen in the play in the department store in which he works as a sales assistant.

One viewer's positive reaction was expressed in a letter published in the *Daily Mirror* (31 August 1968): 'What a profoundly sensitive play. No doubt there will be a lot of unfavourable reaction to it, but to me it was a striking production, intensely emotional and immaculately acted.' Reviews were also favourable, with most critics praising its honesty and successful handling of the 'homosexual' theme. In *The Observer* (1 September 1968), George Melly described the play as 'full of insight and very moving indeed. All the relationships were convincing and the effect of the affair on the man's pregnant wife was remarkably sensitive and yet entirely without sentimentality. Simon Ward managed to suggest how neurosis and unhappiness can carry a powerful erotic charge.'

However, the Audience Research Report (8 October 1968), held at the BBC's Written Archives Centre, revealed that:

> A quarter of the sample [of the audience] thought well of this play, but it mostly had a very cool reception arising from distaste for its theme and from the feeling that this had not been treated very effectively … On the debit side, a common reaction was one of disgust at the central situation, many viewers making it clear that they saw no point in offering, for dramatic entertainment, this 'sordid' story of a nineteen-year-old boy and his relationship with the schoolmaster (a married man, with homosexual tendencies) who is giving him spare-time tuition … In opposition, the minority who thought this a play of quality praised it as a very genuine (and successful) attempt to enter into and portray the feelings of a group of people caught up in a dismal problem.

It is very rare to find examples of the thoughts and feelings of gay viewers at this time. At the BBC Written Archives Centre, a letter to Graeme McDonald, the producer of *Spoiled*, dated 29 August 1968, expressed how a gay viewer felt about the play. Perhaps with the change in the law in 1967, some gay men felt more able to express themselves about such representations. The following is an extract from the letter:

May I thank you and congratulate you for putting on a play about homo-sexuality, a subject which up till now has been badly neglected, and I hope there will be many more forthcoming. As for this play, 'Spoiled', I think it was well produced and directed, and beautifully acted. Thank you.

Spoiled was recorded, because it was repeated on BBC1 on 9 July 1969, but no copy has survived. In order to assess its merits, the last word will go to Mary Malone, the television critic of the *Daily Mirror* (29 August 1968). She recognised the importance of this groundbreaking *Wednesday Play*:

> *Spoiled* was totally absorbing. The problem – latent homosexuality between a teacher and his pupil – was not shirked. There was no hedg-ing. It was stated in looks, glances, and nuances, from the wife's ghastly awakening of her husband's revulsion of her pregnant body to the moment when the two clasped each other in their arms. This was so sen-sitive and honest a play by Simon Gray that there was no sense of shock, only intense sympathy for all four main characters – husband, wife, boy and doting mother – caught in the situation. There were stunning per-formances … I can't remember a television play that dealt so truly and touchingly with the complexities of man's sexual conflicts.

It didn't take long for *Spoiled* to become a victim of the BBC's policy in the 1960s and 1970s to wipe video recordings of their programmes, partly to record over them, partly to save space. *Spoiled* survived long enough to be repeated, and then it vanished forever. In 1975, when Simon Gray discovered that the BBC had wiped the videotapes of almost *all* his tele-vision plays, he expressed his anger in the *Evening Standard* (23 December 1975), adding that some plays by other playwrights had also been lost, including David Mercer 'whose early TV plays were a revolution in tele-vision drama. It is scandalous,' said Gray. He continued: 'I believe that the reason is a matter of storage, but if they are going to be destroyed anyway, why not give them away or sell them to the playwright or director? I'm appalled this should have happened, but I am even more appalled that I was not told.' The BBC responded: 'There is a comprehensive archive policy about which tapes are to be preserved and which are to be wiped. A careful, artistic judgement would be made by someone qualified to do so – namely the head of television drama.' In *The Television Heritage* (1989), Steve Bryant, Television Officer for the British Film Institute, explained that 'The destruction of television programmes by the organisations which produced them was due to a combination of technological, cultural and operational influences.'[1]

In 1976, the controversy flared up again when the National Film Theatre in London presented a season entitled *British Television Drama, 1959–1973*. *New Society* (21 October 1976) reported that one name conspicuous by its absence was Simon Gray. Not one of the eight TV plays Gray had written before 1973 had been included, and *New Society* suggested that they had all been destroyed. Once again, Gray protested publicly. Perhaps his protests were listened to, because in the 1980s the National Film and Television Archive (NFTVA) 'achieved the funding and capacity to systematise its acquisition of television programmes, and what was a small but steady flow became a river … The British Film Institute, no less than the NFTVA, has fully embraced television in its cultural remit.'[2]

The NFTVA, which was part of the British Film Institute, had been known as the National Film Archive (NFA) until television was added in the 1980s. The NFA had, in fact, appointed its first Television Officer as far back as 1959 and concluded a deposit agreement with the BBC in 1960. Agreements were also made with various ITV companies. However, as Steve Bryant explained, there was 'a desperate shortage of funds, combined with a reluctance to accept materials on videotape [which] meant that, throughout the 60s, the rate of acquisition was very low.'[3] Consequently, the opportunity to save many programmes, including Simon Gray's *Spoiled* and his other early television plays, was lost.

Notes

1. Steve Bryant, *The Television Heritage* (British Film Institute, 1989), p. 2.
2. Clyde Jeavons, Curator, National Film and Television Archive in Simon Baker and Olwen Terris (eds.), *A for Andromeda to Zoo Time: The TV Holdings of the National Film and Television Archive 1936–1979* (British Film Institute, 1994), p. ix.
3. Bryant, p. 19.

12

Meanwhile, on the 'Other Side' (ITV)

In 1965, Ken Irwin, writing for the *Daily Mirror*, expressed his concern about a 'kinky' trend hitting British television in a big way, on all three channels. He was shocked by an episode of the ITV drama series *Public Eye* called 'You Have to Draw the Line Somewhere' (tx 24 April 1965) which starred Alfred Burke as the no-nonsense private eye Frank Marker. When he tries to track down a husband's girlfriend, Marker finds the husband is having an affair with a *man*, a shocked Irwin informed his readers. Regrettably the episode hasn't survived in the archives, thus making it impossible to view and assess. Irwin was also upset by the popular ITV series *The Avengers*, with its 'kinky boots and off-beat plots', and he wasn't impressed with BBC1's *Horror of Darkness*, with a gay man at the centre of the drama (see Chapter 10). 'Plays such as these,' he wrote, 'would never be allowed on television in America.' 'Kinky' British television was clearly upsetting Mr Irwin but this was, after all, the 'Swinging Sixties' and television was simply responding to it.[1]

After BBC2 was launched in 1964, it complemented BBC1's ground-breaking and popular *Wednesday Play* series by introducing several anthology drama series of its own. These included *Theatre 625* and *Thirty-Minute Theatre*. In response to this, various ITV companies produced similar cutting-edge drama anthologies. Associated Rediffusion's *Half-Hour Story*, launched in 1967, was one of the best. It provided the producer (and former story editor) Stella Richman with a thirty-minute series format to encourage well-known writers as well as new talent. Cecil P. Taylor contributed *Friends* (tx 6 September 1967), directed by Michael Lindsay-Hogg. Set entirely inside a hotel bedroom in the North of England, the plot centred on a gay couple, middle-aged Cyril (George Cole) and Tom, his young American Air Force lieutenant lover (Stuart Cooper), recently returned from Vietnam. Homophobia surfaces when the middle-aged hotel employee Frank (Bernard Lee) attempts to throw them out of the hotel as 'unsuitable'. The *TV Times* asked: 'But are Cyril and Tom what Frank thinks they are? And what right has Frank – or we, the viewers – to judge them? *Friends* subtly shows how evil, like beauty, is in the eye of the beholder.'[2]

Friends was transmitted shortly after the Sexual Offences Act partially legalised homosexual acts between consenting adults over the age of 21 in private. The Act became law in July 1967. However, before *Friends* was shown, an internal memo was sent from the 'Head of Programme Clearance' to the 'Head of Scripted Series' requesting that there should be a warning given to viewers of the 'homosexual theme' so that the play could be avoided. 'The playing must be very discreet,' it said, 'as the men's situation is so clearly stated, there should be no touches of business in the production to emphasise it since any such would inevitably be regarded as tasteless.'[3] Sylvia Clayton commented in the *Daily Telegraph* (7 September 1967):

> Now that homosexuality is openly discussed in *Mrs Dale's Diary*, it comes as no surprise to find a homosexual love affair as the subject of *Friends*. This brief, nerve-jangling playlet, set in a hotel bedroom, focused on the relationship between a middle-aged British Leftist protester and a blond effeminate American Air Force lieutenant, recently returned with horror from Vietnam. The play raised a nice legal point. Would a manager be within his legal rights in asking two adult guests to leave on suspicion of homosexual behaviour within the privacy of their hotel room?

Stanley Reynolds in *The Guardian* (7 September 1967) described *Friends* as 'a neat piece of writing as you could find anywhere'; however, Max Wilkinson in the *Newcastle Journal* (7 September 1967) was left unimpressed. He felt that the play 'seemed to be making a smutty joke against the audience'. He added, 'I didn't quite see the point of it, but felt I was being obscurely got at.' Wilkinson described *Friends* as 'a sort of marital bicker between two pansies spending the night together. The story made its impact by pretending to treat homosexual intimacies as an everyday subject of peak viewing TV.'

Cecil P. Taylor's stage version of *Friends*, retitled *Lies About Vietnam*, was produced at the Traverse Theatre, Edinburgh in 1969. According to Alan Sinfield: 'Cyril's determination to engage [Frank] Graham on both gayness and Vietnam foreshadows the political impetus of early-1970s lesbian and gay campaigning. Where gay rights were not acknowledged, leftist audiences and performers began to demand them – including in fringe work.'[4]

In 1968, Associated Rediffusion, in their *Playhouse* series, produced *Entertaining Mr Sloane* (tx 15 July). This was Joe Orton's wild, savage and macabre comedy of manners. Orton was a bold, brave playwright who had died in 1967 at the hands of his lover and mentor, Kenneth Halliwell. First presented on stage in 1964, it concerned a middle-aged brother and sister, Ed and Kath, competing for the sexual favours of their young lodger, a strange, beautiful, but dangerous young man called Mr Sloane. By the end of the drama he has successfully destroyed the relationship between the two people. Rediffusion, concerned about screening the play during the usual *Playhouse* slot of 8.30–9.30 p.m., put it back to 10.30–12.00 midnight.

Television critics were impressed. In the *Daily Express* (16 July 1968), Martin Jackson described the play as a macabre epitaph to Joe Orton's 'edgy, uncomfortable genius'. Others praised the performances, including Stanley Reynolds in *The Guardian* (17 July 1968):

> We had brilliant performances from Sheila Hancock, looking just like a middle-aged and rattled Sandie Shaw as the over-sexed Kath; from Clive Francis as the amoral bisexual Sloane; and from Edward Woodward as Ed, the sportsman homosexual who struggled with his sister Kath for possession of the handsome monster Sloane. It was good of Rediffusion to bring us this much talked about stage play no matter at what hour.

Some viewers liked it too. Mrs V. Miles of Margate in Kent had a short but enthusiastic letter published in the *Daily Mirror* (20 July 1968): 'Superb. That is the only word to describe the play *Entertaining Mr Sloane* (ITV, Monday). I wish it could be repeated.'

In *The Observer* (21 July 1968), television critic George Melly asked if the BBC was 'turning yellow' because the commercial channels had taken over producing worthwhile programmes:

> The commercial channels are responsible for a growing number of first-rate serious documentaries and, perhaps more significantly, the production

of plays which, in the past, they would have hesitated to mount. The BBC on the other hand would appear to be entering a cautious and unadventurous phase, especially in the drama department. I should make it clear that this is still only an impression, but it is a strong one. For example, last week, Joe Orton's *Entertaining Mr Sloane* was a *Rediffusion* production. This would have been almost inconceivable until recently, whereas now it's becoming increasingly difficult to imagine it going out under Auntie's aegis.

In *Broadcasting It* (1993), Keith Howes found the television version of *Entertaining Mr Sloane* superior to the better-known film version, made in 1970, starring Beryl Reid:

> Because it sticks to the play and has a less absurd Kath in Sheila Hancock. The Sloane of Clive Francis is perhaps more obviously devious than Peter McEnery's, but Edward Woodward is another blessing as (a younger, fairly attractive) Ed. A landmark play that, for once, was not totally compromised and wrecked on small or large screens.[5]

Entertaining Mr Sloane had been planned for television when Orton was still alive. In his diary, Orton recorded in his entry for 5 February 1967 that the producer, Peter Willes, had informed him that Joan Elman, Associated Rediffusion's 'legal woman', didn't like *Entertaining Mr Sloane*:

> 'Well,' Peter said, 'I've never seen anything like it. She came up to me and flung the book on my desk. 'I think this is a perfectly disgusting play,' she said. 'Joan,' I said, 'I'm not interested in your views on the play. What is the legal position?' 'Disgusting,' she said. 'Horrible.' And she went on and on. 'Perfectly horrible and filthy. I don't know why we want to consider such a play.' So I told her she'd better go and see Cyril [Bennett, Programme Controller, Associated Rediffusion]. So Joan Elman went to him and he said, 'What's the legal position with regard to this play?' 'What a vile play it is,' Joan had said, 'I was shocked and disgusted by it.' Anyway he told her to fuck off and he's going ahead with doing the play. Most unwisely in my opinion. But, there you are. Don't say people aren't nice to you.[6]

Notes

1. Ken Irwin, 'In Search of the Anything-goes Plays', *Daily Mirror*, 24 April 1965.
2. Dave Hanington, 'Playbill', *TV Times*, 2–8 September 1967.

3. Rediffusion Television Internal Memo (30 June 1967) reprinted in *Gay Plays Volume Two*, Michael Wilcox (ed.) (Methuen, 1985), p. 55.
4. Alan Sinfield, *Out on Stage: Lesbian and Gay Theatre in the Twentieth Century* (Yale University Press, 1999), p. 182.
5. Keith Howes, *Broadcasting It: An Encyclopaedia of Homosexuality on Film, Radio and TV in the UK 1923–1993* (Cassell, 1993), pp. 226–7.
6. John Lahr (ed.), *The Orton Diaries* (Methuen, 1986), pp. 78–9.

13

Soap Gets in Your Eyes

Graham Haberfield joined the cast of *Coronation Street* in 1962 as the young apprentice Jerry Booth. He joined forces with the rough builder Len Fairclough and together they made a success of Len's building firm. Jerry's character contrasted with the bullish, hot-tempered Len. He was a kind soul, honest but extremely shy and nervous. A marriage in 1963 to Myra Dickinson ended the following year, following the tragic death of their baby daughter. Softly spoken and gentle, Jerry was sometimes teased, but he did retaliate with his fists when he was pushed too far. In January 1966, Elsie Tanner's son Dennis secretly photographed Jerry when he was half-naked. When the Street's spinster Emily Nugent found the pictures, Dennis was forced to apologise to an embarrassed Jerry. In 1968, in an attempt to keep up with the 'Swinging Sixties' and boost the popularity of the series, executive producer Richard Everitt decided to introduce more social issues into the storylines. Together with Stan Barstow, the writing team's consultant, various controversial stories were planned, including Jerry declaring his homosexuality. The idea was quickly dropped, along with Miss Nugent's pregnancy, Lucille Hewitt's addiction to drugs and plans for the programme's first black family.[1] Almost a decade would pass before a gay character *did* appear in the series, but if viewers had blinked they would have missed the wrist-flapping, swishy hotel waiter who fussed around Stan and Hilda Ogden. That was in 1977. Another *twenty-six* years passed before *Coronation Street* introduced its first regular gay character, Todd Grimshaw (Bruno Langley), in 2003. It had lagged behind other popular soaps for years. As far back as the 1980s, other TV soaps had introduced regular gay characters including Colin Russell in BBC1's

EastEnders (see Chapter 28) and Gordon Collins in Channel 4's *Brookside* (see Chapter 30).

In the 1980s, Colin and Gordon were the first *openly* gay characters in British television's soapland, but it is worth mentioning that there had been a breakthrough as early as 1967 on BBC radio in the Light Programme's daily serial *The Dales*. Weekly synopses of the soap's storyline published in the *Radio Times* revealed that Mrs Dale's sister Sally was married to a homosexual. This was Richard Fulton, the author and Wildean dandy who had a manservant called Fickling and was prone to throwing tantrums. Fulton had been a regular character in the series since 1950, portrayed by Norman Chidgey (1950–58) and David March (1958–67). Eight years after his first appearance in the series, he was described by Mrs Dale in *Mrs Dale: Ten Years in the Life of a Doctor's Family* (1958) as 'intelligent and witty, simple and kind'.[2] Fulton married Mrs Dale's sister Sally on 2 May 1958 but their marriage fell apart when Fulton came out of the closet. The homosexual plot was launched just after the 1967 Sexual Offences Act, and the first indication that all was not well with Sally was published in the *Radio Times* on Monday, 7 August 1967: 'Mrs Dale has learnt that Sally is separated from Richard.' On Monday, 11 September, the *Radio Times* revealed: 'Sally has told Dr Dale that the reason she and Richard have parted is because Richard is homosexual.' The writers spun out the theme for three months until Fulton suddenly left the cosy world of the Dale family and went to live in Paris to explore his homosexuality. The BBC axed the series in 1969. When he died in 1999, David March's obituarist, John Tydeman, revealed that the actor secretly delighted in the fuss caused by his character's sexuality. March's own private life was shared with his partner, Derek Lewis, for nearly forty years.[3]

Throughout the 1970s, the popular ITV soap *Crossroads*, set in the Midlands, had not one but two prissy chefs employed by Meg Richardson in the kitchen of her Crossroads Motel. They were the pompous Mr Booth (David Lawton) and the temperamental Scottish fusspot Shughie McFee (Angus Lennie). The two characters endeared themselves to fans of the programme, and today they are still fondly remembered on social media pages which are dedicated to the series, even though their characters had vanished by the 1980s. The characters of Mr Booth and Shughie McFee may not have been *explicitly* gay, but at times they came very close. Mr Booth was a dapper gentleman, invariably attired in a bow tie. He dabbled in ESP (Extra Sensory Perception) and also fancied himself as an amateur

Sherlock Holmes. In *The Crossroads Story* (2001), Geoff Tibballs described Shughie as 'a bit of a drama queen, he threw many a tantrum over a non-rising souffle. He was also a mummy's boy. Wee Shughie continued to bully beef and harangue meringues until 1981 when, after frequently disappearing for months at a time, he finally vanished for good.'[4]

Notes

1. Daran Little, *40 Years of Coronation Street* (Granada, 2000), p. 45.
2. Jonquil Antony and Robert Turley, *Mrs Dale: Ten Years in the Life of a Doctor's Family* (World's Work, 1958), p. 75.
3. John Tydeman, 'Obituary: David March', *The Independent* (3 September 1999).
4. Geoff Tibballs, *The Crossroads Story* (Carlton, 2001), p. 73.

Part 3

1970s

14

A Handful of Ridiculed Gesticulations

At the end of the 1960s and into the 1970s, Clarence was a popular figure in British television comedy. He was an outrageous queen who referred to everyone as 'Honky Tonk'. He was a stereotype but he was also a winner and *never* the butt of other people's humour. For many years he was brilliantly played by Dick Emery in his BBC1 comedy sketch show *The Dick Emery Show*. For some, Clarence was an offensive caricature, but for others he was a flamboyant gay man who didn't hide his attraction to other men. He was a wonderful character, so happy and contented with life, and nothing phased him. In one classic sketch he is persuaded to join the army. In reality, this was a time when homosexuals were banned from joining the armed forces. When the recruitment officer informs Clarence he will be joining the Queen's regiment, he believes it is full of gay men! With a beaming smile lighting up his cheeky face, he can't wait to sign up. Dick Emery was a pure comic genius and greatly loved by the British public. It is hardly surprising that Clarence is the main character seen on the cover of a DVD reissue of Dick Emery's shows.

Also greatly loved were the characters in *Dad's Army*, one of the most successful sitcoms ever seen on British television. It was launched on BBC1 on 31 July 1968 and ran for nine series until 1977. It is still being repeated. Set in the Second World War, it focussed on the adventures of a disparate group of men, some of them too old for active service. They enrol as Local Defence Volunteers, the 'home guard', also known as 'Dad's Army'. Private Godfrey (Arnold Ridley) was the oldest of the troupe. Ridley was 72 when he started playing Godfrey and 81 at the finish, but why is *Dad's Army* included in a book about playing gay in the golden years of British television? Private Godfrey is a gentle, well-mannered but frail character. Single, he lives with his two sisters in a cottage and is prone to dozing off. For the platoon he makes tea, mends clothes and carries a Red Cross box for emergencies. In an early episode, 'Branded' (tx 20 November 1969), his position in the home guard is undermined when he reveals that he was a conscientious objector (CO) during the First World War. Private Godfrey is immediately ostracised by some of his comrades. Captain Mainwaring (Arthur Lowe) refers to him as a 'damn conchie'. Others in the platoon say he is abnormal and a coward. Frazer (John Laurie) describes him as 'as soft as a cream puff', adding, 'There's an awful queer smell around here.' The Cockney spiv Walker (James Beck) is the only one who defends him, calling him a 'nice old man'. In an emotionally charged scene, when Godfrey makes tea for the platoon and they turn their backs on him, he resigns and leaves in tears. Later, Godfrey saves Mainwaring's life and the platoon find out that in the First World War he had volunteered for the medical corps and received the Military Medal for bravery. All is forgiven and the entire platoon visit Godfrey in his cottage and Mainwaring thanks him for saving his life. This is a magical, beautifully realised episode which touches on the *possibility* of Godfrey being a homosexual but he faces rejection for being a CO in the First World War. Unsurprisingly, 'Branded' has been described by Jimmy Perry, who co-authored the script with David Croft, as his favourite episode.

The 1970s was a decade in which many gay men discovered their identity and gained new confidence. Some found this with political activism and by joining organisations like the Campaign for Homosexual Equality and the Gay Liberation Front. However, positive images of gay men on British television in the early 1970s were rare (see Chapter 15). The dominant images of gay men were comic stereotypes, but sometimes these could be fun to watch. For example, the predatory antiques dealer in *Steptoe and Son*.

After a five-year absence, BBC1's popular sitcom *Steptoe and Son* returned to the screens in 1970, and in the third episode of the new series, 'Any Old Iron?' (BBC1, tx 2 March 1970), innocent Harold is led astray by Timothy Stanhope (Richard Hurndall), an antiques dealer. When Stanhope enters the Steptoes' rag-and-bone yard, Harold seizes an opportunity to make friends with a cultured gentleman who appreciates the finer things in life. Harold is too naive to understand that Stanhope is also a predatory gay and wants to befriend the younger man for more than erudite conversation. Harold's father Albert knows what Stanhope is *really* after and informs his son that the antique dealer is a 'poof'. Harold ignores him, but Albert warns his son, 'He's as bent as a boomerang!' and will want more from Harold than just chit-chat about antiques. Harold accepts Stanhope's invitation to come to his home for dinner, but they are interrupted by Stanhope's partner, a policeman, who has just come off duty. 'Hello,' says Stanhope. '*You're* home early.' When the penny drops, Harold panics and runs off into the night. This is a gem of an episode by writers Ray Galton and Alan Simpson. It occasionally lapses into crude farce, and Harry H. Corbett's performance as Harold goes way over the top, but mostly it is very funny, especially Richard Hurndall's endearing performance as the flirtatious old queen who is smitten by the younger, muscular Harold. Galton and Simpson (and the BBC) are to be commended for portraying a gay police officer, the first time this ever happened in British television. Also funny is a later episode, 'And So to Bed' (BBC1, tx 11 September 1974), in which Harold decides to buy a new bed from the Bayswater Bedorama. The salesman (Angus Mackay) is effeminate, pompous and snooty. When Harold enters the shop, with Albert in tow, the salesman informs them that the betting shop is next door. He changes his mind about the scruffy customers when he sees the colour of their money. The salesman asks Harold if his bedroom is excessively masculine. Harold replies, 'Yes, and so am I' as he removes the salesman's hand from his arm.

Three years later, a typical gay caricature of the time surfaced in an episode of another popular sitcom *Some Mothers Do 'Ave 'Em* ('Have a Break, Take a Husband', BBC1 tx 8 March 1973). The accident-prone wimp Frank Spencer (Michael Crawford) takes his long-suffering wife Betty (Michele Dotrice) to a seaside hotel for their second honeymoon, but Frank finds himself pestered by Kenny (Cyril Shaps), a gossipy hotel guest and a whining sissy who reads *Psychic News* in bed. Kenny makes it obvious that he fancies Frank, but Frank is not impressed and takes care to avoid him.

There was no avoiding Mr Humphries and his catchphrase 'I'm free!' when BBC1's sitcom *Are You Being Served?* was launched on 21 March 1973. Writers Jeremy Lloyd and David Croft created one of the BBC's most popular comedy series, and one of the channel's most criticised gay characters. Set in Grace Brothers, an old-fashioned department store, the series followed the outrageous antics of its staff, who included Mr Humphries, a limp-wristed salesman, and Mrs Slocombe, head of ladies fashion, who not only had ideas above her station but was forever worrying about her pussy (her cat). Critics hated it. They found the seaside postcard humour rude, crude and offensive, but viewers loved it, and laughed out loud – and with affection – at the often-silly antics of the staff of Grace Brothers. One episode in 1979 reached an all-time high audience figure of 22 million. In fact, such was the popularity of *Are You Being Served?* that the BBC kept it going for ten series. It finally ended in 1985.

In 2000, Stuart Jeffries referred to Mr Humphries, played by John Inman, in his entertaining book *Mrs Slocombe's Pussy: Growing Up in Front of the Telly* as someone like Larry Grayson:

> That other seventies TV homosexual … Mr Humphries minced forward across the stage towards the camera as middle-aged women screamed their laughter, and men, I suspect, smiled narrowly. The dapper old queen whose wrist was always limp, and who forever standing on the balls on his feet, could have minced for England. He couldn't even walk straight.[1]

However, Mr Humphries almost didn't make it to the end of the first series. In 1985, John Inman revealed in the *News of the World* ('Are You Being Sacked?', 17 March) that, after just five episodes, a top BBC official told David Croft, the series producer, to 'Get rid of the poof!' Said Inman: 'David told the official, "If the poof goes, I go." And Mr Humphries stayed.'

As far as Inman was concerned, Mr Humphries was not gay. He was a single man who lived with his mother. However, according to an interview with Inman in the *TV Times* (3 September 1981), if Mr Humphries wasn't labelled 'fruity, fluttering, camp, dapper, effeminate, gay, limp-wristed and mincing', he would be disappointed. 'It is quite nice Mr Humphries is mentioned so much,' he said. Throughout the 1970s, when Mr Humphries minced across the shop floor at Grace Brothers, gay activists and campaigners were outraged, especially when Inman publicly denied that his character was gay. In 1977, he told the *Daily Mirror* (7 April) 'I don't think I offend anyone who watches the show … the marvellous thing about [Mr Humphries] is that people never quite know whether or not he's queer. I always say that when it comes to sex, Mr Humphries is nothing really. He's neither one way or the other.' With statements like this, it is not surprising Inman faced a barrage of criticism from the gay community. For example, in 1977, *Gay News* quoted the gay writer Howard Schuman from an interview he had given to *New Society*:

I find the treatment of gay people in British situation comedy a true obscenity. It's one of the things I most hate – John Inman and that school. Even Kenneth Williams whom I think is a genius. I simply don't know why it's tolerated. Gay resistance is really overdue on a whole host of levels.[2]

In 1978, John Inman told Rosalie Shann of the *News of the World* (17 December) that he was upset when several members of the Campaign for Homosexual Equality publicly denounced him for ruining the image of gay men. 'Four or five of them picketed one of my shows,' he said:

I had them round to my dressing room and in fact they were very nice. They thought I was over-exaggerating the gay character. But I don't think I do. In fact, there are people far more camp than Mr Humphries. So, far from doing harm to the homosexual image, I feel I might be doing some good.

The self-delusional, self-oppressed Mr Inman just didn't get it.

It took time, but eventually some gay men began to express their appreciation of Mr Humphries. As Philip Hensher commented in *The Independent* (13 April 2008):

Gay comedians of the new school have often expressed their enjoyment and even admiration of the old-fashioned school, seeing in Frankie Howerd and John Inman not a tragic statement of the closet militant, but men who, in this one setting, were able to revel in their sexuality. Russell T Davies, the creator of *Queer as Folk* and current *Doctor Who* writer, has spoken of his bafflement at what he sees as a politically cor-rect and humourless response to Mr Humphries and the like.

John Inman was not the only actor in a popular BBC sitcom to publicly deny that his character was gay. When BBC1 launched *It Ain't Half Hot Mum* on 3 January 1974, Melvyn Hayes went to great lengths to refute claims that his character 'Gloria' was 'so'. Gunner/Bombardier 'Gloria' Beaumont was a member of a Royal Artillery Concert Party – a theatrical troupe – based in India during the Second World War. 'Gloria' was larger than life, outra-geously camp and flounced around in drag, usually as a Hollywood-style starlet. 'Her' ambition to recreate MGM musicals in the middle of the jungle was overambitious to say the least. Viewers loved 'Gloria' and 'her' antics as much as they enjoyed seeing the mincing Mr Humphries. *It Ain't Half Hot Mum* was a huge success and ran for eight series. When the series was drawing to a close, 'Gloria' and Battery Sergeant Major Williams (Windsor Davies) were featured on the cover of the *Radio Times* (18–24 July 1981). In an interview in the magazine, Hayes, though he didn't exactly 'out' 'Gloria', did finally acknowledge that by constantly declaring his heterosexuality (as he had been doing since 1974) made it *sound* like he was anti-gay:

> It always comes out like you're saying, 'I'm not a poof, I'm not gay.' But that's terrible. It's like saying, 'I'm not a Jewboy, I'm not a Wop.' It sounds derogatory. My father brought me up with one word and that was tolerance ... If my little boy came home and said 'Daddy, I've fallen in love with another boy at school,' I'd say, 'Smashing.'

In 1983, Keith Howes commented that the 'gay' characters who were featured in 1970s sitcoms were 'cherished, but in different ways'. He said that the characters played by John Inman and Melvyn Hayes were 'family favourites, impotent figures of fun for people to "mother" or feel superior towards'.[3]

Another 'family favourite' was 'Lukewarm', beautifully played by Christopher Biggins, in another very popular BBC1 sitcom, *Porridge*, but there was a difference. The writers Dick Clement and Ian La Frenais wrote 'Lukewarm' as an openly gay character who is integrated into the narrative. Off-screen, unlike Inman and Hayes, Biggins did not try to hide the fact that his character was gay. The first series was launched on 5 September 1974. It ran for three series until 1977 and memorably starred Ronnie Barker as the habitual criminal Norman Fletcher. He serves time with a comical group of inmates, including the sweet and ineffectual 'Lukewarm'. In one episode ('Men Without Women', tx 19 October 1974) his boyfriend Trevor is seen on a bus bringing 'wives and sweethearts' to the prison. Although he is one of Fletcher's trusted friends, he avoids becoming directly involved in his schemes, preferring to sit on the sidelines with his knitting. On 15 June 2007, Richard Alleyne reported in *The Telegraph* that fans of *Porridge* had accused the BBC of editing a 'gay slur' when the series was repeated:

> Fans of the sitcom have accused the BBC of giving in to the politically correct brigade after a phrase was removed from the programme. They

claim the comment 'that sort do, don't they' referring to Lukewarm's ability to keep his cell clean, was taken out because it could be offensive to homosexuals. A BBC spokesman said: 'We always endeavour to transmit classic comedies in their original state. However, on rare occasions due to viewer complaints or running time we make a slight edit.' Christopher Biggins said: 'I find it quite extraordinary and one of the most anal things I have ever heard. It was always so well done, the gay thing. Very sensitively handled.'

A gay couple, Rob and Michael, were successfully integrated into *Agony*, a sitcom that was launched by London Weekend Television on 11 March 1979. Maureen Lipman starred as a cosmopolitan radio 'agony aunt' who spent more time sorting out the problems of her friends than her listeners. Rob (Jeremy Bulloch) and Michael (Peter Denyer) were her neighbours and they were a welcome departure from the stereotypical gay men who had been seen in sitcoms throughout the 1970s. Mark Lewisohn described them in the *Radio Times Guide to Comedy* (1998) as the only people to offer Jane real comfort: 'The portrayal of this homosexual couple as non-camp, sensitive, intelligent, witty and generally happy was a notable first in the British sitcom genre, and *Agony* efficiently tackled many other taboos along the way.'[4] *Agony* could also have been the first sitcom to be created and written by a gay man, Len Richmond, who was an American activist. He joined forces with Anna Raeburn, a well-respected magazine and radio 'agony aunt' on which Maureen Lipman's character is based, to script the first series in 1979. However, backstage disagreements led to the second and third series (in 1980 and 1981) being penned by others.

In 1982, Andy Medhurst and Lucy Tuck wrote about the portrayal of gay men in a British Film Institute publication about sitcoms. In relation to the characters in *Agony* and *It Ain't Half Hot Mum*, they commented:

Perhaps the most positive factor in *Agony* is not the presence of Rob and Michael, but the crucial absence of any character mouthing anti-gay prejudices. It would have been only too easy to slip in a few homophobic jibes, but instead it is the gay couple who can smile at heterosexual men's inadequacies … but Rob and Michael are unquestionably an improvement on the indelibly inscribed homophobia of *It Ain't Half Hot Mum* … Even the most positive reading of, say, Gloria would be necessarily undermined by the fact that the character is conceived by and for heterosexuals. Gays have the right to present themselves as camp, since campness is a part of gay culture – but for heterosexuals to reduce gayness to a handful of ridiculed gesticulations is another matter entirely.[5]

Notes

1. Stuart Jeffries, *Mrs Slocombe's Pussy: Growing Up in Front of the Telly* (Flamingo, 2000), p. 102.
2. Keith Howes, 'Uncensored', *Gay News* No. 133 (1978).
3. Keith Howes, 'The Media' in Bruce Galloway (ed.), *Prejudice and Pride: Discrimination Against Gay People in Modern Britain* (1983), p. 206.
4. Mark Lewisohn, *Radio Times Guide to Comedy* (BBC, 1998), p. 23.
5. Andy Medhurst and Lucy Tuck, 'The Gender Game' in Jim Cook (ed.), *BFI Dossier 17 Television Sitcom* (British Film Institute, 1982), pp. 50–1.

15

Early 1970s Drama

Throughout the early 1970s, before *The Naked Civil Servant* was shown in 1975 and helped to change the face of gay men in British television, the majority of popular drama series excluded gays. If they were not found out and imprisoned, many gay men fought bravely in World War Two, but they were conspicuous by their absence in writer John Finch's otherwise superb *A Family at War* (Granada, 1970–72). *Kate* (Yorkshire, 1970–72) starred the popular British film star Phyllis Calvert as an 'agony aunt' on a magazine, but she never received any letters from gay men. In 1970, Daniel (Daniel Massey) was a self-loathing homosexual in BBC2's acclaimed *The Roads to Freedom*. It was based on Jean-Paul Sartre's trilogy, set in Paris from 1938 to 1940. In addition to Daniel's hatred of himself, viewers were subjected to a horrific scene in which he clutches a razor while giving serious thought to castrating himself. However, there were some interesting exceptions, including the BBC's second television version of Christopher Marlowe's *Edward II* which may have included the first gay kiss on the small screen.

This new adaptation of *Edward II* started life as a Prospect Theatre Company production which opened at the Edinburgh Festival in 1969. Ian McKellen starred in the title role. The production was a huge success and McKellen's growing reputation as a new and exciting classical actor strengthened. The following year, BBC2 commissioned a television version which was recorded at London's Piccadilly Theatre, and screened on BBC2 on 6 August 1970. It is an honest and unpretentious recording of the stage production, and preserves McKellen's brilliant performance. It is accepted that *Edward II* included the first gay kiss on British television – in close-up, too – between Ian McKellen and James Laurenson (as Gaveston).

Mary Griffiths in the *Daily Mirror* (6 August 1970) warned her readers that the television production could raise protests, but the play's producer, Mark Shivas, who was interviewed in the same column, explained, 'What theatre audiences will take and accept may give television audiences a shock in the more intimate atmosphere of their living rooms. We don't want to shock people. I sincerely hope people will try to understand that this was a very violent era.' Following the screening, few critics mentioned the gay relationship – and The Kiss. An exception was James Thomas in the *Daily Express* (7 August 1970) who complained that 'Marlowe's *Edward II*, the story of a king embracing his favourites, kissing them on the lips, is a little too much to take in the close-up confines of television', but he also acknowledged that it was 'a considerable chance for TV to take. A good deal of it came off, played with tremendous vigour and passion. But the cameras would have been well-advised to stand a little further back.' Sean Day-Lewis noted in the *Daily Telegraph* (7 August 1970) that:

> Ian McKellen as Edward was most effective while he still had his Gaveston around him. As in the theatre he appeared more committed to sexual lust than to the lust for power which is also part of the character, but with his mannerism toned down I was much moved by the self-pity of his fall as by the horror of his red-hot poker death.

In 1969, W. Stephen Gilbert entered his play *Circle Line* in what the BBC advertised as a 'television play competition for students'. The competition judges included members of the BBC television Drama Group and Script Unit. Among them were Graeme McDonald and Irene Shubik, producers of *The Wednesday Play*, Gerald Savory, Head of Plays for BBC television and Waris Hussein, a drama director in BBC television. In his covering letter to the BBC dated 18 April 1969, which accompanied his script, W. Stephen Gilbert, then a student of English at University College London, described his plot:

> The play primarily concerns a representative of that large body of students who drift thru their college years, inured to and finally oblivious to the 'brains industry' and the seething iconoclasm around them. Tim, the hero of my play, sees no reason to rebel because he acknowledges no moral tenets, no 'rules to life'. He is untouched by the dramas that television and the press present as 'student protest'. He wants only to live his own life and to let others live theirs.[1]

Circle Line won the competition, and although originally conceived and recorded for *The Wednesday Play* series, which ended on 27 May 1970, its transmission was delayed for almost two years. *Circle Line* eventually surfaced on BBC1 in its *Play for Today* series on 14 January 1971. Graeme McDonald produced, and Claude Whatham directed. It is easy to understand why the BBC was nervous about screening the play. In *Circle Line*, Tim lives for the moment. He has no personal morality, no laid-down conduct. He never worries about free sex or drug taking. He accepts them as perfectly normal. However, *Circle Line* was mainly controversial because the sexually experimental student enjoys having casual sex with a 14-year-old lad. When Tim sleeps with the teenager, Tarquin, it is depicted as an experience they both enjoy on a casual basis.

There were some favourable reviews. For example, the critic for *The Guardian* (15 January 1971) described it as:

A fascinating and polished bit of work, one of those tightly talked, argumentative pieces which demands to be seen again so that you can have a go at picking holes in it … The style – both economic and enticingly wordy – was splendid, and it was given impressive life by Claude Whatham's production and the performances, especially of Michael Feast in the trickily ambivalent role of Tim, the central figure.

In the *Telegraph* (15 January 1971), Sean Day-Lewis praised the author: 'Mr Gilbert has an obvious talent. There were moments of exaggeration and gaucherie but his dialogue has a remarkable precision, with some exchanges that Harold Pinter himself would not have disowned.' Some critics hated it. Mary Malone in the *Daily Mirror* (15 January 1971) complained that *Circle Line* was 'a mixture of grotesque images, banality of statement, convoluted dialogue and the youthful desire to shock at any price, combined with a contempt for other people's values'. Some viewers praised it. In a letter forwarded by the BBC to Gilbert, a viewer wrote: 'I can't think of anything that has brought me closer to the student generation. The whole being brought to life quite brilliantly by the actors. Many thanks to all concerned.'

BBC2's *Thirty-Minute Theatre* was an anthology series of short plays. Launched in 1965, the series ran successfully until 1973, and not only provided viewers with some exceptional work, but was used in part as a training ground for new writers. Out of the original 286 episodes, 239 are missing. One of the lost treasures is *The Waiting Room* (tx 29 March 1971).

It was written by John Bowen and starred his real-life partner David Cook as a young man who encounters an older woman, played by Barbara Leigh-Hunt, in a waiting room. They discover that they have both been involved with the same man who has died.

When the writer E.A. Whitehead researched his play *Under the Age* (tx 20 March 1972) for *Thirty-Minute Theatre*, his dialogue came directly from a tape recording he made in his favourite Liverpool pub. The landlord of the grotty, Liverpool pub depicted in *Under the Age* is Susie (Paul Angelis), a gay man who takes more time over painting his face at the bar than attending to his customers. He bullies a young barman into serving a couple of scousers who are anxious to down a few pints before christening a new mattress with a couple of teenage girls in the back of their van. Though he wears make-up, Susie does not wear drag. Instead he is seen wiggling his arse in tight jeans. He is depicted as sharp-tongued and vicious, constantly bullying the young barman. It is made clear that he uses a local men's lavatory to meet men for sex and he is keen to have his way with Mike, one of the scousers. Mike does not rebuff Susie's advances, but in the end Mike pairs off with one of the girls. In 1972, British television hadn't seen anyone quite like Susie, and there is no reason why Whitehead should have made Susie a tart with a heart. Susie is hard as nails, spiteful even. Presumably a Susie existed in the real-life Liverpool pub where Whitehead recorded his dialogue.

John Mortimer's *Thirty-Minute Theatre: Bermondsey* (tx 19 June 1972) was an adaptation of his 1970 stage production. It is a superb, bitter-sweet drama set in a pub in Bermondsey in south London run by the working-class Bob and Iris (Dinsdale Landen and Rosemary Leach). On Christmas Eve, Bob has decided to leave his wife and children for Rosemary who is described as a 'brainless dolly bird'. He is persuaded to stay when his oldest friend, the upper-class Pip (Edward Fox), intervenes. Bob and Pip have been friends for eighteen years. They met when they were serving in the army. They have also been lovers for all that time. They are tender towards each other. They also kiss on the lips, probably the first time a male couple had been seen kissing on television since Ian McKellen and James Laurenson in *Edward II* (1970). At the conclusion, Rosemary discovers the truth about Bob and leaves. Iris reveals that she has always known about the relationship between her husband and Pip. The three characters look forward to enjoying the rest of Christmas together.

Bermondsey was a breakthrough in the portrayal of gay men on British television. It was well written by John Mortimer and unselfconscious in its portrayal of same-sex love. It was beautifully acted by the three leads. Landen is particularly memorable in the emotionally charged 'confession' scene when he recalls how he and Pip met and started their relationship. In 2009, when *Bermondsey* was rediscovered and screened during the British Film Institute's Lesbian and Gay Film Festival, the audience applauded at the end. They had not expected to see a British television play from the early 1970s being so positive in its depiction of a loving gay couple. When *Bermondsey* was first shown, gay men were, almost without exception, portrayed on television in comedy programmes as the butt of the joke. When the wheelchair-bound Mortimer entered the cinema after the screening, and was introduced to the audience, he was applauded and cheered.

In *Total Eclipse* (BBC2, tx 10 April 1973) the passionate but destructive relationship of two nineteenth-century French poets Verlaine and the younger Rimbaud was explored by Christopher Hampton. It was an adaptation of his explosive stage play, first produced at the Royal Court in 1968. Critics were unanimous in their praise for Ian Hogg's intense, passionate portrayal of the troubled Paul Verlaine. As Michael Ratcliffe commented in *The Times* (11 April 1973):

> It was a splendid idea to cast Mr Hogg, an actor of tigerish tenacity usually assigned to dull heavies or peasant oafs … He gave the bourgeois lyricist and wife-basher not merely a proper masochism and indecision but also the terrific sexual drive without which he might never have attempted to escape in the first place: there could be no peace among these elements, although a shell of shrewd dignity remained to the end.

In the same review, Mr Ratcliffe also praised Joseph Blatchley's portrayal of Arthur Rimbaud: 'the accuracy of Mr Blatchley's impersonation was astonishing … he listened to Verlaine with glittering eyes and a deceptively mocking mouth; he was plausibly under 20, yet blown with every experience under the sun.'

Notes

1. W. Stephen Gilbert, letter to the BBC, 18 April 1969. Thanks to W. Stephen Gilbert for sharing this information and other background information on *Circle Line.*

16

Roll on Four O'Clock and *Penda's Fen*

In the early 1970s, two television dramas focussed on troubled youths who grappled with their sexuality. However, Granada's *Sunday Night Theatre: Roll on Four O'Clock* (tx 20 December 1970), written by Colin Welland, and BBC1's *Play for Today: Penda's Fen* (tx 21 March 1974), written by David Rudkin, couldn't have been more different. The former was set in a tough inner-city secondary modern school for boys and filmed entirely on location in the industrial district of Miles Platting in Manchester. The latter had a rural setting, with the beautiful Malvern Hills in Worcestershire as its backdrop. *Roll on Four O'Clock* centred on the teenager Peter Latimer (Frank Heaton), whose life is made intolerable by his teachers and classmates because he is perceived to be homosexual. In *Penda's Fen*, Stephen Franklin (Spencer Banks), about to turn 18, is a detached, almost robotic young man from a middle-class background who is bullied at his grammar school for the same reason as Peter Latimer. Visually the two plays couldn't be more different. The grim, urban setting of *Roll on Four O'Clock* is light years away from the gorgeous landscape of *Penda's Fen*. Yet there are similarities in the themes of the plays because they are the likeliest candidates for the first television dramas to expose the homophobic bullying of gay teenagers who find they have no way out. Both plays are engrossing and disturbing.

In *Roll on Four O'Clock*, Latimer is an ideal candidate for persecution. He is despised by his fellow pupils because he prefers art and English to sport. In the playground he is repeatedly ridiculed. When a group of boys are confronted by the headmaster for physically assaulting him, they give the following excuse: 'He keeps looking at us.' Latimer is the butt of schoolboy jokes and, in the classroom, he is the victim of a sadistic teacher who is fiercely homophobic. The teacher says, in the staffroom, 'He's a poof, an embryo queen. He needs putting away. In every school you have one or two. We don't cater for poofs. A lad like him, what chance has he got around here? He'll have to hide.' The headmaster, Mr Crampton (George A. Cooper), is also unsympathetic. He holds the view that Latimer should be more willing to join in school activities in order to be toughened up, because life on the factory shop floor after he has left school will be even tougher. Latimer doesn't stand a chance of survival in this rough house.

Colin Welland brilliantly conveys the boy's sense of isolation and desperation, though he does receive tea and sympathy from the kindly art teacher, Mr Fielder (Clive Swift). Older, wiser and gay, Mr Fielder is comfortable with his sexuality. His wise words of advice to Latimer are: 'As you get older, you'll find other boys and men who'll be a great comfort. You're not alone. You will learn to live with it.' Mr Fielder tells him he is a brave lad, but ultimately, he fails to get through to him. Afterwards Latimer steals a motorbike and crashes it into a wall, hoping to be 'put away' to avoid returning to school.

Welland sensitively and accurately explored a number of social issues, such as teenage angst, poverty and the class system. The surprise is that Welland acknowledged that homosexuality existed in the working classes at that time, and amongst working-class schoolboys. Unsurprisingly, he was singled out for praise. According to Richard Last in the *Daily Telegraph* (21 December 1970):

> If any doubts still lingered that Colin Welland now belongs in the front rank of television playwrights, they were blown away last night by his latest opus *Roll on Four O'Clock* ... the central, inner story of the school victim and the sympathetic art teacher (a beautifully sensitive performance by Clive Swift) had as many smiles as tears.

George Melly, in *The Observer* (20 December 1970), acknowledged that Welland 'is a brilliant anatomist of the human failure to connect'. For his script, Welland received an award from the Writers' Guild of Great Britain for Best British Original Teleplay. *Roll on Four O'Clock* was also one of four plays for which Welland was awarded the Best Script prize by the Society of Film and Television Arts, now known as the British Academy of Film and Television Arts (BAFTA).

Poetic and anarchic, writer David Rudkin's *Penda's Fen* is considered one of the most original dramas ever screened on British television. According to Terry Metcalf in the *Birmingham Daily Post* (23 March 1974), 'the play reaches out and draws the viewer into total involvement'. Stephen, the adopted son of a village rector, subscribes to the sanctimonious Tory ideal of Olde England, but finds himself plagued by visions of angels, devils, King Penda (the last Pagan king of England) and nightmarish visions of the nation's political corruption. He also experiences homoerotic feelings and dreams of a sexual encounter with a bullying fellow pupil at his school. In his notes to the British Film Institute's DVD reissue of the drama, Sukhdev Sandhu describes writer Rudkin as 'both an insider and an outsider'.[1]

However, Sandhu's assertion that the play is not about homosexuality is questionable because Stephen's homosexuality is referenced all through the story. Sandhu is correct in stating that 'it doesn't depict it as a sub-culture, a lifestyle, a social category, far less a cause,' and that it is 'long before the term was first used to describe the work of directors such as Todd Haynes and Isaac Julien, a queer film',[2] but when Stephen's sexuality becomes the focus it is explicit and, for its time, challenging. For example, when Stephen excitedly greets the sexy but indifferent milkman at the front door, he says to his mother: 'I wish Joel would like me. He can be so cutting.' His father, the Reverend, overhears, and says to his wife: 'Milk lad. Hardly original.' Stephen's parents agree that, at this stage in his life, their adopted son is unaware of his attraction to young men.

A dream sequence begins with Stephen staring at the buttocks of his fellow pupils who are engaged in a rugby scrum. Then the blond, attractive class bully, Honeybone (Christopher Douglas), appears. He is naked, standing over Stephen who strokes and caresses Honeybone's chest, including his nipples. It is a sexually charged sequence, and one that broke new ground with its explicitness in 1974. However, Stephen's erotic dream turns into a nightmare when he 'awakes' to find a demon sitting on his bed. It is a terrifying image. Once seen, never forgotten. Afterwards, Stephen realises he is gay and sexually desires other men.

In one of his many editions of *Biographical Dictionary of Film*, David Thomson included Alan Clarke, the director of *Penda's Fen*. He described Clarke as a 'genius of TV … He believed TV was an opportunity for looking beneath the rocks of the social order and giving voice to the anonymous, the wretched – the scum, even.'[3] Yet, when Thomson wrote about Clarke in the *Independent on Sunday* in 1998, he said that 'There's no need to sentimentalise the quality of British television in the 1960s, 1970s and 1980s. Much of it was awful: pathetically polite and clinging to a world that never was.'[4] This demonstrates the lack of knowledge and imagination that some *film* scholars, even those as brilliant as Thomson, have for British television drama. He includes a *television* director in a film reference book, and then denigrates the medium in which the director excelled. According to Lez Cooke in *British Television Drama: A History* (2003):

> Both the subject matter and treatment of *Penda's Fen* mark it out as a rare non-naturalistic drama within the history of *Play for Today*. Striking imagery, an impressionistic narrative involving a boy's growing awareness of his homosexuality, fantasy sequences, the evocation of myths and legends, all of these combine to make *Penda's Fen* a remarkable and unique film.[5]

Notes

1. Sukhdev Sandhu, 'Penda's Fen', *Penda's Fen*, DVD, British Film Institute, 2006.
2. *Ibid.*
3. David Thomson, *The New Biographical Dictionary of Film* (6th Edition) (Alfred A. Knopf, 2014), pp. 189–90.
4. David Thomson, 'Made in Britain, and bleak as hell,' *Independent on Sunday*, 23 August 1998.
5. Lez Cooke, *British Television Drama: A History* (BFI Publishing, 2003), p. 119.

17

Upstairs, Downstairs

When London Weekend Television's *Upstairs, Downstairs* made its debut on 10 October 1971, it became one of British television's most popular costume drama serials. Set in an upper-class Edwardian household in London's grand Eaton Place, it cleverly interweaved the dual narrative threads of the upstairs Bellamy family with their downstairs servants. The head of the domestic staff was Mr Hudson (Gordon Jackson), a dour Scottish butler who knew his place and ensured the rest of the staff knew theirs. However, he didn't have any trouble with the cook, the gruff Mrs Bridges (Angela Baddeley), or level-headed Rose (Jean Marsh), the chief housemaid. Jean Marsh, who won an American Emmy award for her portrayal of Rose, also created the series with Eileen Atkins.

Alfred Harris (George Innes) was the original footman at Eaton Place but in the fifth episode, 'A Suitable Marriage' (tx 7 November 1971), set in 1905, he is caught in a compromising situation which leads to his disgrace and instant dismissal. Baron Klaus von Rimmer (Horst Janson), a German visitor to London, is befriended by the young, impressionable but head-strong Elizabeth Bellamy. Her mother, Lady Bellamy, is appalled when he informs them that his lodgings are inadequate, and promptly offers him a room at Eaton Place. Elizabeth is thrilled, and so is Alfred, especially when he is told he will be the baron's valet during his stay. Downstairs, Hudson expresses his suspicion of 'foreigners' but Alfred doesn't take any notice. He is very attentive to the baron's needs. Then Alfred falls in love with the German aristocrat and begins an illicit sexual liaison with him. However, tensions surface when the baron angrily confronts Alfred about his indiscretions, such as using his eau de cologne. The situation calms down when the baron forgives Alfred and permits him to kiss his hand while stroking the valet's hair. There follows one of the most shocking scenes on British television. Rose enters the baron's room without knocking and, to her horror and distress, finds Alfred in a compromising position, sitting bare-chested on the bed with the baron leaning over him! It isn't made clear *exactly* what has happened, and what Rose saw, but what the distressed Rose tells Hudson is enough for the butler to inform Lord Bellamy. All along the baron has lied to the family about his reason for visiting London (to study banking). At the end of the episode Albert and the baron have vanished and it is revealed that the baron is actually a German spy who is on the run from the police. Lady Bellamy is upset about having put a roof over the head of what she calls a 'pervert'. 1905 was only a decade after the trials of Oscar Wilde. The famous playwright's downfall was swift and he became the most infamous and despised homosexual towards the end of Queen Victoria's reign.

Two years later, in the third series of *Upstairs, Downstairs*, Alfred unexpectedly returns to Eaton Place in an outstanding but distressing episode set in 1913 entitled 'Rose's Pigeon' (tx 24 November 1973). Poor Alfred is discovered by Rose at the bottom of the steps outside the basement door. It is foggy, and he is in a terrible state, bedraggled and soaking wet. After hiding him in a room in the basement near the kitchen, Alfred spins Rose a yarn about his time in Germany with the baron. Rose takes pity on him and, extremely gullible, she believes his story. However, when Hudson discovers Alfred, he reminds Rose, 'This young man brought shame and disgrace on the house it took a long time to recover from. I'd sooner have forty thieves in here than see him back!' Hudson reports Alfred's presence to Lord Bellamy and the truth about him is discovered. Alfred had been sent back to England by von Rimmer to work for his friend in Brighton, but Alfred has murdered the man and is on the run from the police. The victim is described by a detective inspector as an 'unmarried man of some age … effeminate'. Alfred described him as a serpent who used him when all he wanted to do was lead a decent life. When the man went too far, Alfred butchered him with a meat axe.

In this highly charged and melodramatic episode, there was a danger that Alfred would lapse into the stereotype of the gay man as an evil psychotic killer. However, in Jeremy Paul's sympathetic writing and the superb performance of George Innes, Alfred is depicted as a pathetic victim from the lower classes. He is a servant who is used and sexually abused by wealthy, sophisticated and selfish men. In desperation (and retaliation) he kills one of them. Alfred is then hunted like an animal by the police, and seeks refuge at Eaton Place. When the truth is revealed there is no sympathy for him whatsoever but, at the end of the episode, when Alfred is hung for the murder, Rose protests against the sentence. She argues that it is wrong to hang a person who is not right in the head. It is unlikely that Rose understands that Alfred's 'mental state' has been caused by being a persecuted outsider because of his homosexuality and the victim of other men's exploitation. Jean Marsh later described George Innes as an actor who brought a 'gothic' presence within the cast and for memorably giving Alfred 'his unpredictable and often bitter temperament'.[1]

On a lighter note, in 1976, when Keith Howes interviewed Angela Baddeley for *Gay News*, she recalled Stanley Baxter's memorable impersonation of her character, Mrs Bridges, in one of his popular television specials. 'He was *hilarious*,' she said:

> He had a costume made just like mine with an *enormous* bosom and a huge teapot in his hand. He played Rose as well. Rose said: 'Oh Mrs Bridges, do you remember the night I came to you and told you the old Queen had gorn?' And Mrs Bridges replied: 'Yes, and I told you not to speak so disrespectful of Mr 'udson!' I thought it was *gorgeous*.

When Keith tried to engage Miss Baddeley in a discussion about the inclusion of gay characters in the series, including 'Rose's Pigeon', she replied, 'It was rather a failure. I don't think people liked it very much.' Then the penny dropped and the formidable Miss Baddeley suddenly realised that she was being interviewed for a gay newspaper. 'Oh heavens!' she gasped, 'are you bringing *me* into *this*?'[2]

Notes
1. Owen Emmerson, 'Downstairs Queers: Homosexuality Within Domestic Service Dramas 1968–2015', 16 November 2014. https://headmasterrituals.wordpress.com.
2. Keith Howes, 'No Gays in Mrs Bridges' Kitchen', *Gay News*, No. 87 (1976).

18

At Home with Larry Grayson?

The variety artiste and drag queen Larry Grayson was getting on a bit. He had his 50th birthday on 31 August 1973 and had been treading the boards for over thirty years when he was finally 'discovered' and given his own television series. Before he became famous, he was known professionally as Billy Breen. Grayson recalled: 'in a white suit and straw hat, doing a song and dance with a few jokes to finish. I toured all the halls in the early 1950s – you *could* say I was there the day variety died. I got to the theatres just before the bulldozers!'[1] The television series that made him famous was *Shut That Door!* Launched by ITV (ATV) on 18 August 1972, its title was taken from one of his catchphrases. However, Grayson didn't appear on television as a female impersonator. He dressed conservatively in a suit and tie, and he captivated viewers with an inoffensive camp persona. His stage act was cosy and intimate and yet it could be subversive too. Mostly Grayson remained conservative with a small 'c' in the sexually ambiguous 'glam-rock' era of David Bowie and Elton John.

Grayson's act consisted of nothing more than dragging a chair across the stage to the music of Judy Garland's song 'The Man That Got Away'. He made his audiences howl with laughter with sayings like 'Look at the muck in 'ere', 'What a gay day!' and 'Seems like a nice boy' as he gazed at a young gentleman in the audience. Grayson's daft but hysterically funny comedy routines included references to his hypochondria: 'I was a weak child. I had everything twice'; 'I get it all down here,' he said, pointing to his left leg; 'I feel as limp as a vicar's handshake.' He also told stories about his imaginary friends Everard Farquharson, the coalman's daughter Slack Alice, Apricot Lil (a tart who worked in a jam factory), Brenda Allcock and his postman: 'My postman is called Pop-it-in-Pete. When he's got something too big to put through the letter box he knocks on the door. He really is a joy.'

Publicly, Grayson denied he was gay. In an interview in the *TV Times* (10–16 June 1972) he explained: 'When I'm on stage I look down and see the women screaming at me. All my fan-letters are from women. Now, if they thought I was homosexual, immediately they would switch off a light. And, I mean, I'm not.' But some television critics just took it for granted that Grayson was a friend of Dorothy's. According to Alan Coren in *The Times* (29 March 1973): 'Mr Grayson is both stooge (I almost said straight man) and comic: he plays himself off against his own freakishness, in this case, homosexuality.'

Grayson's rise to fame was meteoric, but not everyone was impressed. In 1977, following a period of unemployment, the popular comedy actor Kenneth Williams expressed his resentment for Grayson when he wrote in his diary, 'That Grayson TV show is a complete crib of my stuff, and that Inman is doing the same thing on the BBC! It hadn't *hit* me before! Of *course*! they've found other people to do it, and cheaper people in every sense.'[2] However, nothing could have been further from the truth, for Grayson and Williams were completely different personalities. The only thing they had in common was concealing their homosexuality from the public. Williams was not only a fine character actor, but a superb raconteur. Grayson didn't act but audiences warmed to his on-stage persona, even though he had his limitations. Williams had been working successfully since the 1950s. The popular *Carry On* films made him a star. At the same time poor Grayson, as a drag artiste, was languishing in run-down music halls, working-men's clubs, and as a pantomime dame in third-rate theatres. Grayson was on the brink of chucking it all in when his big break came.

Throughout the 1970s, Grayson's television career went from strength to strength and, after two series of *Shut That Door!*, his many shows included *The Larry Grayson Hour of Stars* (1974) and a brief guest appearance as Meg Richardson's chauffeur in an episode of his favourite soap *Crossroads* (1975). In 1978 he enjoyed his biggest success when he replaced Bruce Forsyth as the presenter of *The Generation Game*, then one of the most popular shows on television. 'I'll never be as fast as Brucie,' he said. 'because I wear surgical stockings.'[3]

Grayson remained with *The Generation Game* for four series. However, not everyone was happy with Grayson's way of playing gay. In *Gay News*, Robin Houston expressed his unhappiness with Grayson taking over from Forsyth in a feature entitled 'The Generation Shame': 'If we'd tried to work out the worst possible thing that could happen to gay rights on British television, we would never have thought of that one.' He criticised Bill Cotton, head of BBC TV's Light Entertainment Group, for 'instilling a breath of stale air into his schedules in the hope of finding the lowest common denominator' and, he added, 'they do not come much lower than Larry Grayson'. As far as Houston was concerned, Grayson had little personality, charm or talent, 'unless you count the ability to expose our effeminate brothers – gay and non-gay – to derision and hatred'. He described Grayson's catchphrases as 'cliches of oppression … The prospect of Grayson fronting *The Generation Game* is depressing as well as distasteful.'[4]

When *The Generation Game* ended in 1981, Grayson semi-retired from showbusiness. In 1993, to coincide with Grayson's 70th birthday, London's National Film Theatre presented a special event called 'At Home with Larry Grayson?' Andy Medhurst, a lecturer in Media Studies at Sussex University, assessed the popularity of Grayson and his problematic screen persona in the context of debates around gay politics. According to Medhurst:

You wouldn't have wanted to shag Larry, even at the height of his fame. You'd have had far more fun settling down together with a Joan Crawford film on the telly, for the truth is that Larry was a sister, or, if you want to be ageist about it, an auntie. He was also an auntie that for years and years the gay family wanted to disown. In the dear-old po-faced 1970s, his name was mud. He stood for everything that we were supposedly getting away from. We wanted (grit your teeth) positive images, fair representations, and this clapped-out ex-drag-queen swishing around, swooning about Judy Garland, was anathema. Homosexuality was about liberation and homosexual men were bearded and moustached and check-shirted and most of all Were Not Like Larry. Except, of course, some of us were, some of the time (and a few of us were *all* of the time). I don't want to play down all the enormous and crucial gains made by gay politics in the 1970s; without them it's very unlikely that I'd be writing this or you'd be reading it. But as in any battle there were casualties, and one of the most regrettable ones was that whole, brave, pansified tradition of which Larry was so clearly a part.[5]

By the time Grayson died in 1995, the gay community was still divided about him. Some continued to disparage him. In a letter to *Capital Gay* (20 January 1995), Nicholas Loeb wrote, 'He never did anything positive for us, so why the hell should we put him on a pedestal now?' Others gave him the status of a camp icon, comparing him with Quentin Crisp and Julian Clary. The showbusiness journalist Patrick Newley, who knew Grayson for over twenty years, revealed that the comic's denial of his sexuality was in reality a joke at the expense of heterosexuals: 'It was his way of taking the piss out of the straight world,' Newley told *Capital Gay* (13 January 1995). 'He said it very tongue-in-cheek and the straight press used to fall for it over and over again. He couldn't stand gay activists picketing outside his theatres but he loved talking to queens in his dressing room. He took all his gay secrets to the grave.'

In a letter to *The Pink Paper* (10 February 1995), David Nott defended Grayson:

> Please world, gay or straight, stop sniping at the late and wonderful Larry Grayson. There was no need for him to come out – as it was obvious who he was and what he was. The key to him was truth which shone through all he did and said. It was no accident that he became a star.

In *Capital Gay* the author of this book recalled how, as a closeted teenager growing up in the 1970s, he was embarrassed by Grayson:

> But by the end of the 1980s, I realised many of us had misjudged him, and I began to appreciate his comic genius and the breakthrough he made in the 1970s. Last year I met Mr Grayson. He was approachable, charming and witty. He talked non-stop about the golden years of Hollywood, so I asked him if he had ever appeared in a film. 'Oh, no', he replied. 'They didn't want me. But I did try out for a West End musical when I was very young, thin and blonde. I auditioned for one of the Red Indians in *Annie Get Your Gun* but when I walked on stage everybody just fell about laughing.'[6]

One of Grayson's final television appearances was one of his funniest. Interviewed by Judi Spiers on BBC1's *Pebble Mill* on 28 January 1992, he was on form:

'Slack Alice works behind the bar at the Cock and Trumpet. She's not too well. She slipped on a satsuma and she had her leg up all over Christmas.'

'I don't see much of Everard these days. He's got his friend, Michael Bonaventure, and they go winkle picking in Brixham.'

On afternoon television: 'Only dogs and cats watch. It all fades after two o'clock. I go to sleep. I put my legs in tin foil and rest in the afternoon.'

On his friend Arthur Marshall, the broadcaster and raconteur: 'I miss him terribly. We used to talk about the old stars. Arthur would say "I must go now, Larry dear. I've got Anna May Wong coming for tea." And I'd say, "Well, Clive Brook is coming to see me this afternoon." This is how we used to go on.'

Notes

1. *Radio Times*, 16–22 July 1983.
2. Russell Davies (ed.), *The Kenneth Williams Diaries* (HarperCollins, 1993), p. 533.
3. 'Larry Grayson', obituary, *The Daily Telegraph* (9 January 1995).
4. Robin Houston, 'The Generation Shame', *Gay News* No. 143 (1978).
5. Andy Medhurst, 'Icons: Wilde About Larry', *Attitude* (April 1995).
6. Stephen Bourne, 'Lay off Larry!', *Capital Gay* (13 January 1995).

19

The Naked Civil Servant

In 1975, *The Naked Civil Servant* was the first television drama to portray the life of a gay man which was acceptable to the majority of its viewers. This may have been helped by its historical setting, London's Soho in the 1930s and the Second World War, when it was against the law to be homosexual. The gentle effeminacy of its subject, Quentin Crisp, appealed to most viewers. Philip Mackie adapted it from Crisp's autobiography, published in 1968, and his brilliant script helped enormously to make this a landmark in British television, as did John Hurt's outstanding portrayal of Crisp. Keith Howes has described Crisp as:

> The most visible – and therefore the most despised, beaten and spat upon – gay man in Britain ... His crusade was to make people understand that effeminate homosexual men like himself existed. His weapons were hennaed hair, long finger nails, mascara and lipstick. His philosophy was total self-absorption and passivity. His Holy Land lay between Soho and Chelsea.[1]

Not all gay men were sympathetic towards Crisp. When 'John' was interviewed in *Between the Lines: Lives of Homosexual Men 1885–1967* (1991), he claimed that Crisp was the bravest man in the world, but revealed that gay men would cross the road and walk on the other side when they saw him coming towards them:

> It's a terrible thing to say, but he was persecuted by us as much as he was persecuted by everybody else. If we came upon him in a covered place,

like a pub or a club, we would talk to him, but I can only talk about myself. There was a Bloomsbury character, a woman, and she was a great friend to all the gays, the original faggots' moll ... he was her friend. If anybody insulted him they insulted her and she used to lash out with her handbag.[2]

According to a survey conducted by the Independent Broadcasting Authority (IBA), when *The Naked Civil Servant* was first shown, only 18 out of a sample of 475 viewers switched it off because of the content. Eighty-five per cent said that the production was 'not shocking'. Few felt that Quentin Crisp's story 'encouraged' homosexuality. However, some time later, it was revealed that the IBA were concerned about the play's content. They even censored a line of Philip Mackie's script. Out went 'Sexual intercourse is a poor substitute for masturbation.' In its place went 'Wasn't it fun in the bath tonight?' When it was first proposed for television, *The Naked Civil Servant* was rejected. According to its executive producer, Verity Lambert, in Channel 4's documentary *100 Greatest TV Characters* (tx 5 May 2001), both the play and Hurt had faced a great deal of opposition. She said: 'Everybody had turned it down. It had been everywhere and the BBC had turned it down twice. John Hurt's agent rang me up and he said "I don't want John to do this. This is going to ruin his career."' Hurt, however, saw it as an opportunity that was too good to miss:

> Robert Bolt [the screenwriter] probably put it best when he wrote to me and said, 'The shocking material aside, this is a portrait really of the tenderness of the individual against the cruelty of the crowd, and no better subject could there have been.' And, in a sense, that was what the piece was about, even though its content was about something quite different.[3]

Hurt, who first read it in 1970, recognised in Philip Mackie's script a stunning piece of writing but he also understood that it was something that was very risky for an actor to do, but it didn't deter him. Hurt, Mackie and the director Jack Gold joined forces, determined that nothing would prevent this production from being made. According to Hurt: 'We'd sworn, like the Three Musketeers, that if we got this going, we'd drop everything and make it. Well, suddenly Verity Lambert took it up with Jeremy Isaacs at Thames Television, and we had to drop everything.'[4]

Hurt was supposed to be going to New York with Tom Stoppard's play *Travesties*:

the director Peter Wood tore *strips* off me. Those were the days when directors *were* directors – they were big beasties. He said, 'How *dare* you take a poxy little English television instead of a third lead on Broadway.' I said, 'I'm terribly sorry, but I don't think it is a poxy little English television. I think it's a terrific piece, and I have to do this.'[5]

When *The Naked Civil Servant* was shown on 17 December 1975, television critics were unanimous in their praise. In his preview in *The Guardian* (15 December 1975), Peter Fiddick described it as 'one of the very best, wittiest, most honest, least offensive, and above all, most entertaining pieces of television drama you are likely to have seen this year.' Three days later in her review in *The Guardian* (18 December 1975), Nancy Banks-Smith heaped more praise on the production:

> It was as enchanting as it was inoffensive and that, I think, was due to Jack Gold's direction. He stylised the subject … It was artificial, which was reasonable as Crisp himself is an artefact. Playing Crisp … John Hurt was outstandingly good. Sounding, looking at times like a double exposure of Marlene Dietrich and Fanny Craddock.

Other critics were also impressed. As Margaret Forwood commented in *The Sun* (18 December 1975):

> *The Naked Civil Servant* was a breakthrough in television … it was the first time the subject has been treated so openly in a play – and worth watching for that reason. It was also amusing, moving, and had a lot to say about the way attitudes to homosexuality have changed … Those who find the subject distasteful probably switched off when Crisp met a group of outrageous male prostitutes. But many more probably found him instantly likeable and sympathetic, with his flippant bravery in the face of the violence so often dished out to his kind.

Peter Lennon in the *Sunday Times* (21 December 1975):

> John Hurt tackled this dramatically excessive character in the only sensible way possible: he reproduced, and very effectively, Crisp's camp mannerisms, but his characterisation emphasised the patience, compassion and implacable distance of Crisp's relationship to people. Jack Gold

handled this potentially disastrous subject (one shudders at the thought of what Ken Russell would have done with it) with understanding, humour and skill, aided by an excellent script by Philip Mackie.

Peter Bennett in *Gay News* No. 86 (1976):

The prejudice and downright hatred he faced were what gave the film its momentum and, though less stunning, the hostility of other homosexuals, the virtually universal censure of society must have made it a tough life. Yet I felt sure he enjoyed every minute of it and if England in the '30s, '40s and '50s had not hated homosexuals then I'm sure Mr Crisp would have been something else. Perhaps a witch, in an earlier age.

John Hurt:

The whole business of *The Naked Civil Servant* was quite astonishing. We thought we'd done something pretty well, but we didn't expect the massive reaction we got. I'd never seen a mailbag like it, and you wouldn't have thought – what with all those homophobes and bigots – that the letters would be from people who said the film had made them change their minds and their attitudes. I couldn't get into a taxi and pay the fare: the drivers wouldn't accept my money. It was extraordinary, a real watershed at the time. I think people realized that *The Naked Civil Servant* wasn't just about homosexuality. I think the whole business of the unloved – all those rather difficult and grey areas – seemed to touch a lot of people.[6]

To say that *The Naked Civil Servant* changed the life of Quentin Crisp would be an understatement. In the audio commentary for the Network DVD release, recorded in July 2005, Hurt recalled that, before it was screened on television, he went to see Quentin Crisp's show at the King's Head, Islington. 'There were about five people in the audience,' he recalled. 'When the film came out, he moved to the Duke of York's and you couldn't get a seat!' However, for Crisp, though the success of *The Naked Civil Servant* brought him overnight fame and celebrity status, it also attracted virulent homophobia. This was something he was used to by the 1970s. Even when he was in his 70s, strangers would ring him up, threatening, 'You queer, I'll kill you.'[7]

Crisp told Hurt it was difficult for actors to play victims. 'But he has specialised in victims,' Crisp later reflected. 'When he stopped playing me, he played Caligula, which was only me in a sheet. Then he played The Elephant Man, which was only me with a paper bag over his head.'[8] Throughout it all, Crisp never lost his sense of humour and resilience.

For his remarkable performance, John Hurt deservedly received the Best Actor award from the British Academy of Film and Television Arts (BAFTA) in the television category. *The Naked Civil Servant* was also nominated for Best Single Play but it lost to Jack Rosenthal's nostalgic *The Evacuees* (directed by Alan Parker). In America, *The Naked Civil Servant* received an Emmy (American television's equivalent of the Oscar) in the Fiction category of International Award Winners.

Home video recorders were not widely used in the 1970s. Video and DVD releases hadn't been invented. So, if anyone had missed it or wanted to see it again, opportunities did not exist. However, due to its success, both with television critics and with the awards it received, Thames Television decided to give viewers a second opportunity to see *The Naked Civil Servant* on 30 May 1976. As Philip Purser commented in the *Sunday Telegraph* (6 June 1976): 'on a second viewing, Philip Mackie's script was even more cunning, Jack Gold's picture-making even more luminous, John Hurt's performance even more uncanny, than I had supposed. Not a single scene dragged.' When Thames screened it for the third time on 13 December 1977, Quentin Crisp was given a two-page spread in the *TV Times*, which he wrote himself and called 'My love affair with the world'. Just before the third showing, W. Stephen Gilbert commented in *The Observer* ('Littered with despair,' 11 December 1977):

Garlanded with awards, it deserves to be seen again. For it *is* a marvellous film, marvellously filmic. And John Hurt's portrayal of its subject, Quentin Crisp, is certainly the best any actor could have realised … Yet the film is littered with despair. Although Crisp was able to make the basic leap that every gay needs to make – 'I learned that I was not the only one in the world' –and to pinpoint the gay's fundamental problem of social ignorance – 'people hate when they don't understand' – he perpetually sees himself as being outside … the film is ambiguous. Made by as heterosexual a production team as you'd find anywhere in television, it's real effect is to appeal to everyone's liberalism while leaving non gay people free to despise *every other* gay in the safety of Crisp's particularity … It *is* possible to be gay and to live more comfortably than that. But how often does TV reflect such security?

In 1981, the openly gay American film historian Vito Russo observed in his acclaimed book *The Celluloid Closet: Homosexuality in the Movies* (1981):

> Although Quentin Crisp's story ... was not the dream of a gay liberationist, gays admired and respected Crisp's defiant lifestyle enormously. Crisp makes public hay of the fact that he is not a gay militant, but he may in fact have been one of the first gay activists in his own passive way. A man who dyed his hair, wore eye makeup and painted his lips and nails, a man who refused to deny his homosexuality, Crisp was a revolutionary soon after the turn of the century. In revealing his life and opinions in print and on film, he is himself an implicit challenge to the myth; the stereotype speaks. *The Naked Civil Servant* said that flamboyant, overt homosexuality was heroic and the struggle to remain different in a conformist world was admirable.[9]

The early television screenings also had a big impact on the writer and media lecturer Andy Medhurst, who was a teenager at the time. He later recalled:

> It had an incredible impact. I watched it while my parents were at a works dinner. I knew they would be back at midnight and it didn't finish until 12.30. I sat near the on-off switch in case they came back. By the third showing I had come out, so we watched it together. It was tense-making because I wanted them to like it.[10]

At the time of its first screening, Britain's popular bi-weekly newspaper *Gay News* continued to provide a platform for analysis and criticism of gays on television, and one of its most vocal critics was Robin Houston. In 1977, Houston acknowledged that, in the 1960s, any publicity for gays was considered to be good publicity, and to have the subject talked about or enacted on radio or television was considered a triumph in itself. However, by the time *The Naked Civil Servant* was first screened in 1975, Houston pointed out that there had been a maturity in the political thinking of gay men:

> We now understand that *bad* publicity – of which oppressive gay humour is an example – is nothing more nor less than bad publicity. Unfortunately that concept isn't at all widely understood yet, even amongst many gay activists. Because of this the majority of gays still feel

that the mere appearance of someone openly gay on radio and television – regardless of the circumstances surrounding that appearance – is a leap forward in public acceptance.[11]

Houston welcomed the transmission of *The Naked Civil Servant* for its portrayal, at peak viewing time, of an 'out' gay man: 'It was a brilliant film. It reached millions of people, it won repeats, it was transmitted in New York, it won international prizes, and it won fame for Crisp.' But, added Houston, Crisp's life story was an apology for being gay, boasting his self-oppression, his self-hatred and his lack of pride. Crisp had predicted, before the film was made, that 'Homosexuals of the world will say that the cause of homosexuality has been taken back a *thousand years* through identification with this terrible pained creature prancing through the streets.' Houston agreed: '*The Naked Civil Servant* brought the unhappy, mincing, self-deprecatory unloving "queer" right into millions of living rooms, telling viewers that as one of the stately homos of England he is the god-image for all gays.' Houston asked that, if he had not done this, had the film not been self-oppressive and sad, would it have been transmitted? Houston doubted it would have been. The film required the Independent Broadcasting Authority's approval before it could be shown.[12]

After the New York transmission, America's popular television chat show host, Dick Cavett, asked the IBA's Chair, Lady Plowden, how the Authority had come to approve the film. She replied: 'We viewed it, and we considered it to be an excellent film, beautifully shot, very sensitively handled, and above all it was *sad*, so we allowed it to be shown.' Houston asked, 'Do we take it that if the film had been happy – if it had shown homosexuality in a positive light – it wouldn't have been approved?'[13]

In the British Film Institute's *bfi TV 100* list, published in 2000, *The Naked Civil Servant* ranked fourth in the Top 100 list, after *Fawlty Towers*, *The Wednesday Play: Cathy Come Home* and *Doctor Who*. In the Single Drama list it was placed second after *Cathy Come Home*. It is also worth noting, as a testament to its enduring appeal, that *The Naked Civil Servant* was repeated at least six times from 1976 to 1991. Today it is still a candidate for the *only* television drama to have been screened on three channels: ITV, Channel 4 and BBC. Thames repeated it in 1976 and 1977, and in 1989 they screened it again for their 21st anniversary celebrations. Channel 4 showed it twice, in 1983 and 1986, and in 1991 BBC2 included it in *Saturday Night Out*, an evening devoted to lesbian and gay programmes.

In 2009, Hurt revisited the role of Crisp in *An Englishman in New York*, an acclaimed television sequel to *The Naked Civil Servant* which covered Crisp's life (and popularity) in New York. However, not everyone was impressed. In a press release dated 28 December 2009, the day of the transmission on ITV1, the human rights activist Peter Tatchell acknowledged that Crisp was 'astonishingly brave and defiant as an out gay man in the 1930s and 1940s,' but that he was also a 'contradictory, infuriating figure' who became defiantly self-obsessed, homophobic and reactionary. Crisp denounced the gay rights movement and slammed homosexuality as a 'terrible disease'. Tatchell felt that the new television drama, though good, 'sanitises Crisp's ignorant, pompous homophobia … Quentin hated the fact that he was no longer unique'.[14]

In 1981, Crisp adopted New York as his home. He died in 1999 at the age of 90, days before embarking on another British tour of his one-man show. According to James Cary Parkes in *Gay Times*:

> It was never said of him that he was a kind man, and kindness was never expected of him. Admired as a survivor, as a testimony to endurance in the face of seemingly insurmountable hate, Crisp was a victim who practised being pathetic with boundless enthusiasm. But whatever he was, he wasn't what he was often mistaken for – a typical queer.[15]

When Crisp died, the pop star Boy George told *The Pink Paper*:

> Despite his often-contentious views on the gay lifestyle, I have always loved and admired Mr Crisp. I think of him as a gay suffragette, he was out on the front-line in rouge and henna and he provided a light at the end of the tunnel for us more freaky queers. God bless his soul.[16]

Fittingly, in his last interview two days before his death, Crisp explained: 'I had no alternatives. I lived among the only people who could bear the disgrace of me. No alternatives, and so nothing to regret.'[17]

Notes

1. Robert Aldrich and Garry Wotherspoon (eds.), *Who's Who in Contemporary Gay and Lesbian History: From World War II to the Present Day* (Routledge, 2001), p. 96.
2. Kevin Porter and Jeffrey Weeks (eds.), *Between the Lines: Lives of Homosexual Men 1885–1967* (Routledge, 1991), p. 140.

3. Paul Bailey (ed.), *The Stately Homo: A Celebration of Quentin Crisp* (Bantam Press, 2000), pp. 159–62.
4. Simon Hattenstone, 'God save the queen', *The Guardian Weekend*, 21 November 2009.
5. *Ibid.*
6. Bailey, pp. 159–62.
7. Simon Hattenstone, 'Miracle on 3rd Street', *The Guardian*, 12 December 1998.
8. Hattenstone, 'God save the queen'.
9. Vito Russo, *The Celluloid Closet: Homosexuality in the Movies* (Harper and Row, 1981), pp. 224–5.
10. Keith Howes, *Broadcasting It: An Encyclopaedia of Homosexuality on Film, Radio and TV in the UK 1923–1993* (Cassell, 1993), p. 536.
11. Robin Houston, 'The Distorting Mirrors', *Gay News* No. 118, (1977).
12. *Ibid.*
13. *Ibid.*
14. Peter Tatchell, 'Quentin Crisp – No hero to gays' (28 December 2009) www.petertatchell.net.
15. James Cary Parkes, 'The mother of all queens', *Gay Times*, January 2000.
16. Cary James, 'The queen is dead', *The Pink Paper*, 26 November 1999.
17. Patrick Newley, *The Stage*, 25 November 1999.

Douglas Byng in *The Television Festival Dinner* (BBC, 1938). (Alexandra Palace Television Society)

Basil Langton as Charles Granillo in *Rope* (BBC, 1939). (Alexandra Palace Television Society)

Oliver Burt as Wyndham Brandon in *Rope* (BBC, 1939). (Alexandra Palace Television Society)

Vivienne Bennett as Queen Isabella, David Markham as Edward II and Alan Wheately as Gaveston in *Edward II* (BBC, 1947). (BBC)

Peter Wyngarde and Graydon Gould in *Play of the Week: Youth* (Granada, 1959). (ITV/Shutterstock)

Micheal MacLiammoir in *On Trial: Oscar Wilde* (Granada, 1960). (ITV/Shutterstock)

Tony Warren (Author's Collection)

John Hopkins (Author's Collection)

lfred Lynch and Nicol Williamson in *The Wednesday Play: Horror of Darkness* (BBC, 1965). (BBC)

an Marsh, George Innes, Gordon Jackson, Christopher Beeny and Angela Baddeley in *Upstairs, ownstairs* ('Rose's Pigeon') (London Weekend Television, 1973). (ITV/Shutterstock)

Noele Gordon and Larry Grayson in *Crossroads* (ATV, 1975) (ITV/Shutterstock)

Michael Cashman and June Brown in *EastEnders* (1986). (Lord Michael Cashman)

Quentin Crisp and John Hurt in 1975. (Fremantle Media/Shutterstock)

Drew Griffiths in 1977 (Robert Workman Archive, Bishopsgate Institute)

Sam Dale and Karl Johnson in *The Other Side: Only Connect* (BBC, 1979). (BBC)

nthony Andrews and Jeremy Irons in *Brideshead Revisited* (Granada, 1981). (ITV/Shutterstock)

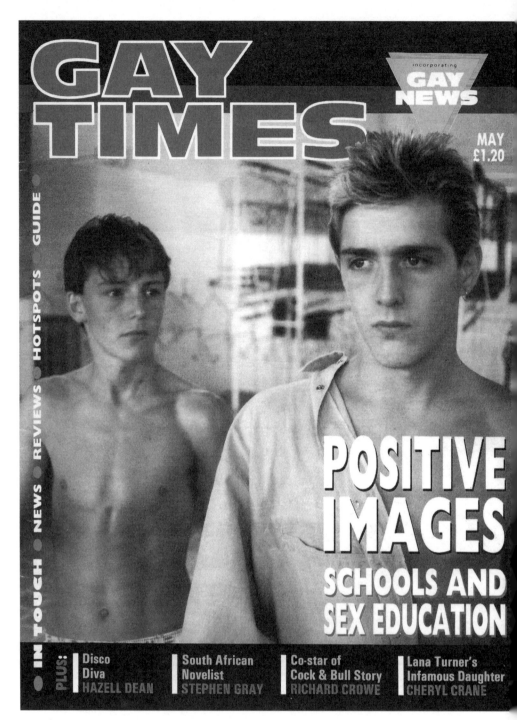

Two of Us on the cover of *Gay Times* (1988). (*Gay Times*)

20

The Year of the Big Flood

In his excellent *Gay News* survey 'Gays on Television 1960–1977', Keith Howes described 1976 as the year of the 'Big Flood'. He was referring to a number of gay-themed documentaries and dramas which surfaced throughout the year.[1] Howes acknowledged that, following the success of *The Naked Civil Servant*, gay visibility increased on British television screens. Some of the programmes were disappointing and at least one, 'For Queer Read Gay', made for the BBC series *Sex in Our Time*, was produced but not screened. However, there was some interesting and occasionally outstanding work to be seen. The times they were a-changing.

The 1976 'flood' began with writer Frederic Raphael's acclaimed six-part series *The Glittering Prizes* (BBC2, tx 21 January to 25 February). It followed the lives of a group of Cambridge students who meet as undergraduates in 1952. Raphael's six 'plays' looked at their individual successes and failures, right through to middle age in the 1970s. The only gay student is the exhibitionist Denis Porson, played by a very young, slim and attractive Nigel Havers. He appeared only briefly in the first episode, but in episode two he is seen to be successfully integrated into the group, and flirtatious with the other male students, who are not bothered. However, he only exists on the periphery of the group. Porson has to draw attention to himself by talking loudly and waving his arms. Before episode two is over, he has been arrested for cottaging, found guilty of 'gross indecency' and imprisoned for two years. He tells his sympathetic friends Adam and Barbara (Tom Conti and Barbara Kellerman) that he was happy at Cambridge: 'A three-year lease on paradise.' Porson then vanishes until episode four, set in 1964, when he reappears as the owner of a country pub in Norfolk. However, he is barely seen. Porson is a marginal, under-written character and it is regrettable that Raphael did not make him more central to the drama, because Nigel Havers is a fine actor and managed to give some depth to the character and draw attention to himself in his few scenes. If only Raphael had given Porson more scope. One thing that Raphael did do was draw attention to the post-war homosexual 'witch hunt' which resulted in an escalation in the victimisation, criminalisation and imprisonment of gay men.

ITV's inclusion of a gay couple in *The Crezz* (Thames Television, tx 16 September–2 December 1976) should have been a major break-through. In some respects it was, thanks to the actors who played them. In this twelve-part comedy-drama series, Terry and Denny are accepted by the inhabitants of 'Carlisle Crescent' in North London and seem to have the most stable relationship of all the couples in the series, but this antique-dealing couple were portrayed in terms of husband and wife. 'He' (Terry), played by Roland Curram, was a straight-acting, pipe-smoking, moustached antique dealer; 'she' (Denny), played by Paul Greenhalgh, was an effeminate screaming queen, who wore a silk kerchief round his neck. Regrettably, there were times when *The Crezz* relied on this pair of bitchy queens for comedy relief, but there were also times that they took centre stage. In 'Bent Doubles' (tx 4 November), the neighbours rally round and support Terry when Denny abandons him and runs off with the gardener.

At the press launch, Paul Greenhalgh explained to *Gay News* that the characterisation of the gay couple improved as the series progressed, and that he and Roland Curram *had* changed the script considerably. 'It was full of "petals",' he explained. 'We took those out.' Greenhalgh also hoped that the gay couple would be allowed to kiss on screen.[2] In the next issue of *Gay News*, a review condemned the series: 'There is no excuse for Thames Television to spend £700,000 on what is almost a replica of an early sixties' Sunday afternoon serial tricked out with the odd four-letter word. Too twee for satire, too sophisticated for soap opera, *The Crezz*, at prezz, is a mezz.'[3]

Three issues later, Jeff Grace interviewed Curram and Greenhalgh in *Gay News*. Curram explained that someone of his character's age (45) would have grown up in an atmosphere where homosexuality was unacceptable: 'It was illegal, right, so he had to keep it underground, be very careful. He always wore a shirt and tie and didn't flap his wrists, especially in front of the next-door neighbours and in public. So, I thought that a man whose upbringing would have been fairly proper wouldn't scream around.' Greenhalgh drew attention to his wardrobe and what the producer and director expected a gay man to wear:

> They wanted me to wear the most extraordinary things and the wardrobe lady who took me shopping was terribly disappointed that I didn't choose brushed nylon fur, beads and high-heeled clogs. She said: 'Oh, I am so disappointed. I was really looking forward to dressing you up.' Actually, I did compromise over the first episode. They wanted me to wear a knitted waistcoat and no shirt. I said, 'not with my body!' but I gave in over that dreaded paisley silk kerchief round my neck.[4]

In the same issue, when Keith Howes reviewed the episode 'Bent Doubles', he said that he liked it:

> Alick Rowe's script provided a string of amusing, if obvious situations … It was fun in a simple-minded way with conservative and permissive attitudes used as Aunt Sallys. Unfortunately, Terry and Denny's relationship was little more than a catalyst and it was their bitching which was highlighted rather than any real emotional and physical feelings, but Roland Curram as the pernickety, stolid Terry gave an excellent and touching performance of hurt pride and resignation – and affection.[5]

Greenhalgh described *The Crezz* as 'a very brave failure' but, by the time Curram and Greenhalgh were interviewed in *Gay News*, the series was almost over. For good. Poor ratings meant that ITV shunted it from an early evening slot to after the ten o'clock news because *The Crezz* could not compete with the American crime drama *Kojak* on BBC1. When the series ended on 2 December, it was not recommissioned.

In 1976, two contrasting single plays starred two of Britain's finest and most celebrated classical actors playing gay: BBC1's *Play of the Month* adaptation of Oscar Wilde's *The Picture of Dorian Gray* with Sir John Gielgud, and Granada TV's *The Collection* by Harold Pinter starring Sir Laurence Olivier. *The Picture of Dorian Gray* (tx 19 September 1976) was dramatised by John Osborne. Some critics found Peter Firth (as Dorian Gray) beautiful in the looks department but wooden in his performance. Nicholas de Jongh described Firth in *The Guardian* (20 September 1976) as 'looking like a very prim, slightly androgynous Scottish governess – shades of Maggie Smith's Jean Brodie.' De Jongh added that Jeremy Brett, as the painter Basil Hallward, who falls in love with Dorian, 'seemed dwarfed by the furniture'. De Jongh thoroughly approved of Gielgud, who spoke the Wildean epigrams and truisms 'with the nonchalance and natural- ness of a man thoroughly at home in the period'. In fact, television critics were unanimous in their praise of Gielgud's portrayal of the hedonistic Lord Henry Wootton. His biographer Jonathan Croall described it as one of his most subtle performances:

> Hampered by a startling red wig, he poured forth a stream of epigrams with perfect *fin-de-siècle* nonchalance and wit. The over-elaborate production kept the homosexual nature of the characters' relation- ships implicit, allowing him to play 'the love that dare not speak its name' with subtle restraint, and put over the old roué's sadness with great poignancy.[6]

James Murray couldn't contain himself in the *Daily Express* (18 September 1976). He declared that Gielgud's magnificence and skill as an actor had created:

> An immortal piece of television with his performance ... For a glorious hour, Sir John dominates the screen picking up Wilde's verbal fireworks, and scoring goal after goal while the rest of the players are still wait- ing for the referee's whistle for the start of play – if you'll forgive the mixed metaphors.

Murray then listed some of Wotton's best 'one-liners' including: 'Men marry because they are tired. Women because they are curious. Both are disap- pointed.' Stewart Lane observed in the *Morning Star* (22 September 1976): 'It was, for me, the elegant diction of John Gielgud, delivering Oscar Wilde's epigrammatic wit with panache, which gave true strength to John Osborne's dramatisation.' Lane added, 'There was no surprise in Osborne underlining, with a gesture here and there, the homosexual undertones of Wilde's mannered fable of the handsome young man whose sins and ageing are registered on his portrait, and only transferred to him at the moment of death.'

Granada TV's series *Laurence Olivier Presents* included an adapta- tion of Harold Pinter's acclaimed 1960 stage drama *The Collection* (tx 5 December 1976). Laurence Olivier described the play as one of the best ever seen on the British stage. He played Harry, a wealthy gay dress designer, and Malcolm McDowell was cast as his young lover, Bill. They come under attack from the menacing James (Alan Bates) when he accuses Bill of sleeping with his wife (Helen Mirren). Bates's biographer Donald Spoto described *The Collection* as 'a spare, witty but disturbing treatment of people suddenly caught up in suspicions of infidelity and the tangle of a gay relationship'[7] The (unidentified) critic of *The People* (5 December 1976) was full of praise, especially for Olivier: 'If you've never really watched a great actor catch Laurence Olivier in *The Collection* and have something to tell your grandchildren. He is simply superb – towering over the near-perfect performances of Alan Bates and Helen Mirren.'

Granada TV launched its popular courtroom-based daytime drama serial *Crown Court* on 18 October 1972 and it enjoyed a long and successful run until 1984. It was shown as a series of three-part, half-hour stories (on three consecutive afternoons). A new case was presented each week and homosexuality was just one of the many 'controversial' subjects tackled by the writers. Others included heroin smuggling, indecent assault, illegal abortion, murder, arson and racism. It was gripping stuff, made even more compulsive by the inclusion of a jury made up of real people, not actors. They delivered their verdicts at the end of episode three.

In 1976, *Crown Court* included not one but two of the most outstanding television dramas about gay men. In 'Beyond the Call of Duty' (tx 4/5/6 February), Keith Drinkel played Colin Tyler, a popular and respected teacher at a comprehensive school. Tyler finds himself in court charged with the indecent assault of one of his pupils, a 15-year-old who comes from a troubled background. The prosecution claims that Tyler took the lad under his wing, and then took advantage of him. In the dock, Tyler confirms that he is gay but insists that he would not engage in sexual conduct with one of his pupils and that any inappropriate contact was accidental. Tyler was found not guilty. The superb script of 'Beyond the Call of Duty' was written by Michael O'Neill and Jeremy Seabrook. The actor Keith Drinkel, then best known for his role as the university-educated Philip Ashton who joins the army in the Granada TV series *A Family at War* (1970–72), gave a memorable performance. In 1976, Seabrook published his acclaimed book *A Lasting Relationship: Homosexuals and Society*, a collection of interviews he conducted with a diverse range of gay men, both single and couples.

Other sympathetic depictions of gay men in *Crown Court* included 'Meeting Place' (tx 10/11/12 January 1978) in which Leslie Simon (Derek Smith), an introverted middle-aged bachelor, is accused of assaulting a cocky, extrovert 19-year-old Barry Gems (Gerry Sundquist) in a public lavatory. Cross-examined, Gems describes Smith as a 'rotten queer, he makes me feel sick' but it is Gems who is found guilty of grievous bodily harm and sentenced to three months in a detention centre. According to Keith Howes in *Gay News*, this story was 'gripping and frequently witty' and dealt with a difficult case 'in a penetrating way with Kathleen Potter's script making the most out of the hypocrisies and the humour to be squeezed from a modern-day variant upon something nasty in the woodshed'.[8]

The best of all the *Crown Court* 'gay' three-part stories is undoubtedly 'Lola' (tx 8/9/10 December 1976). Philip Sayer gave a magnificent performance as Lola Martin who identifies himself as a gay transvestite. He finds himself in the dock after being accused by a 'plain clothes' police officer of importuning in a gay club. The officer is the dodgy Detective Sergeant Jeffrey Lent (Nicholas Ball) who has also accused Lola of assaulting him. The 'plain clothes' worn by the undercover cop were made of black leather with silver charms around his neck. David Yallop's script cleverly brought together a number of pro-gay attitudes like the trouncing of Lola's woman psychologist who believed in aversion therapy, and the exploitative attitudes of newspaper journalists towards gays and, especially, transvestites. Yallop presented Lola as someone who had realised that guilt and fear are wrong, not homosexuality. These were serious issues for an afternoon's viewing on British television in 1976, and 'Lola' did not shy away from confronting some viewers with situations they had never encountered. Added to these was the police entrapment of gay men, or, in Lola's words, their attempts to 'roll over a few queers'. *Dixon of Dock Green* was never like this and *Z Cars* didn't go this far. The story had a shocking finale too. When Lola enters the witness box to give evidence, he wears full drag (until then he has conformed and worn a plain suit and tie). He declares he is a transvestite who is proud to be gay. In a passionate and moving speech, Lola explains that, in his view, the persecution of gays is larger than that of other groups, such as Jews and Catholics. He claims that he has been exploited by the police officer, and that is why he became a 'raving, screaming queen' and assaulted him, but that is not all. The policeman's sexuality is also questioned, by Lola's barrister, and Lola himself. Lola asks the court to consider why he kissed him. 'Why he did this is his problem or maybe he thought I was a woman – or maybe he is a closet queen?' The jury found Lola not guilty.

Notes

1. Keith Howes, 'Gays on Television 1960–1977, Part 2: The Fat Years, 1975-77', *Gay News*, No. 132 (1977).
2. 'Paul and Roland cut out the "petals"', *Gay News*, No. 103 (1976).
3. 'On the box', *Gay News*, No. 104 (1976).
4. Jeff Grace, 'Terry & Denny & Roly & Pauly', *Gay News*, No. 107 (1976).
5. *Ibid.*
6. Jonathan Croall, *Gielgud: A Theatrical Life 1904–2000* (Methuen, 2001), p. 484.
7. Donald Spoto, *Otherwise Engaged: The Life of Donald Spoto* (Hutchinson, 2007), pp. 150–51.
8. Keith Howes, *Gay News*, No. 135 (1978).

21

Schuman's *Follies*

Thames Television's *Rock Follies* is one of the most original television productions seen in Britain. Critically acclaimed, it became one of the most
popular television series of 1976. *Rock Follies* was the brainchild of writer
Howard Schuman and his satirical and often savagely funny musical drama
explored the cutthroat side of the UK music business. Schuman focussed
on a trio of women who were formed into the Little Ladies rock band by
a composer who groomed them for stardom. The band's career highs and
lows captured the imagination of British viewers, and the series made such
an impression on members of the British Academy of Film and Television
Arts (BAFTA) that they voted it that year's Best Drama Series/Serial over
such classics as *I, Claudius* and *The Glittering Prizes*. Schuman was commissioned to put together a sequel. However, in the first series he hadn't
included any major gay characters, and for the sequel he was determined
to change this.

Meanwhile, 'The Show Business' (tx 24 February 1976), the first episode
of the first series, did feature a gay character called William Bishop (Jeffrey
Gardiner). He was a theatrical but dainty director/choreographer of a
hopelessly out-of-date stage musical called *Broadway Annie*. He was inept
but had a high opinion of himself. In his 60s and past it, Bishop is incapable of holding *Broadway Annie* together. His direction is extremely limited.
'Think Peter Pan,' he says. 'Make it light, delicate, gay. Remember you're a
delicate little soap bubble.' He lives in the past and amuses the bored cast
of the show with anecdotes from his career in the theatre. He is introduced
as 'a man of great talent who gave us some memorable revues in the forties
and fifties'. However, Bishop points out that his career ended in the 1960s

when satirical stage and television productions like '*Beyond the Fringe* and *TW3* came along'. Unsurprisingly, *Broadway Annie* is a disaster. In addition to Bishop, there is a brief appearance by Frank Williams, who would have been recognised by viewers as the vicar from *Dad's Army*, as an effeminate makeup man on the set of a porn film starring Q (Rula Lenska), before she becomes one of the Little Ladies.

Rock Follies of '77 (tx 4 May–6 December 1977) repeated the success of the first series and Schuman realised his ambition to integrate fully rounded and realistic gay characters into the story. One of them is Harry Moon (Derek Thompson), a footloose, cocky young Northerner who becomes the manager of the Little Ladies. Harry's flatmate Ken Church (Denis Lawson) contributes occasional articles to *Gay News*. When Q makes a pass at Harry, he turns her down by explaining that Ken is his flatmate *plus*. The two final episodes in the series showed Harry's brief (and enjoyable) affair with Q and Ken's reaction to it. In *Gay News*, when Keith Howes reported on this breakthrough (an openly gay writer creating openly gay characters in a popular television drama), he commented that the actors playing the gay characters were heterosexual and 'trepidacious' about essaying their first gay roles.

Denis Lawson felt that Ken was 'the sort of South London boy who is quite camp but I haven't played him camp'. Physically, Denis based Ken on Howard Schuman: cropped hair and glasses. Derek Thompson describes himself as a 'token Left-wing, fist-raising gay sympathiser' who knew nothing about gays on a one-to-one basis. The nervousness began to fade as the two actors worked together, and for the final episode Derek says that 'we were flinging in as much mouth-to-mouth contact as we could, hoping that 10% would get through the editing.'[1]

Thompson was quite upfront with Howes about compromises made in the new series of *Rock Follies*. Though it was still one of the most innovative and pro-gay series on television at that time, he said: 'the show hasn't got the guts to say things it should about politics and social issues. It's been put through the media mincer.'[2] A few months later, Schuman reflected:

The only thing I'm sorry about is that I didn't show Harry and Ken in bed together. I thought that it was important to have one informal physical scene between them and I actually wrote it but we didn't feel it worked so it was scrapped. But if anything has been successful in *Rock Follies of '77* I'd like to think that it is the character of Harry. If kids, for example, like

Harry and really respond to him then, in theory, it should make them less afraid or uptight about being gay. But it's an opening volley. It's only useful in the larger context if different strands are picked up and developed by other people.[3]

Acknowledgement of Schuman's dazzling television work of the 1970s, including two series of *Rock Follies* and a number of single plays, was swift. In 1981, Paul Madden celebrated the writer with a retrospective called *Schuman's Follies: The TV Plays of Howard Schuman* at the National Film Theatre. Madden described Schuman as a writer whose work 'triumphantly breaks through the barriers of television's run-of-the-mill naturalism ... the camp and the comic disguise serious purposes. Above all he is a social satirist who takes a sharp scalpel to the follies and foibles of the rock generation.'[4] In 1996, the National Film Theatre celebrated the work of Schuman again with a special event in *Out of the Archives*, a lesbian and gay television retrospective. Schuman was interviewed onstage by Stephen Jeffery-Poulter, who described the writer in his introduction as:

One gay man who has undeniably made a unique contribution to British television for almost a quarter of a century. One of Howard Schuman's greatest dramatic gifts is his ability to inject a quirky, warm and, above all, gentle humour into every one of his dramas ... he is a playwright who has always revelled in experimentation – mixing genres, exploiting the latest technology, creating new and unique TV drama forms, while invariably offering a critique and commentary on the evolution of television itself ... A Howard Schuman drama is always energetic, original and amusing, invariably challenging and subversive.

When Schuman was interviewed by Russell T Davies, writer of *Queer as Folk*, for *The Observer* (16 June 2002), he reflected on what he was trying to do with *Rock Follies*:

I wanted to deal with the current decadent era in which rock music and bands were being manufactured. It seemed to mirror what was happening socially at the time. Men had all the power in the rock industry and I wanted to look at men and women. I had this idea about three actresses who would be in a show. One would have a rock background, one would be a chanteuse and the other a Shakespearean actress who had never sung anything and they would become a group who would be manipulated by this guy … It was also a chance to be as funny as possible and use music, and see how much serious stuff you could get beneath it.

When Davies alluded to the lack of imagination in television drama in 2002, Schuman responded with an answer that would be relevant now:

The bane of British drama is condescension to the audiences. Genre is an important part of contemporary drama but there's too much of it, and too much soap-opera influence. When I began [in the 1970s] the competition was to find the most idiosyncratic voice. Dennis Potter could describe television as our true national theatre, but TV allowed for different points of view then. Now, with exceptions like Paul Abbott or Caroline Aherne, there's no ambiguity in either the writing or the acting. I always believe the talent is out there, it's just a question of where it goes. The trouble is, you and I in our different eras were inspired by simply watching television. But kids now, what are they watching, what are they going to aspire to?

Notes

1. Keith Howes, 'Rock Follies a Deux', _Gay News_ No. 120 (1977).
2. _Ibid._
3. Keith Howes, 'Uncensored', _Gay News_ No. 133 (1978).
4. Paul Madden, _Schuman's Follies,_ National Film Theatre programme booklet, May 1981.

22

Burgess, Blasphemy
and Bennett

ITV Playhouse's production of Ian Curteis's spy thriller *Philby, Burgess and Maclean* (Granada, tx 31 May 1977) starred Derek Jacobi as the flamboyant gay traitor Guy Burgess. It was Jacobi's first television role since his acclaimed appearance in BBC2's *I, Claudius*. Set in the twilight world of espionage, reviews were favourable. According to Paul Byrne in *Films and Filming* (March 1985):

> That the film works well is due not only to the actors, but to [director] Gordon Flemyng's ability to keep up a level of tension throughout. There is no suspense, no surprises (because we know the story) – but we are made to feel the awful nervous anguish of the professional spy, the strain of being on guard 24 hours a day, of never letting the mask slip.

The role of the extrovert, over-the-top Guy Burgess was suited to the screen, as Alan Bennett later recognised in his brilliant television film *An Englishman Abroad* (1983) (see Chapter 26). Jacobi rose to the challenge and for his memorable performance he was nominated for a BAFTA. The production was nominated for Best Single Play but lost to *Play for Today: Spend, Spend, Spend*.

In 1977, the Old Bailey saw the first trial for blasphemy in the United Kingdom for over half a century. Instigated by Mary Whitehouse against *Gay News* for its publication of James Kirkup's poem 'The Love That Dares to Speak its Name', it ended in a conviction, heavy fines and

a suspended prison sentence for the newspaper's editor, Denis Lemon.
Kirkup's poem gave the viewpoint of a Roman centurion who graphically
describes having sex with Jesus after his crucifixion. Only ten weeks later,
the BBC's *Everyman* team produced *Blasphemy at the Old Bailey* (BBC1,
tx 18 September 1977), one of the fullest 'dramatic reconstructions' of
a criminal trial ever shown on television in Britain. The programme set
out to question whether the prosecution was an attack on free speech or a
necessary defence of the principle that, even in a sexually liberated society,
some things must remain sacred. Interviews with Lemon, Whitehouse and
others were included, with an enactment of the trial played entirely by
professional actors. In *Gay News*, Alison Hennegan was impressed:

> Courtroom battles have become a cinematic cliché, but here the tension
> was inescapably real. Mine weren't the only guts which knotted during
> that total stillness which accompanied the bemused jurors' first read-
> ing of the poem, or during those moments awaiting their verdict … the
> real Mary Whitehouse was clearly as shaken as I was – albeit for different
> reasons – by Geoff Robertson's intensely moving and compelling clos-
> ing speech. And, all the time, cutting and flashing through the barbed
> sobriety of the Old Bailey were the real people – accused and his accuser,
> a Mrs Whitehouse who was oh-so reasonable, with just the odd hint of
> an ingenuousness so great as to be entirely unconvincing.[1]

Hennegan added that the *Everyman* series was planning to screen a second
programme at a later date which would tackle the issues involved but,
she said, 'paradoxically, the re-enactment of the trial itself allowed many
of the basic questions to emerge with unmistakable clarity'.[2] *Everyman:
Blasphemy – A Law on Trial* was shown on BBC1 on 19 March 1978. Robin
Houston commented in *Gay News*: 'It was a sincere, comprehensive and
educative programme on the law of blasphemy', but 'The presence of
Mary Whitehouse, her stuttering astonishment, interviewer-patronage,
declarations of no malevolent intent and Cheshire Cat smile overshadowed
the programme and bode ill for us all. By contrast, Denis Lemon could
barely raise a smile at all. Which was a pity, because his, at least, is honest.'[3]
Blasphemous libel ceased to be a common law offence in England and
Wales with the passing of the Criminal Justice and Immigration Act 2008.

BBC2's *Premiere* series gave opportunities to new directors to direct
their first dramas for television. The enjoyable series of thirty-minute plays

included Richard O'Brien's *A Hymn from Jim* (tx 29 September 1977), directed by Colin Bucksey, and *The Obelisk* (tx 13 October 1977), directed by Giles Foster, based on a short story by E.M. Forster. *A Hymn from Jim* was a bizarre, stylised thriller in which Jim Tayo (Christopher Guard), a pretty but psychotic gay pop star, murders his black one-night stand Sugar (Reg Tsiboe) by smashing him over the head with his solid gold, million-selling disc. The acclaimed television dramatist Dennis Potter described O'Brien's high camp, humorous and moving melodrama with songs in the *Sunday Times* (2 October 1977) as 'dazzling … a precious parody of a parody', while Colin Pavlow in *Variety* (28 September 1977) considered it 'extremely adventurous and refreshing'. In complete contrast, *The Obelisk*, set in 1938, was an engaging piece about a middle-aged couple's brief encounter with two young sailors at the seaside. It was filmed entirely on location in Weston-super-Mare. Peter Sallis was superb as Ernest, a pompous schoolmaster who dominated his wife Hilda (Rosemary Martin). In *The Guardian* (14 October 1977), Nancy Banks-Smith explained to her readers that Forster's short story, written in 1939, was never published in his lifetime (he died in 1970), because he believed it would be considered indecent. 'It was the word he used,' she said, adding that 'saucy' is the strongest possible word one would use to describe Forster's:

> Lovely little seaside joke, a literary man's Donald McGill. It is almost pure postcard material … but it would never have been printed even as a postcard between the wars for the joke is homosexual … the *Premiere* production was light, delightful, ironic and, well yes, I suppose the word is gay. A fussy pedantic school teacher and his common, cowed wife go for the day to the seaside … They go for a walk to the obelisk, two by two, with a couple of chance-met sailors and right out of the blue, the wife enjoys one of those surging purple passions so highly thought of by lady novelists of the time. She never reaches the obelisk. Nor does the husband and his sailor.

Scum was made for BBC1's *Play for Today* series in 1977, but it remained on the shelf for fourteen years. It was a different channel, Channel 4, which dusted it off and screened it on 27 July 1991 in their *Banned* season. Writer Roy Minton set his drama in a borstal, but it was considered too realistic and hard-hitting for television viewers. Alasdair Milne, the BBC's Director-General, deemed the play unsuitable for transmission because he believed that Alan Clarke had directed something so naturalistic viewers could easily mistake it for a documentary. Ray Winstone was featured as Carlin, a rebellious inmate who invites an angelic-faced inmate to become his 'Mrs' and share his bed. In *Alan Clarke* (Faber and Faber, 1998), a collection of interviews edited by Richard Kelly, various personnel who worked on *Scum* made some interesting observations about Carlin's sexuality. They included Winstone, who commented, 'In the original [banned television version] he becomes a prison poof, and that's true, that happens in prisons. They're prison poofs when they're inside, outside they're straight as a die – I can't work that one out myself.' According to Minton:

> One of the guys I met during research, a professional villain, he told me that once you're in a dormitory, the public-school element prevails. It's not a homosexual thing, he made the point I gave to Carlin, 'I'm no fucking poofter.' But it's not unusual for professional criminals to engage in a bit of that. I thought the gay scene opened all sorts of areas up and said a lot about Carlin, his flexibility – and also the problem about being a pretty boy, which is the same in adult nicks.

When *Scum* was remade for the cinema in 1979, the relationship between Carlin and his 'Mrs' was almost entirely eliminated, thus making the new version less honest than the television version banned by the BBC.

Granada TV's *The Last Romantic* (tx 12 March 1978) starred Michael Jayston as James, a gay ex-BBC Drama Department producer who has been sacked for alcoholism. Writer Kerry Crabbe based this on his stage play and it was described by Richard Last in the *Daily Telegraph* (14 March 1978) as 'a tense but often extremely funny study in desperation'. James is the son of 'Old Gantry' (André Morell), an overbearing but literate retired army brigadier. Crabbe's play included a battle of words between the father and son, but Last felt that 'in the end it didn't get anywhere and you felt the rather obvious stage origins; the author badly needed an audience to respond to the hurled insults'. In *Gay News*, Keith Howes revealed that Jayston's gay character was portrayed as self-hating and faint-hearted, but 'the point was quite nicely made that his emotional life had been blasted by a combination of his father's militaristic bombast and the proscenium arch emotions of his work in drama'.[4]

Will Shakespeare (ATV tx 13 June–18 July 1978), the creation of writer John Mortimer, was an engaging comedy drama about the life of the playwright William Shakespeare. Mortimer's largely fictitious six-part series upset the purists because of its lack of historical facts but, in reality, facts about Shakespeare's life were thin on the ground. The series was great fun for those viewers who didn't care about historical accuracy. In early episodes, before the story becomes dark and sombre, Tim Curry portrayed the bard as bawdy, romantic and bisexual, someone who didn't hold back from exploring his desires for men and women. In episode two, 'Alms for Oblivion' (tx 20 June), set in London in 1593, he falls for handsome 'Hal' (Nicholas Clay), a seductive, ebullient thief. When Shakespeare discovers that 'Hal' is actually Henry Wriothesley, the wealthy 3rd Earl of Southampton, he accepts an invitation to move in with him. 'Why do you rather drink in a thieves kitchen?' asks Will. 'Hal' replies: 'Because I love the company of thieves, rogues and poets better than councillors, seated Lords and the pale green girls my mother would have me marry.' As portrayed by Nicholas Clay, love was written all over the face of his character, the Earl. The two men become lovers. Says 'Hal': 'I want a man such as you – a poet to draw me as I am in your verses.' Though the two men barely touch on screen, the characters are clearly devoted to each other. Shakespeare scholars have acknowledged that Shakespeare attracted patronage from the Earl, to whom he dedicated much of his poetry. Clay portrayed the Earl as a man who is not only sexually attracted to Shakespeare, but deeply in love with him. The relationship continues into episode three, 'Of Comfort and Despair' (tx 27 June), but the union falls apart when Shakespeare finds himself attracted to the 'Dark Lady' of the sonnets and the Earl becomes jealous. Shakespeare moves on.

Mortimer's (unauthorised) biographer Graham Lord revealed that the writer 'loved doing it because he had always idolised Shakespeare and knew a great deal about his plays'. Lord added that ATV built at Elstree the most expensive British television scenery ever on sets, that included a cobbled street flanked by exact models of Elizabethan houses and a replica of the Globe Theatre.[5]

The year ended on a high note with Alan Bennett's gentle and beguiling *Me, I'm Afraid of Virginia Woolf* (tx 2 December 1978). It was shown in London Weekend Television's anthology series *Six Plays by Alan Bennett*. Bennett's study of a 35-year-old college lecturer called Trevor Hopkins (Neville Smith) and his relationship with his formidable, critical mother (Thora Hird) was superbly handled. Hopkins has a problem relating to other people. He feels they disapprove of him and he hates his own name

– Trevor. Unmarried, he is uncertain about his future. Challenged – and frustrated – by the ineptitude of his adult students (he teaches evening classes in English Literature) he falls in love with a student, Dave Skinner (Derek Thompson), who is married with a young child. Skinner has energy and wit, and a sense of mischief. The physical attraction between the two men is subtly acknowledged by the exchange of looks between them, and the unexpected use of Richard Rodgers and Oscar Hammerstein II's glorious, exuberant song 'I'm in Love with a Wonderful Guy' from their musical *South Pacific*. Critics loved it. Michael Ratcliffe described it in *The Times* (30 November 1978) as 'one of the most touching and certainly the funniest play I have seen this year'. Referring to its 'gay' ending, Bennett's biographer, Alexander Games, says: 'The final moments are touchingly erotic. The screen directions are: "In the final credits sequence, Hopkins shares the frozen frame with Skinner, who is also smiling." But it is Hopkins whose smile is wicked. Skinner looks rather fond … It is the first happy ending in Bennett's work.'[6] However, for Bennett, the upbeat, exhilarating ending to this marvellous play was sabotaged on its first transmission, as he explained in his introduction to the publication of the script in 2003:

> I can never watch a tape of *Me, I'm Afraid of Virginia Woolf* without cringing at its final minute. It's not at all plain where the action is going (and wasn't plain to me when I was writing it) but five minutes from the end (when Hopkins gets it together with his student, Skinner) it turns into a love story. As they both grin cheekily there is a wonderful swelling (on the sound track, at least) and in comes *South Pacific* … climaxing with 'I have found me a wonderful guy.' Back in 1978 this was rather bold, except that in transmission the sound was (as I've always thought deliberately) faded down at this point for one of those needless announcements (since discontinued) saying, 'Hugh Lloyd is currently appearing in *Run for Your Life* at the Vaudeville Theatre.' So no danger there, and the nation's moral sensibilities remained unassaulted. It wouldn't happen now, of course, and maybe in its small way the play and others like it (though more explicit) are part of the reason why.[7]

For gay viewers, *Virginia Woolf* was meaningful because gay love stories had rarely been seen on television before. An exception was John Mortimer's *Bermondsey* (see Chapter 15). The love that dare not speak its name had finally been expressed. It is a liberating play, because it acknowledges a physical attraction between two men which is not just sexual. Though the build-up to the revelation of Hopkins's gayness is slow, it is subtle and understated, but clearly expressed. There might not be any *physical* contact between the two men, but Dave *does* flirt with Hopkins, and Hopkins *does* respond at the end, in the knowing look he gives Dave.

Notes

1. Alison Hennegan, 'Faith-saving', *Gay News* No. 127 (1977).
2. *Ibid.*
3. Robin Houston, 'Boding ill', *Gay News* No. 140 (1978).
4. Keith Howes, 'Parent trap', *Gay News* No. 139 (1978).
5. Graham Lord, *John Mortimer: The Devil's Advocate* (Orion, 2005), pp. 186–7.
6. Alexander Games, *Backing into the Limelight: The Biography of Alan Bennett* (Headline, 2001), p.136.
7. Alan Bennett, *Me, I'm Afraid of Virginia Woolf* (Faber and Faber, 2003), xii.

23

Play for Today: Coming Out

When it was announced that *Coming Out* was going to be screened in BBC1's popular *Play for Today* series on 10 April 1979, the *Evening Standard* (26 January 1979) informed its readers that the BBC was prepared 'for a storm over its first explicitly gay play'. The 'storm' mainly focussed on the writer James Andrew Hall's inclusion of a scene in which two men – one of them a black prostitute – are seen in bed together. The *Evening Standard* also noted that 'several prominent actors have turned the play down because they do not want to be seen playing homosexuals'. Fortunately, Anton Rodgers was not one of them and he accepted the lead role of Lewis Duncan, a closeted gay 'Agony Aunt', with a reputation for being the author of a number of bestselling tough he-man thrillers. Duncan is faced with the prospect of having to 'come out' in public after publishing a pro-gay article in a non-gay magazine (under a pseudonym). Nigel Havers, who had already played gay in *The Glittering Prizes* (1976), was cast as Duncan's young lover Richie. Hall's play questioned whether a gay man's private life is his own affair, or whether he owes it to the gay community to declare himself.

Mary Whitehouse, the activist who believed in Christian morality and was the media watchdog/figurehead of the National Viewers' and Listeners Association (NVALA), was incensed by the pre-publicity. Even before the play was screened, she expressed her anger in a letter (5 April 1979) to the BBC governor George Howard: 'any such play could only give great offence'. Howard advised Whitehouse to see the play before judging it. So, she watched it and, on 12 April, wrote to the BBC again, this time to the chairman Sir Michael Swann, and stated on behalf of the NVALA that *Coming Out* should never have been broadcast: 'it is difficult to believe that the play did anything to help homosexuals who are looking for genuine help and understanding – rather the reverse ... and one has certainly been left with the impression that the "Gay" lobby has very powerful friends at the BBC.'

While *Coming Out* included a number of gay stereotypes (predator, bitchy older queen) and character traits some heterosexuals associated with gays (unfaithfulness, loneliness, self-loathing), it had some breakthrough moments. The gay couple, Duncan and Richie, are seen in bed together, possibly a first for British television and, according to Robert Cushman in *Radio Times* (28 April–4 May 1979), 'the hero's session with a black male prostitute was explosive ... not for anything it said, but for the mere fact of its appearing on a television screen'. Reviews were generally favourable. Richard Last described it in the *Daily Telegraph* (11 April 1979) as a 'sympathetic view of homosexuality'. But letters to the *Radio Times* (5–11 May 1979) were mixed:

> I would like to congratulate the BBC and the cast for the most accurate portrayal of gay relationships yet produced by a television company.

> Thank heaven for a well-made play ... thank heaven for a little real *wit*, instead of vulgarity which so often passes for the same thing. Above all, thank heaven for a play about recognisable human beings that one wouldn't be ashamed to know!

> The public were presented with the usual gay caricatures (bitchy ageing queen, heartless pretty young thing), staggering through lives of depression and decay ... I am an operator on Gay Switchboard, and one of the first questions callers always ask is if gay people are 'like they're shown on the telly'. It would be nice if the BBC took a more responsible view in their depiction of gay people.

> Why were those who watched this play (and who were presumably considered to be adults) subjected in the following programme (*Tonight*) to Valerie Singleton rushing to inform viewers that all the cast of the play were heterosexual? This gratuitous reassurance seemed extremely patronising and insulting to both homo and heterosexual viewers, and was surely one of the attitudes that the play was criticising.

Kenith Trodd, the producer of *Coming Out*, replied:

> *Coming Out* was never intended as an attempt to make a comprehensive or even typical 'statement' about contemporary homosexuals. It was

one writer's view and one producer's endorsement of that view – offered above all for its entertainment value and only secondarily for such psychological or sociological insight it might contain ... Any play with so large an ambition would be bound to fail.

Keith Howes, television critic for *Gay News*, blasted it:

Even the bitching was tepid as well as shallow – blunt and plodding instead of sardonic, cutting and athletic and giving us too much time to ponder the plot's improbabilities ... At no point were we shown the very real pressures on a man like Lewis Duncan to stay in the closet ... the play was incapable of tackling the 'coming out' theme it had set itself ... This was the gay world seen through pebble-thick glasses with all the self-deprecation and mendacity that television viewers have been conditioned to expect.[1]

Fourteen years later, Howes viewed the play again for his encyclopaedia *Broadcasting It* (1993) and made the following observation:

Ambitious, relatively frank (Lewis in bed with his lover and with black prostitute Polo – played by Ben Ellison), it was sunk by its totally improbable premise (an article on homosexuality causing such a tidal wave of interest in 1979) and by its negative attitude towards gay men in particular and gay political action in general. Its central theme was never fully confronted: damned if he remains untrue to himself, hopelessly compromised if he reveals he's been telling lies or leading his readers on. The BBC crowed about this production ... The play was popular, and was repeated the following year. It received a generally favourable press, though not from *Gay News* – I *hated* it. The BBC doubtless felt very pleased with itself, though a production from the Corporation a few weeks later – *Only Connect*, which was not ballyhooed, widely praised, or repeated – was *Coming Out*'s superior in every way.[2]

After *Coming Out* was repeated in 1980, John Russell Taylor, who had missed the first screening, reviewed it for *Gay News*. 'Despite all I had been told,' he commented:

The play was not all that bad. In fact, it struck me as serious, worthy and unsensational, suffering mainly from its own good intentions in trying to stuff a quart of information about male homosexuals into a pint pot of playing time … Gay drama on television has to start somewhere, and I can think of many less creditable ways to start than this. Now let us hope it will go on to better things.[3]

Polo (Ben Ellison), the prostitute picked up by Duncan at Piccadilly Circus, was one of the first black gay characters to be seen on British television. 'Black Polo's a good lay,' he tells Duncan. 'Clean sheets, no clap, get your rocks off in style.' He earns £5,000 a week, doesn't pay tax, but tells Duncan angrily, 'I *earn* my money. I went with forty-two last week, and all of them dogs.' But Polo wants to show Duncan that he has a 'heart of gold' by offering him 'one on the house'. In spite of this gesture, Polo is as hard as nails, bitter and angry. In the 1970s, apart from Polo, the only other black gay characters in television dramas were Norman (Thomas Baptiste) in Alun Owen's *Play for Today: Pal* (BBC1, tx 2 December 1971), which no longer exists, and Sugar (Reg Tsiboe), the one-night stand in *Premiere: A Hymn from Jim* (BBC2, tx 29 September 1977) (see Chapter 22).

In 2017, James Andrew Hall was interviewed by Darren Slade in the *Bournemouth Daily Echo* (2 July) about his writing career. He had retired to Bournemouth with his partner Raymond. Hall recalled that he had written 'quite a few' early episodes of *Crossroads* in 1964–65: 'It was a bit silly at times but I really loved it, and things multiplied after that. The novel I had published in 1965 helped enormously because it added a bit of class.' He recalled that *Coming Out* was controversial and upset a lot of people including Nigel Havers's father, Sir Michael Havers (later Baron Havers), a barrister. He was also the shadow Attorney General in the Margaret Thatcher-led Conservative party at the time *Coming Out* was shown. Said Hall: 'He was really upset that his son was appearing in this TV play which garnered all these headlines in the papers like "Gay sex shocker".' Havers, described as married with an 18-month-old daughter, told *The Sun*: 'I suppose the play is a little adventurous.' It was the *Daily Mirror* (10 February 1979) that described *Coming Out* as a 'Gay sex shocker' and included a quote from Anton Rodgers: 'I'm sure it will horrify Mary Whitehouse!'

Notes
1. Keith Howes, 'Play for Today?', *Gay News* No. 165 (1979).
2. Keith Howes, *Broadcasting It: An Encyclopaedia of Homosexuality on Film, Radio and TV in the UK 1923–1993* (Cassell, 1993), p. 135.
3. John Russell Taylor, 'Suffering from good intentions', *Gay News*, No. 194 (1980).

24

Only Connect

When the theatre company Gay Sweatshop was founded in 1974–75 it committed itself to staging positive plays, and to touring these around Britain. They quickly established a reputation for the high standard of their productions, both in the gay movement and in the world of political theatre. In addition to theatres, it reached out to universities, trade union venues and Campaign for Homosexual Equality groups. The company toured extensively in Britain and Europe, but they faced criticism wherever they travelled. One of the founder members was Drew Griffiths. In 1976, when he was interviewed about a Sweatshop production called *Mister X,* which he had written with Roger Baker, Griffiths agreed that it had offended far more homosexuals than heterosexuals: 'They don't like it [homosexuality] being brought out into the open and discussed. The show is about this sort of self-oppression. About accepting second-class status. And before they can do anything about how society treats homosexuality, they have got to do something about how they treat it themselves.'[1]

Lancashire-born Griffiths studied at the Birmingham School for Speech Training and Dramatic Art. From 1967 he pursued a career in 'straight' theatre, but then he heard about 'painted freaks in the south wearing silly clothes and saying ridiculous things and assumed it was part of the queenery I found so unappealing'.[2] When he arrived in London in 1973, he saw them for himself and decided that what they represented was not for him, 'But there was a nagging doubt,' he said. 'Perhaps these people were having a better time than I was; perhaps my weekend gay status was incompatible with the hard-working, a-sexual, professional actor image I presented during the rest of the week.'[3] The doubt remained until he co-founded Gay

Sweatshop in 1974–75. He said: 'I joined with great fear and trepidation – after all, I could be ruining my career but somehow found the courage to direct two of the plays in the first season. At the end of the first six months I knew that the previous seven years had been preparation for this.'[4]

In 1976, Griffiths made an early television appearance when he was seen in an excerpt from the Sweatshop play *Mister X*. This was recorded for 'For Queer Read Gay', an edition of the seven-part Thames Television series *Sex in Our Time*. However, though the programme was scheduled for a late Monday night slot between eleven and midnight, the Independent Broadcasting Authority (IBA) panicked and the entire series was not transmitted. In November 1976 a letter appeared in *The Times* signed by fifty programme makers, headed by Jonathan Dimbleby, which said, in part, that the decision to ban the series *Sex in Our Time* should 'profoundly disturb all those who are concerned to preserve the freedom of communication in Britain'. 'For Queer Read Gay' eventually surfaced as part of Channel 4's *Banned* season in 1991. Regrettably, Tony Bilbow's patronising interview with Griffiths and other actors from Gay Sweatshop's production of *Mister X* hadn't stood the test of time. With other members of the Gay Sweatshop collective, Griffiths took part in an edition of BBC2's 'access' programme *Grapevine* (tx 11 July 1979). They were seen on tour in Belfast and participated in a studio discussion.

When the actor, director and writer Noel Greig joined Gay Sweatshop in 1977, he collaborated with Griffiths on the groundbreaking play *As Time Goes By*, one of the first 'historical' gay plays. It showed repression in three different timeframes: Victorian Britain at the time of Oscar Wilde's trial (1896), Berlin under the Nazis (1929–1934) and New York on the eve of the Stonewall riots (1969). The success of this production (which premiered at the Campaign for Homosexual Equality's conference in Nottingham) led to Greig's solo *The Dear Love of Comrades* (1979), the story of the nineteenth-century Utopian socialist Edward Carpenter. Greig took the role of Carpenter.

In spite of critical acclaim and their popularity, none of Sweatshop's productions were adapted for television. Andy Kirby's *Compromised Immunity* (1986) was the only Gay Sweatshop play to be broadcast on radio: BBC Radio 5 Live in 1991. Michael Cashman co-starred. However, in 1979, Sweatshop members Griffiths and Greig co-authored *Only Connect*, one of the finest television plays ever produced. This was an original drama written for an anthology series on BBC2 called *The Other*

Side. It was commissioned by W. Stephen Gilbert, an openly gay BBC television producer based at Birmingham's Pebble Mill.

Only Connect didn't go out with a lot of fuss. It was screened quietly on BBC2 on a Friday night, which, according to Gilbert, 'we regretted'. He also explained that he was able, as a young producer at Pebble Mill:

> To decide who I wanted to commission, and go right ahead. I had six slots to fill [for the series *The Other Side*] back to back in a year for transmission on BBC2, which sounds a lot, but twenty years earlier Sydney Newman, for *Armchair Theatre*, would have done thirty-six in a year, but of course they all went out live. Now, of course, if a producer has two projects in three years, he's thought to be a great empire builder. But then they have to jump through hoops that we never had to! My boss, who was David Rose, simply told us to 'fill these slots, off you go.'[5]

Gilbert immediately went to Drew Griffiths and asked, 'Can you write something for us?' He knew Griffiths well and had seen a number of Gay Sweatshop productions. Griffiths asked if he could collaborate with Noel Greig. Neither had worked as writers in television before, but Gilbert had a feeling they could do something positive and probably rather affecting. 'And they did exceed my wildest hopes', he said.[6]

The screening of *Only Connect* on BBC2 on 18 May 1979 coincided with the 100th anniversary of the birth of the novelist E.M. Forster, the 50th anniversary of Edward Carpenter's death, and the 10th anniversary of the Stonewall riots and subsequent founding of the Gay Liberation movement. All three events are celebrated in the play, in which Graham Johnson (Sam Dale), a research student who, in tracing 'The Roots of the Labour Movement', rediscovers the forgotten figure of Carpenter (1844–1929), a socialist pioneer and campaigner for gay rights. Graham tracks down 70-year-old John Bury (Joseph O'Conor) who met Carpenter when he (Bury) was 21 and Carpenter 80. The play also draws on a real-life BBC radio broadcast made by E.M. Forster in 1944 as a tribute to Carpenter.

The portrayal of Graham's relationship with his partner, Colin (Karl Johnson), was a breakthrough. Rarely had young gay couples been shown on television. Tensions in their relationship surface because of their class differences. Graham is a middle-class student. Colin is a working-class bus driver. Dale and Johnson made a convincing couple. The scene in which they lie in bed, after making love, is beautifully handled. When they kiss, and cuddle, it is a natural thing.

W. Stephen Gilbert, interviewed in *Gay News* just prior to the screening, made the following comments:

> I think it's the first time gays have been presented in their own terms …
> The most heartening thing about it was that people who aren't gay read
> the play and understood something quite different but equally valuable
> from it. But I don't mind saying that I don't give a fuck what straights
> think of *Only Connect* when it is shown. It will get an enormous audience
> of gays. If non-gays start picking things up from it that's fine. But if they
> don't like it then they can go back to watching Larry Grayson![7]

Reviews were positive. Sean Day-Lewis commented in the *Daily Telegraph* (19 May 1979): 'The piece was as well knitted as it was acted, decidedly touching in a sentimental sort of way, but it was propaganda and as such made no progress towards the millennium when homosexuals have equal dramatic treatment with the rest of humanity and are not burdened with special pleading.' Keith Howes described *Only Connect* as:

> A sensational work in the truest sense: changing our perceptions, stimulating
> our minds, stretching us. Although it was … completely accessible to non-gay
> people, it was ultimately ours. All we were required to do was to adapt to its
> pace and structure and watch it. I hope we haven't seen the last of it.[8]

Though it was not repeated on television, Howes got his wish some years later when *Only Connect* was revived twice at London's National Film Theatre in *Out of the Archives*, a lesbian and gay television retrospective, first in the opening season on 28 July 1992, and then with a repeat on 11 July 2000. W. Stephen Gilbert introduced the screening in 2000. He told the audience that the BBC made a tremendous fuss about *Coming Out*, its *Play for Today* production. When it went into production, the BBC put a page on its internal video system that informed its staff, right across the country, where BBC people gathered, in foyers, bars, and so on, how progressive, brave and liberal it was for doing it, how it was the first openly gay television play. Stephen recalled how his production team watched this fuss wryly, pleased because they had a feeling that *their* play, *Only Connect*, was going to be more honest and to the point than *Coming Out*.

Only Connect is a masterpiece, though it has not been acknowledged in any histories of British television, except those written by Keith Howes, or histories of gay men. Noel Greig and Drew Griffiths somehow managed to become one voice – a bewitching combination of two very different gay men – and yet they came from totally different perspectives. Griffiths was very warm, chaotic, and political, but in a sweet, gentle way, whereas Greig was hard-driving, very involved in gay rights and other political activism. Greig had also been an actor. He played Edward Carpenter in Gay Sweatshop's *The Dear Love of Comrades*, which should have been televised. *Only Connect* is beautifully crafted and satisfying on every level. While listening to the quality of the dialogue there is a realisation what great talents the writers were. There is not one hint of patronage in *Only Connect*. Each of the characters is fully rounded. The fact that they're gay is, of course, integral, but it's not the only thing about them.

What makes *Only Connect* special is that Gilbert produced it with great love and care. He allowed two gay writers to have a voice, which they'd never have got in television anywhere else. It was cast very carefully. Joseph O'Conor was not associated with gay roles. He was a veteran character actor who was best-known for playing Old Jolyon in the BBC television classic *The Forsyte Saga* (1967). O'Conor doesn't play his role in *Only Connect* with that subconscious thing of 'I'm a straight man playing a gay role'. That must have come from Greig and Griffiths, because they worked very closely with the cast, and Gilbert must have encouraged them to be very involved with the production. It was a labour of love.

The Naked Civil Servant and *Only Connect* are two sides of the same coin. The former is all about oppression, individuality, fighting, and *Only Connect* is about loving, but this was the breakthrough. According to Keith Howes: 'This was the turning point in gay television history that failed to turn. It is its beginning and its end. The publicity around *Coming Out* completely submerged *Only Connect* and, because it isn't seen, or acknowledged anywhere, nobody will ever know what we have really lost.'[9]

Notes

1. Paul Valley, 'Drama of being gay is just a way of life', *Yorkshire Post*, 30 June 1976.
2. 'Recording the History of Alternative Theatre', www.unfinishedhistories.com.
3. *Ibid.*
4. *Ibid.*

5. W. Stephen Gilbert in his introduction to the screening of *Only Connect* in *Out of the Archives*, a lesbian and gay television season curated by Stephen Bourne for the National Film Theatre on 11 July 2000.

6. *Ibid.*

7. W. Stephen Gilbert interviewed by Keith Howes, 'Carrying the Can', *Gay News* No. 166 (1979).

8. Keith Howes, 'Well-connected', *Gay News* No. 168 (1979).

9. Keith Howes, by email, 27 February 2019.

Part 4

1980s

25

Drew Griffiths
and *Something for the Boys*

The 1970s ended on a high note with Noel Greig and Drew Griffiths' *Only Connect* on BBC2. Afterwards, Noel, who was a dedicated political practitioner, continued to work successfully in community theatre. The 1980s more or less began on a high note when Griffiths went 'solo' and contributed *Something for the Boys* to the anthology series *House on the Hill*. It was made by Scottish Television (STV) and broadcast nationally on all ITV networks on Saturday, 1 August 1981.

It came about after *Only Connect* when Griffiths was approached by the producer Robert Love at STV. In addition to writing some episodes of a popular soap opera called *Take the High Road*, he was also commissioned to write *Something for the Boys*. It was an engaging comedy-drama about Dougie (James Telfer), a gauche young Scottish soldier, who enjoys a romantic encounter with Dusty (Raymond Thompson), a devil-may-care, self-possessed, sexy American GI in an unofficial gay club in wartime Glasgow. Dougie loses his virginity to Dusty, but they part the next morning, never to meet again. Research into the period brought no evidence that a gay club existed in Glasgow in 1944, the year in which the play is set, but Griffiths pointed out that there were gay clubs in other cities at that time, so why not Glasgow? In *Gay News* in 1981, in a feature about Griffiths, Emmanuel Cooper offered readers some insights into the writer's character:

> As far as writing goes, Drew finds the solitariness of it much more difficult than acting: there is not the support of fellow actors, as well as a great deal of emphasis on 'creativity'. Drew finds he tends to be bad at

self-discipline and avoids writing until the last minute. Then he goes off to his aunt's house in Manchester and works solidly and without interruption for two to three weeks ... Ironically, his success as an actor and writer has taken him out of the class in which he feels most at home, and now, to use Richard Hoggart's phrase, is 'uprooted and anxious', being neither working or middle – but stuck in between.[1]

In the next issue of *Gay News*, Emmanuel Cooper reviewed *Something for the Boys* and described Griffiths as:

Surely one of our most talented and promising playwrights: not only can he evoke a feeling of 'period', but he can deal with sexuality – particularly homosexuality – with honesty, freshness and subtlety ... *Something for the Boys* is a happy blend of romance and excitement, as well as a gentle lesson in how people, gay or heterosexual, can be kind, generous and accepting.[2]

W. Stephen Gilbert also appreciated the play. He described it in *Broadcast* (7 September 1981) as:

Warmly written, indeed suffused with human warmth. Griffiths writes such good, real dialogue, especially for Northern English working people, and the best characterisation here was Jean, the English keeper of the house, a beautifully rounded portrait, full of rich and precise detail and cherishably acted by Rachel Davies ... James Telfer's rookie was appealingly played but, sadly, Raymond Thompson was inadequate to the task of the older man, missing the right sort of charm.

In the *Oxford Dictionary of National Biography*, Mick Wallis described what Griffiths was like at this time: 'despite an inner fragility, Griffiths liked risk: he was a heavy drinker and smoker, treated shoplifting as a minor hobby, and aggressively affected a theatrically glamorous off-stage appearance that sometimes provoked hostile reactions ... A slight, quietly spoken man, plagued by self-doubt, Griffiths always seemed vulnerable.'[3]

Griffiths wrote another television play, this time for *ITV Playhouse*. It was called *Something's Got to Give* (tx 19 June 1982) and starred Ian Charleson as a straight-laced young businessman. He finds his life has changed when he literally bumps into the clumsy but attractive

Ann Mitchell (Charlotte Cornwell). However, in 1983, the stress of writing *Nicola Johnson*, a daily soap opera for Capital Radio, may have brought on an emotional crisis and a breakdown. According to Mick Wallis: 'After he set his flat on fire, friends unsuccessfully attempted to get him assigned to a psychiatric social worker; then, in desperation, they tried to get him sectioned. This too failed. He stopped paying rent, burned furniture in the garden, drank all day, and hardly slept.'[4] Griffiths was murdered at the age of 37 on 18 June 1984 at his flat in Brixton, London, after taking home a man he had picked up on a drinking spree in the Elephant and Castle. Mick Wallis observed: 'He had been seen flashing large wads of money about, and when he was eventually found, naked and stabbed through the heart, the cash was gone … In retrospect it might be thought that in his self-destructive behaviour he was looking for his "angel of death".'[5] W. Stephen has described him as 'a lost talent. He had much more talent than he ever knew. Had he lived longer he would have written some more fine work for television and theatre.'[6]

When Noel Greig was interviewed in 2008 for the *Unfinished Histories* website, he remembered the good working relationship he had had with Griffiths on *As Time Goes By* and *Only Connect*. He described Griffiths as someone who was:

> So lovely really. Very very fragile. Steely as well. Passionate about theatre, a brilliant actor, a lovely writer. He never recovered from the indignities of being gay. Gay Sweatshop was a mission for him. Sort of a revenge, a creative revenge. And his relationships with people were very intense. Too intense.[7]

Noel Greig died at the age of 64 in 2009.

In 2018, Keith Howes remembered Griffiths as 'a sprite, an elf, he reminded me of a wandering troubadour of the medieval period.'[8] Howes remembered how they would meet in the Salisbury pub in St Martin's Lane when it used to be a gay pub:

> He would have a beer and I would have a port and lemon, something rather sissy like that. We'd talk about musicals and coming out and changing the world and getting rid of the ridiculous age of consent, then twenty-one years old in Britain. Gay men were treated as less than human. It was always open season for gay men … I was in the bank the other day and I

said to the male teller 'Oh, I do like your nails! What colour is the polish?' And he said 'Over the top.' And I thought Drew would have loved that.[9]

According to Mick Wallis, Griffiths was remembered at his funeral for being 'compassionate, easy-going, and caring, as someone loved by all who met him, even though he could never bring himself to believe this'. Wallis added:

> Griffiths established Gay Sweatshop as the prime artistic expression of a politicised lesbian and gay identity. His personal and creative life reflects poignantly the larger social process, and to some extent the social pressures upon him – particularly the pressures of homophobia. In a short period, Drew Griffiths produced a body of work – as writer, actor, and director – that was marked by an intense honesty and considerable bravery.[10]

Yet, in spite of his accomplishments, with the exception of the work of Keith Howes, Drew Griffiths is barely acknowledged in histories of gay men or the LGBTQI+ communities.

Notes

1. Emmanuel Cooper, 'Drew Connects Again', *Gay News* No. 220 (1981).
2. Emmanuel Cooper, *Gay News* No. 221 (1981).
3. Mick Wallis, 'Drew Griffiths (1947–1984)', *Oxford Dictionary of National Biography* (Oxford University Press, 2004).
4. *Ibid.*
5. *Ibid.*
6. W. Stephen Gilbert in his introduction to the screening of *Only Connect* in *Out of the Archives*, a lesbian and gay television season curated by Stephen Bourne for the National Film Theatre on 11 July 2000.
7. www.unfinishedhistories.com.
8. 'The Unsolved Murder of Drew Griffiths' by Keith Howes (https://www.youtube.com/watch?v=ygNYe7GKKJ8). Published on 23 March 2018.
9. *Ibid.*
10. Wallis, *ibid.*

26

And the Winner is ...

In the early 1980s, the British Academy of Film and Television Arts (BAFTA) bestowed three of their Best Television Actor awards on actors who played gay roles. The first was Anthony Andrews as the teddy-bear-carrying, upper-class alcoholic Sebastian Flyte in *Brideshead Revisited* (1981). Then Alan Bates as the real-life spy Guy Burgess in *An Englishman Abroad* (1983). Finally, Tim Piggott-Smith won for playing the sadistic policeman Merrick in *The Jewel in the Crown* (1984). These characters couldn't have been more different and yet they all had something in common. They were troubled, self-destructive gay men who either ended up dead (Flyte, Merrick) or alone (Burgess). So, they were hardly going to further the cause of gay self-affirmation and empowerment. Nevertheless, gay characters were taking centre stage in critically acclaimed, award-winning dramas.

John Mortimer adapted *Brideshead Revisited* (tx 12 October to 22 December 1981) from Evelyn Waugh's novel in eleven episodes and thirteen hours of screen time. Spanning three decades from the early 1920s to the end of World War Two, the series chronicled Charles Ryder's obsession with a wealthy, aristocratic family. The aristocracy have lots of money, so the series had to be expensively mounted. It cost Granada Television more than twice what it had budgeted. However, this was not a happy tale but one of decadence, decay and despair in England between the wars. In spite of its leisurely pace (the cast were told to speak slowly), 9 million viewers were hooked on this high-class soap opera which moved between Brideshead, a magnificent English stately home, and scenes in Oxford, Venice, London, Paris, North Africa and New York. It had a glittering cast led by Anthony Andrews and Jeremy Irons (Charles Ryder) as the young lovers; Laurence Olivier; John Gielgud; Claire Bloom and Stephane

Audran. Nickolas Grace had the scene-stealing supporting role of Anthony Blanche, the decadent gay friend of Sebastian.

The first five episodes focussed on the same-sex relationship between Sebastian and Charles, and dealt quite openly, for 1981, with their passion for each other. According to Hilary Kingsley and Geoff Tibballs in *Box of Delights: The Golden Years of Television* (1989): 'they helped to make the homosexuality something viewers could accept – part of the English process of growing up.'[1] However, as Sebastian disintegrates, while clutching 'Aloysius' (his teddy bear), Charles turns 'straight'. First, he falls for Sebastian's sister Julia (Diana Quick) but later on he marries Celia (Jane Asher), but neither relationship seems to generate the youthful passion and romance of the one he enjoyed with Sebastian at Oxford.

Brideshead Revisited helped set the tone of a 1980s British film and television genre described as 'White Flannel' dramas. These included *Chariots of Fire*, which won the 1981 Oscar for Best Film the same year that *Brideshead* won a host of BAFTAs including Best Drama Series/Serial; *The Jewel in the Crown* (1984); David Lean's *A Passage to India* (1984); and Merchant Ivory's *A Room with a View* (1986). These productions represented a yearning for an England that no longer existed but they did co-exist alongside dramas that captured the brutal reality of 1980s Britain under the leadership of the right-wing and reactionary Tory Prime Minister Margaret Thatcher. These included Alan Bleasdale's brilliant BBC drama series *Boys from the Blackstuff* (1982). The longing for a bygone 'Englishness' and the nostalgia for the British Empire as expressed in 'White Flannel' dramas was widely attacked in cultural criticism. The 'White Flannel' film and television dramas were seen as products of Thatcherism and part of a resurgence of regressive nationalism.

Brideshead Revisited was criticised for its 'slow, reverential pace, for wallowing in inherited wealth, for being a glorified "soap". Nevertheless, the production is seen internationally as an example of what the British do best, a large-scale "quality" production of television drama.'[2] The outspoken gay filmmaker Derek Jarman loathed *Brideshead*: 'There is nothing more excruciating than English Historical Drama, the stuff that is so successful in America and is usually introduced by Alistair Cooke as Masterpiece Theatre; in which British stage actors are given free rein to display their artificial style in period settings.'[3]

While *Brideshead Revisited* took thirteen hours to tell its story, *An Englishman Abroad* (BBC1 tx 29 November 1983) took just 65 minutes. It is a gem, at once tremendously moving and droll and laugh-out-loud funny.

The story was based on a real-life incident in the life of Coral Browne, an elegant and witty actress who, in 1958, visited Moscow with the Royal Shakespeare Company. During a performance of *Hamlet*, Browne was visited in her dressing room by Guy Burgess, a homosexual spy who had defected to the Soviet Union in 1951 and later died there, in exile, in 1963. Interviewed by Henry Fenwick in the *Radio Times* in 1983, Browne recalled the origins of *An Englishman Abroad*:

> I was discussing spies one day with Alan Bennett ... and I happened to say to him: 'Oh, I met Guy Burgess in Russia!' We discussed it for about five minutes; no more than that. Several months later he sent me the script and said he'd written up the things that I'd told him and would I mind if he went on with it or would I rather he didn't. I said I didn't mind at all. I was delighted. I thought it was a very good script.[4]

According to Bennett: 'The picture of the elegant actress and the seedy exile sitting in a dingy Moscow flat through a long afternoon listening again and again to Jack Buchanan singing "Who Stole My Heart Away?" seemed to me funny and sad.'[5] Bennett sent an early draft of the script to the director John Schlesinger who was drawn to the story of Burgess towards the end of his life, isolated in Moscow, desperate for news of England. Schlesinger described Bennett's writing as 'Witty and sad at the same time. It's an anecdote, we're not trying to do a great spy story.'[6]

From the start it was agreed that Browne would play herself in *An Englishman Abroad*, but the casting of Burgess took a bit longer. It needed someone special to play the paunchy, dishevelled, eccentric and almost broken outsider. When Robert Stephens, the first choice, was unavailable, Noel Davis, the casting director, made a 'shopping list' that included Jeremy Kemp, Ronald Lacey, Alec McCowen, Denis Quilley, Anthony Hopkins, Keith Michell and John Standing. Davis's final shortlist had the following names and notes:

> Alan Bates: I believe he would be great, appearance?
> Michael Caine: CAN do the accent
> Tom Baker: is very debauched
> Edward Fox: can be made to look less handsome?
> Dirk Bogarde: prissy – self pity. NOT JUICY.

Alan Bates was cast.[7]

The gay American writer and film historian Vito Russo observed that the real Guy Burgess was less serious-minded about gay politics than he was about his Marxism:

In 1950 he was posted as Second Secretary of the British Embassy in Washington, D. C. On his first day, a superior warned him, 'Guy, there are three basic "don'ts" to bear in mind when you're dealing with Americans. The first is communism, the second is homosexuality and the third is the color bar.' 'What you're trying to say in your nice long-winded way,' replied Burgess, 'is "For God's sake, Guy, don't make a pass at Paul Robeson."'[8]

It was Alan Bates's belief that Burgess never tried to hide himself: 'Quite the opposite. He was drunk in front of everyone, he was homosexual in front of everyone and he went around telling everyone he was a spy, though no one believed him ... He had a dreadful time in Moscow, and I'm sure he thoroughly regretted going there.'[9] Bates's biographer Donald Spoto described the actor's portrayal of Burgess as one that is 'laced with moments of inventive brilliance' and Spoto acknowledged Bates's 'refusal to indulge in any of the clichés so often brought to the portrait of a slightly effete, middle-aged homosexual. Most of all, his portrait of Guy Burgess is of a man who sees no reason to beg forgiveness.'[10]

When *An Englishman Abroad* was premiered at the London Film Festival on 21 November, and eight days later was shown on BBC1, television critics applauded. Nancy Banks-Smith described it in *The Guardian* (30 November 1983) as 'extremely beautiful and funny and sad and marvellous and silly'. However, Richard Ingrams was not impressed. As he commented in *The Spectator* (3 December 1983):

The film did not come to life. Alan Bennett reminds me nowadays of a sort of intellectual Russell Harty, giggling over references to inside legs, kedgeree and Leeds, but not really capable of getting under the skin of a man like Guy Burgess, who in Alan Bates's version, came over as more of a delightful old queen than the dreadful monster he was.

In spite of what Ingrams felt about *An Englishman Abroad*, it collected Best Single Drama, Best Actor and Best Actress awards from the Broadcasting Press Guild *and* BAFTA.

Vito Russo included *An Englishman Abroad* in the 1987 revised edition of his 1981 success *The Celluloid Closet,* his classic study of gays in the movies. Even though the book was primarily about cinema representations, Russo made exceptions for two British television productions: *The Naked Civil Servant* and *An Englishman Abroad,* which he described as 'a model of sophistication and wit. Aside from being the best hour of television seen in a decade, *An Englishman Abroad* is an excellent example of how the sexuality of a celebrated figure is second nature to the project instead of the problem.'[11]

In 1987, Anthony Hopkins played Guy Burgess in *Screen Two: Blunt* (BBC2 tx 11 January). Jonathan Sanders commented in his *Gay Times* review (February 1987) that Ian Richardson portrayed Blunt, the art historian/Soviet spy and lover of Burgess, as an 'aloofly formal aesthete (in the Oscar Wilde tradition of gay men), even when in the bedroom with Guy Burgess. Perhaps this is accurate ... Still, the play could have stood a little more bluntness about Blunt's sexuality. At least Anthony Hopkins's blustery Burgess was disarmingly frank.' There were no BAFTA nominations for Hopkins or Richardson.

Granada TV's epic fourteen-part saga and BAFTA-laden *The Jewel in the Crown* (tx 9 January–3 April 1984) was based on Paul Scott's *Raj Quartet* novels. It focussed on the closing years of British rule (1942–47) in India. The story had two contrasting gay men: the envious, sadistic and inadequate policeman (later army officer) Ronald Merrick (Tim Pigott-Smith) and Corporal 'Sophie' Dixon (Warren Clarke), a cockney orderly. Early in the story, Merrick despises Hari Kumar (Art Malik), an Indian newspaper reporter who has been raised and educated in England, but it is likely that Merrick secretly desires Kumar. In an act of spite, he frames Kumar for the rape of Daphne Manners (Susan Wooldridge) and punishes him with beatings. Later, when Merrick is convalescing in hospital, he is looked after by 'Sophie'. For a gay character in this setting (British army) and in this era (1940s), 'Sophie' is a revelation. In addition to winning a medal for risking his life to save wounded soldiers, he is bitchy, quick-witted and funny. He goads Merrick into asking him: 'Are you a hero or a bloody pansy?' to which 'Sophie' gleefully gives as good as he gets: 'I don't think that's a question *you* ought to be asking, sir.' Always on the lookout for a bit of the other, 'Sophie' tries it on with the handsome Guy Perron (Charles Dance), a Cambridge graduate and a scholar of Indian history. 'I suppose you wouldn't fancy a little "Victory Day" celebration?' asks 'Sophie'.

Guy says that he has arranged to meet an old school friend. 'Sophie' responds: 'That's what they all say.'

When Sunil Gupta considered David Lean's *A Passage to India* and *The Jewel in the Crown* in *Coming on Strong: Gay Politics and Culture* (1989), he observed that *Jewel* was practically a reworking of *Passage* with a more popular audience in mind, 'but also with a much more overt gay theme'. In his chapter 'Black, *Brown* and White', Gupta looked at Ronald Merrick's homosexual desire for the 'Other' (Hari Kumar):

> Caught up in his own class contradictions and repressed sexuality he [Merrick] is finally murdered in native costume by local rent boys. It is the most powerful gay image dealing with the impossibility of fulfilling desire across racial boundaries that I have come across. Again, for obvious reasons, *Jewel* does not do justice to Paul Scott's books, but for a work dealing with the big issues surrounding homosexuality – of race, SM and desire – one need look no further. It is very easy to dismiss these works as mere colonial stereotypes, but I think that they have left us with the few serious works that attempt a discourse around the colonial white/Brown homosexual relationship.[12]

Notes

1. Hilary Kingsley and Geoff Tibballs, *Box of Delights: The Golden Years of Television* (Macmillan, 1989), p. 200.
2. David Oswell and Guy Jowett, 'Bridehead Revisited', Horace Newcomb (ed.), *Encyclopaedia of Television*, (Fitzroy Dearborn, 1997), p. 218–19.
3. Derek Jarman, *Dancing Ledge* (Quartet Books, 1984), p. 14.
4. Henry Fenwick, 'Coral Browne as herself', *Radio Times* (26 November–2 December 1983).
5. Donald Spoto, *Otherwise Engaged: The Life of Alan Bates* (Hutchinson, 2007), p. 178.
6. *Ibid.*
7. Rose Collis, *Coral Browne: 'This Effing Lady'* (Oberon Books, 2007), p. 238.
8. Vito Russo, *The Celluloid Closet: Homosexuality in the Movies* (Harper and Row, 1981; revised 1981), p. 306.
9. Spoto, p. 178.
10. *Ibid.*
11. Russo, p. 306.
12. Sunil Gupta, 'Black, *Brown* and White' in Simon Shepherd and Mick Wallis (eds.), *Coming on Strong: Gay Politics and Culture* (Unwin Hyman, 1989), pp. 170–1.

27

Auntie's Dramas

In 1992, when the singer Elisabeth Welch was interviewed about her radio and television appearances in the 1930s, she recalled that 'The BBC was called "Auntie" because it had a reputation for being prim and prissy.'[1] It was a popular view of the BBC that remained until the 1960s and 1970s. It only began to fade when the corporation made cutting-edge dramas and documentaries and changed the BBC's image. If the campaigner Mary Whitehouse had had her way, the 'Auntie' image would have remained. However, with only a few exceptions, the BBC held back from putting realistic gay characters in its television dramas. In the 1960s, they were tortured souls like Robin in plays like *Horror of Darkness*. In the 1970s, in spite of gay liberation, self-affirmation and the publication of *Gay News*, limp-wristed comic caricatures like Mr Humphries were the 'norm' in sitcoms like *Are You Being Served?* In the 1970s, 'Auntie' turned down *The Naked Civil Servant*, but by the end of the decade she did turn a corner with Drew Griffiths and Noel Greig's *Only Connect*, one of the best gay-themed plays ever made for television. Yet, in the 1980s, as far as gay-themed plays went, the BBC was slow to push the boundaries until it made *Two of Us* (see Chapter 29). This may have had something to do with the onset of HIV/AIDS and Margaret Thatcher's reactionary, oppressive Tory government. It could also have had something to do with homophobic attitudes being expressed in the tabloid newspapers by the likes of Garry Bushell in *The Sun*. Whatever the reason, Britain's gay community was under attack in the 1980s and the BBC could and should have done more to provide drama that reflected the reality of their lives.

Early in the decade, the *Play for Today* series included Rose Tremain's *A Room for the Winter* (BBC1 tx 3 November 1981) which, according to Mary Kenny in the *Daily Mail* (4 November 1981), contained 'fairly unabashed homosexual scenes of naked chaps in bed together'. She added that the play was well written and 'presented with a certain refinement'. Jack Shepherd played the lead, James, an exiled white South African saboteur pining away in a dingy London bedsit. An attempted suicide by James's boyfriend didn't exactly lighten the load. When Emmanuel Cooper reviewed it for *Gay News* he commented that: 'Disillusionment and despair was the recurring theme and was pursued with a relentless, joyless intensity.'[2]

In David Clough's *Belles* (BBC2 tx 27 May 1983) a pair of drag queens, Michael (Martyn Hesford) and Lenny (Robert Gary), are booked by mistake to perform their act for an audience of 'twin-set and pearls' at a run-down South Coast resort. Michael is the younger of the two. Bitchy and sulky, he drinks a lot while listening to his Judy Garland tape. Lenny is older, sensitive, fussy and protective of Michael. Hostility surfaces between the two men as they realise they are reaching the end of their professional and personal life. The situation is not helped by Phil (David Calder) who is the 'entertainments' compère. The sight of Michael's wig and slap does something to Phil and he cannot resist sexually harassing the young man. In the shattering climax, Michael snaps and directs his anger and frustration at the elderly audience. According to Michael Church in the *Times* (28 May 1983): 'Unfortunately, it was just not dramatic. The characters were stereotypes: that would have been acceptable if their interaction had not been equally predictable.'

It was only a matter of time before the long-running *BBC Television Shakespeare* series included someone playing gay. The series was launched with much fanfare on BBC2 on 3 December 1978 with *Romeo and Juliet*. It ended on 27 April 1985. *Coriolanus* (tx 21 April 1984), starring Alan Howard as the Roman general Caius Marcius (later Coriolanus), upset a few critics. The director Elijah Moshinsky couldn't resist giving an undercurrent of homoeroticism to the drama. Caius Marcius fights the Coriolian soldiers with his shirt on, but when he fights Tullus Aufidius (Mike Gwilym) in one-to-one combat, the shirt comes off! John Wain was not impressed. In his review in *The Listener* (3 May 1984) he described the play as one that:

Fell apart into self-indulgent, opinionated foolishness with the director's frantic insistence that Tullus Aufidius has a homosexual crush on

Coriolanus. The relationship of two men who have given years to fighting with each other may, or may not, contain a streak of this as one ingredient – the play does not specifically contradict it, and if it makes the homosexual lobby happy to have it indicated, I'm no killjoy. But it is not the same as … turning the death of Coriolanus, which is specifically shown in the play as a mob lynching, into a sexually charged single combat. Rubbish like this does nothing to serve the reputation of the BBC.

One month before the BBC axed its acclaimed *Play for Today* series, it made an attempt to portray a contemporary gay couple in *The Groundling and the Kite* (BBC1 tx 24 July 1984). In addition to writing it, Leonard Preston also co-starred (with John Duttine) and contributed original music and lyrics. In *Time Out* (19–25 July 1984) Martyn Auty observed that the 'BBC are rumoured to work to a ration of only three plays on a gay theme per year. This must be one of them.' Duttine played Jimmy, a moody pop music executive who commissions and then produces a record by his boyfriend, played by Preston. In *Time Out*, Auty observed that 'the dramatic conflict centres around whether the relationship can survive the rigours of the record business, but both seem slightly distant from reality and in consequence the play strains credibility … don't expect anything earth-shattering.' For some, the BBC had moved ahead in its depiction of a gay couple. In the *Daily Express* (25 July 1984), Judith Simons commented: 'as a play about a loving and giving relationship, this piece could not be faulted'. Hilary Kingsley was also complimentary in *The Standard* (25 July 1984):

> Don't spread it around. But the BBC came out of the closet last night. With a touching, cheering play. Auntie confessed, gay relationships exist. Exist, crack, mend and change … Part of the success was due to the talented John Duttine … The play never quite flew high and free like the kite. But without a limp-wristed moment, it lifted me several inches from the ground.

In John Peacock's *More Lives Than One* (BBC1 tx 18 December 1984), David (Michael N. Harbour), happily married with two sons and running a successful business, finds himself attracted to Steve (Daniel Webb), a sexy, confident young electrician who is politically aware. A tense scene had David and Steve trapped in the back of Steve's van where they hide from the police to avoid being caught 'cottaging' in a gent's toilet in a park. Maureen Paton commented in the *Daily Express* (19 December 1984): 'The play roundly condemned the unsavoury activities of the police in spying on hapless individuals in public conveniences, with one young constable vehemently protesting at the Peeping Tom role thrust upon him.' The disgruntled young officer spoke for many of his colleagues up and down the country when he complained: 'I didn't join the police force to sit in a roof space watching some poor unsuspecting sod having a shit.' The degrading 'cottaging' duties of the police, still common in the 1980s, were generally accepted as a waste of valuable police time. *More Lives Than One* made it possible to sympathise with David's predicament. He had to remain in the closet, because he had a wife and children. Consequently, he looked for same-sex companionship in the park's public convenience, but in doing so he risked being arrested and charged with 'indecency'. There is a suggestion in John Peacock's writing that David will one day find it in himself to be gay and become a happier, more giving and interesting man. According to Keith Howes in *Broadcasting It* (1993): 'David is probably the last of television's pre-AIDS no-man's land gays, searching, searching and almost finding.'[3]

Portrayals of black gay men were conspicuous by their absence in television dramas of the 1980s. None had surfaced since Polo in *Coming Out* (1979) (see Chapter 23). One that jumped out of the closet in 1985 was seen in *In Sickness and in Health*, a situation comedy series in which writer Johnny Speight resurrected Alf Garnett, his East End bigot from *Till Death Us Do Part*. Older now, and in need of a home help, he is dismayed by the arrival of Winston (Eamonn Walker), his worst nightmare: black, named after his hero Winston Churchill, and gay (with a white boyfriend). Alf calls him 'Marigold' but Winston hits back, taunting Alf with lines like: 'I'm British with a *gorgeous* tan. So, eat your heart out.' 'Marigold' was embarrassing but he lasted for three series into 1987. For Jonathan Sanders in *Gay Times* (December 1986):

However much people defend Johnny Speight's Alf Garnett in *In Sickness and in Health*, I shall continue to view him as an endorsement of prejudice rather than a condemnation. Winston/Marigold is doubly offensive: a lisping black home help who just about manages to get enough over on the awful Garnett to keep the character marginally on this side of caricature.

Gay characters rarely appeared on the cover of the BBC's weekly listings magazine, the *Radio Times*, but an exception was made for Alan Bates when he appeared in *An Englishman Abroad* (26 November–2 December 1983). *Radio Times* also featured Michael Gambon and Robin Lermitte on its cover as Oscar Wilde and Lord Alfred Douglas (23–29 March 1985). The actors were starring that week in the three-part series *Oscar*, shown on BBC2 from 26–28 March. Oscar Wilde had previously been the subject of at least two television dramas: Granada TV's *On Trial* drama in 1960 with Micheal MacLiammoir (see Chapter 7) and London Weekend Television's acclaimed series *Lillie* (1978), based on the life of Lillie Langtry with Peter Egan as Wilde.

John Hawkesworth, the writer and producer of *Oscar*, concentrated on the final, tragic years of the writer's life. In the same issue of the *Radio Times* that featured Gambon on the cover, Jim Hiley noted in a three-page spread entitled 'The Importance of Playing Oscar' that 'What emerges in Gambon's performance is a powerful, sensitive figure, astonishingly similar to surviving pictures of Oscar, but with barely a hint of camp or caricature.' Gambon told Hiley: 'I didn't cultivate mannerisms or anything like that. I mean, I knew Oscar wouldn't stand how I usually stand – like a wreck. But with every part, how you look and move comes from how you feel inside. It's all about feelings – and in Oscar's case, the words. His words made me feel light.' The actor brought a similarly unprejudiced view to Oscar's homosexuality: 'To my mind, gay men don't fall into categories. It is said that Wilde was effeminate, but I never smelt that in what I read about him.' In the same article, Hawkesworth described Wilde as 'a sweet, kind man. He was also incredibly naïve, to get caught up in the Queensberrys' family battle. What's more, I've a feeling attitudes haven't changed too much since.'

Notes

1. Elisabeth Welch interviewed by Stephen Bourne in Jim Pines (ed.), *Black and White in Colour: Black People in British Television since 1936* (British Film Institute, 1992), p. 24
2. *Gay News* No. 228 (1981).
3. Keith Howes, *Broadcasting It: An Encyclopaedia of Homosexuality on Film, Radio and TV in the UK 1923–1993* (Cassell, 1993), p. 519.

28

EastEnders

John Hawkesworth, the writer and producer of BBC2's *Oscar* in 1985, was correct in asserting that attitudes hadn't changed too much since the persecution of Oscar Wilde in the 1890s. *EastEnders*, a new BBC soap, launched the month before *Oscar*, generated some disturbing hostility and homophobia when a regular gay character was introduced in August 1986. Tabloid newspapers were ruthless in their attacks on the BBC.

EastEnders made its debut on BBC1 on 19 February 1985. Its first producer, Julia Smith, told the press that the setting, Albert Square, Walford in London's East End, had been chosen for the diversity of its past and the multi-racial community that had developed. From the start, *EastEnders'* mix of social realism and melodrama was consistently popular with viewers but it took almost a year for a gay character to appear.

Meanwhile, once the series was underway and attracting millions of viewers, especially teenagers, the campaigner Mary Whitehouse warned anyone who would listen that: 'It is at our peril that we allow this series. Its verbal aggression and its atmosphere of physical violence, its homosexuality, its blackmailing pimp and its prostitute, its lies and deceit and its bad language, cannot go unchallenged.'[1] As a 'Bible-bashing' Christian, Whitehouse also attacked the decision to repeat the show on Sunday. Julia Smith defended *EastEnders* vigorously:

> I think I'm just as moral as Mrs Whitehouse. And I care possibly more deeply. The difference is she generally believes in sweeping things under the carpet and pretending they don't exist. I believe in showing what does exist and preparing people for the world they live in. My prime aim is to entertain, my second is to inform. I do not preach.[2]

It was the real-life drag artist David Dale who played the first gay character in *EastEnders*. He had been the subject of *If They'd Asked for a Lion Tamer*, an excellent Channel 4 documentary shown on 5 April 1984. The highlight of this programme was a devastating cabaret performance by Dale who provided a great deal of humorous and ironic comment on the society in which he grew up. In *EastEnders* Dale was perfectly cast as a drag queen who is employed by Angie Watts at the Queen Vic, the pub she runs with her husband Den. He made his first appearance on 28 January 1986, but the character only lasted for eight episodes. A few years later, Dale told Marianne McDonald in *The Independent* (23 May 1993):

> The job was going to be this big, loud East End drag queen, very confi-dent, very bossy, with advice for everyone. In rehearsal the character's name, which was something like Butterfly L'Amour, got changed to John Fisher because they felt it was too extrovert. My lines got cut and when I was camping it to the hilt as a drag queen, they told me to tone it down. When they asked me back I turned them down.

When another gay character appeared in *EastEnders* a few months later, he couldn't have been more different from John Fisher. The graphic designer Colin Russell (Michael Cashman) was a quiet, introspective, middle-class 'yuppie' with a kind heart. He made his first appearance on 5 August 1986 and lasted for 133 episodes. He left Albert Square, having been diag-nosed with multiple sclerosis, on 19 January 1989. When Cashman joined the soap, *The Sun* (13 August 1986) declared – on its front page – 'IT'S EASTBENDERS – Gay men to stir up TV soap' with a photo of a smiling Michael Cashman.

Colin Russell may not have been a screaming queen like John Fisher, but he still managed to make waves in Walford. For example, Albert Square's Bible-bashing gossip, Dot Cotton (June Brown), is mortified when she discovers that Colin is not only gay, but sharing his bed with a younger boyfriend, the chirpy Cockney barrow boy Barry (Gary Hailes). Dot spreads rumours that Colin has AIDS, and some of the residents of Albert Square shun him. However, all's well that ends well when Colin and Dot forge a close friendship.

In the magazine *City Limits* ('Café Society', 23–30 April 1987), Tim Robinson expressed his relief that gay characters like Colin and Barry were an improvement on Mr Humphries: 'However flawed these represen-tations of gays may be – and they certainly are – at least none are weak, contemptible, camp caricatures … They certainly improve on the past, but improvement doesn't mean perfection.' Gay television critics also kept a close eye on Colin and Barry. In *Sunday Today* (31 May 1987), Mark Finch wrote a critical article about gays in broadcasting entitled 'We're either game for a laugh on TV or low-lifes in nightclub shadows'. Finch described Colin as *EastEnders'* 'nouveau homo' who was:

> A bit of a stereotype. He's a graphic designer (the modern aesthete) and he's friendless, except for his boyfriend Barry (gays on TV never have any other gay friends). But at least Colin is boring. Slowly, in liberal soaps like *EastEnders* and *Brookside*, the message is getting across: gays are almost as ordinary as everyone else.

Later that year, in the December 1987 issue of *Gay Times*, Jonathan Sanders was pleased to report that Colin and Barry had made some progress:

> A year ago, the couple were very marginal characters, lacking clear identities as gay men and regarded with suspicion by the other Albert Square inhabitants. Now they are 'out' and much more involved with the rest of the community. The scene where they were allowed to embrace (which caused Mary Whitehouse to squeak at top pitch) was a landmark for popular TV. However, the lack of development in the couple's relationship during the last few months suggests that the BBC is running scared of right-wing censorship.

It didn't last. Right-wing censorship intensified with the Tory government's introduction of Clause 28 of the Local Government Act of 1988. This prohibited local authorities from 'promoting' homosexuality or gay 'pretend family relationships'. Colin and Barry provided the tabloids with months of stories, mostly homophobic. By the end of 1988, the scriptwriters turned Barry straight and put the now-solitary Colin through a gruelling 'am I HIV positive?' storyline. Happily, he wasn't and then Colin finally found true love with Guido Smith (Nicholas Donovan), who first appeared on 15 November 1988.

Then came The Kiss. In an episode shown on 19 January 1989, Colin informed Guido that he has been diagnosed with multiple sclerosis. A letter from a viewer in the *Radio Times* (4–10 February 1989) was favourable: 'A gentle kiss of comfort between the two men was performed beautifully, with taste and understanding. I defy anyone to be offended by this very tender scene.' The couple then packed their bags and left Albert Square for good.

There had been an outcry about Colin's appearance in *EastEnders* and another outcry when he shacked up with Barry. The Kiss was too much, as reported by Helen Gould in *The Stage* ('No Gay Sex Please Says Whitehouse', 16 March 1989). Gould acknowledged that the 'gay community' was living in the shadow of Clause 28-style broadcasting censorship, but Mary Whitehouse was adding to this. Whitehouse had warned the National Viewers and Listeners Association that the on-screen relationship between Colin and Guido, and their expression of intimacy, was a 'dangerous, propagandist message, encouraging children to believe gay is normal. It is one thing for adults to treat homosexuals with understanding, as we all should. It is something entirely different to leave the young without the support which it is our duty, and that includes broadcasting personnel, to provide.' When Gould asked Whitehouse if she was trying to get homosexuality banned from the airwaves, the old campaigner hotly denied it.

Meanwhile, Michael Cashman, also interviewed by Gould, had become a forceful campaigner for gay rights, especially around the time of Clause 28. He accused Whitehouse of:

> Seeking to reinforce a narrow, prejudiced, minority view, holding up children as an emotive shield. The best thing we can do for our children is educate them as to how the world really is … We have to encourage loving relationships and not tolerance and prejudice. Any programme that goes out of its way to show lesbian and gay relationships in their usual, boring, mundane fashion can only be good.

A BBC spokesman defending *EastEnders* pointed out that homosexuality was a fact of life.

Notes
1. Hilary Kingsley, *Soap Box: The Papermac Guide to Soap Opera* (Papaermac, 1988), p. 229.
2. *Ibid.*

29

Two of Us

In 1987–88, the BBC had to cope with a drama over the inclusion of a gay couple, Colin and Barry, in *EastEnders* (see Chapter 28), but nothing could have prepared Auntie for the shockwaves that hit her over *Two of Us*. This was a sensitively made hour-long television film about two 17-year-old lads who fall in love. The production had a tumultuous history, having been filmed during the summer of 1986 for the BBC series *Scene* which was aimed at young people from the age of 14 upwards in secondary schools. The intention was to screen it in 1987 during school time in two half-hour parts. This would give it maximum exposure to teenagers in their schools all over the country. The teaching of homosexuality in classrooms was a controversial and unpopular subject. Teachers needed guidance; teenagers needed to learn about sexual diversity. However, in 1987–88 the moral climate changed dramatically, with the media and Margaret Thatcher's Tory government whipping up public fears about homosexuality being 'promoted' in schools. Trouble started when the right-wing media learned about the making of *Two of Us* and the BBC's plan to screen it during schooltime.

A BBC spokeswoman told the *Times Educational Supplement* (TES) (14 November 1986) that since the programme had been made, 'there has been a heated public debate about sex education in schools. As a result, we believe it would now be difficult for many teachers to use these programmes in the manner intended.' The BBC denied that it had a 'rocky relationship' with Margaret Thatcher and her Tory government but it was understood that the campaigner Mary Whitehouse knew about *Two of Us* when it was being filmed and had written to the BBC about it. Alasdair

Milne, the Director-General of the BBC, had responded to Mrs Whitehouse defending the programme makers with assurances that the subject would be dealt with responsibly. The *TES* (14 November 1986) also included a report by Nick Baker, who believed that it was BBC Education's indecision, rather than cowardice, which was to blame for this sorry state of affairs. He added that the idea for *Two of Us* had come about after the popular agony aunt Claire Rayner had 'briefly mentioned homosexual stereotypes' when she presented her 'Personal View' in an edition of *Scene* back in 1981. Baker commented: 'The response was sufficiently favourable to look at the possibility of doing a *Scene* on homosexuality. The School Broadcasting Council agreed that the subject warranted research.'

The first option, a documentary, was jettisoned in favour of a drama, and Leslie Stewart, a writer who was popular with the *Scene* production team, was drafted in to script it. Stewart wrote the script in consultation with the *Scene* producer-director Roger Tonge. When the BBC decided not to screen the film, Stewart was understandably shocked and told the *TES*:

> The idea of writing the play wasn't to make life awkward for teachers but to get people in the school environment to face up to the facts that homosexuality does exist among teenagers, does cause a lot of grief and can lead directly to suicide and massive unhappiness. The idea was to make teachers and teenagers feel more comfortable about discussing it, and to make teenagers who are gay not feel so desperate about it.

It was a hostile climate that led to the BBC withdrawing *Two of Us* and cancelling the 1987 screening. Several cuts were ordered by Alan Rogers, head of BBC School TV. A kiss between the gay teenagers vanished and a new ending was imposed. The lads were supposed to remain together, but one of them chooses to return to his girlfriend. Thus heterosexuality became his preferred lifestyle. It was this 'cleaned up' version of *Two of Us* that the BBC finally screened for one hour (instead of two half-hour episodes) on BBC2 on 25 March 1988 at 11.30 p.m. Teenagers, at whom it was partly aimed, were tucked up in bed. The BBC believed that teachers who were interested would video record the drama and screen it in their classrooms, with the gay kiss omitted, and the new 'choose straight' ending.

Some of the hostility directed at *Two of Us* came from the Conservative MP and former deputy headmaster Harry Greenway. Shortly before the screening, he demanded that Kenneth Baker, Britain's Education Secretary, intervene and force the BBC to withdraw *Two of Us* 'immediately and unreservedly'. Greenway described *Two of Us* as 'deplorable and outrageous'.[1] In spite of Greenway's objections, the BBC went ahead with the screening.

Those who stayed up late to watch *Two of Us* were shown an inoffensive, romantic and uplifting story of loyalty and love and of being true to one's self. Matthew (Jason Rush) knows he's gay, but Phil (Lee Whitlock) is unsure of his sexuality. He has a girlfriend, but he finds himself drawn to Matthew both as a loyal friend and romantic partner. The compromised version shown by the BBC in 1988 still made an impact and showed that teenage lads who are playful *and* sexually attracted to each other are normal, not freakish or unnatural.

Interviewed in the *Morning Star* (25 March 1988) on the day of the screening, Leslie Stewart explained that *Two of Us* should not be thought of as a gay play:

> It is a teenage love story, mildly tragic, nothing special, except that it is about two boys. In one London survey of gay youth, one in five had attempted suicide – each believed he or she was the only young gay person in the world. Perhaps if the nine in ten knew more – the one in ten might lead happier lives.

The day after the screening Mark Lawson, television critic for *The Independent* (26 March 1988), praised *Two of Us* but criticised the Tory MP and ex-deputy headmaster Harry Greenway who objected to the screening:

> It would be fascinating to know what advice Mr Greenway, in his teaching days, would have given to students of confused sexuality. At a time when such young people are faced with a renewed climate of emotional suspicion and a *Sun* newspaper which cheerfully uses terms like 'poof', 'woofter' and 'queer' – on Page 1 this week, you could read of a man who changed his surname from Gay to Straight – *Two of Us*, directed by Roger Tonge, was a brave and responsible piece of education, not just for schoolchildren.

Shortly after the screening, the *Radio Times* (16–22 April 1988) published several positive and moving letters from viewers:

Even though it has taken two years to make the decision to transmit *Two of Us* it is heartening to see the BBC finally living up to its obligation to spread information without fear or favour. This can only help to dispel the bigotry and prejudice that stem from ignorance.

I am only sorry the BBC found it necessary to put on such a thought-provoking, well-balanced and entirely inoffensive play in the middle of the night.

'So why all the fuss in Britain?' asked Jonathan Sanders in his *Two of Us* feature in *Gay Times* (May 1988): 'Perhaps the play implicitly "promotes" gayness by presenting its teenagers as very confident and happy about their sexualities. On a beach they whirl about, arms round each other, to a soundtrack chorus of "Shall We Dance?" in a joyous, naturalism-breaking moment worthy of Derek Jarman.' Sanders added that the 'cheerful simplicity' of Phil's bisexuality, without invalidating Matthew's gayness 'blurs the boundaries on which laws like Section 28 depend'. Sanders concluded by stating:

Whether many teachers will be allowed to use the programme, even if they wish, remains to be seen, but at least the battle to broadcast *Two of Us* has been won. In view of the circumstances, however, it has been a Pyrrhic victory which forebodes the heavy losses we may sustain in the war against Section 28.

Almost two years later, when the dust had settled, BBC2 screened *Two of Us* again as originally planned, in two half-hour parts, during the school day at 12.15 p.m. (tx 2/9 February 1990). However, Peter Dawson, the head of the 45,000-strong Professional Association of Schoolteachers, called this decision 'disgraceful'. Dawson believed that *Two of Us* promoted homosexuality and could contravene Clause 28 of the Local Government Act which banned material in school promoting homosexuality. Dawson then said that BBC employees wanted to screen *Two of Us* again because 'a large number of people working in television and radio have a vested interest in justifying their own behaviour. The film could cause arrested development by suggesting to children experiencing an adolescent homosexual phase that their feelings were an adult norm.'[2] In response, the BBC acknowledged that the repeat had been endorsed by the Education Broadcasting Council and the National Union of Teachers.

In 1988, in spite of its midnight screening, over 2 million viewers tuned in to *Two of Us*. In 1992, with the BBC's consent, Dangerous to Know, a gay and lesbian video distribution company, released the original, uncut version. So, many more millions were able to see it. It has remained in the public domain ever since, including a DVD release in 2004. *Two of Us* continues to educate, inform and entertain, which is in keeping with the aims of the BBC's founder, John Reith (1889–1971).

Notes
1. 'Film Row Over Homosexuality', *Irish Independent* (22 March 1988).
2. 'Homosexual Play a Disgrace', *The Daily Telegraph* (12 January 1990).

30

Are We Being Served?

It was with great fanfare that Britain's fourth television channel, Channel 4, was launched on 2 November 1982. Under the direction of Jeremy Isaacs, its first chief executive (1981–88), a veteran of documentary and current affairs television, Channel 4 promised to give a voice to minority groups. It would provide 'alternative' programmes by making products new to British television including access, community, youth and minority groups. It even appointed a commissioning editor for multicultural programming and promised to give opportunities to independent programme makers. So, at first, things were looking up.

Two months before the launch, Jackie Marcus, the television critic for *Gay News*, interviewed Paul Madden, Channel 4's (wait for it) Commissioning Editor of Single Documentaries, Media Programmes and Animation. Regarding gay programming, Madden told Marcus: 'What we're *not* going to do is put out programmes specifically aimed at gays which focus on gayness as a problem. As soon as you start identifying you start ghettoising and that's what we want to avoid.'[1] Madden convinced Marcus that Channel 4 was very aware of its potential gay audience, and what they thought, felt and said would have a bearing on future decisions. Marcus was happy: 'I felt, after speaking to Paul Madden, that the gay community had a decent chance of fair and balanced representation on Channel 4, and I don't think, once it starts, that I shall find myself after a fortnight of viewing with nothing to say.'[2] Sadly, this was not to be, for Jackie Marcus found very few Channel 4 programmes to write about in *Gay News*. Then, in January 1985, Madden became the first commissioning editor at Channel 4 not to have his contract renewed.

In 1988, Channel 4 carried out a survey with its supposedly liberal, enlightened viewers and discovered a large disparity between proffered acceptance of the lesbian and gay community and what, to a significant majority of the channel's clientele, constituted acceptable viewing. Lesbians and gays were *not* wanted in people's living rooms on Channel 4, even by heterosexual liberals.

Meanwhile, in December 1982, one month after Channel 4 launched, it found itself in hot water when it purchased the rights to three films made by Derek Jarman, the openly gay independent filmmaker and activist. One of the films was his homoerotic *Sebastiane* (1976), a beautifully shot drama set in the fourth century AD featuring male nudity. According to Tony Peake, one of Jarman's biographers, the tabloid *Daily Star* (30 December 1982) condemned the acquisition of Jarman's films as well as Ron Pecks's gay film *Nighthawks* (1978):

> In a diatribe that stretched across two pages … the paper fulminated against Channel 4 for buying a film [*Sebastiane*] which, it claimed, 'the Latin dialogue is used to disguise a script packed with pornographic language.' It quoted one 'TV insider' as saying: 'I know Channel 4 is keen to cater for minorities, but homosexual gladiators must be the smallest minority of the year.' A Tory MP called for the withdrawal of the station's right to broadcast.[3]

Channel 4 responded by explaining that Jarman's three films and *Nighthawks* had been bought as part of a package and they had no intention of screening them. Later, Jeremy Isaacs revealed that it was always Channel 4's intention to show the films, and they were just trying to throw the tabloids off the scent. However, Jarman was incensed and in 1984 he retaliated in his published journal *Dancing Ledge*:

> Then came Channel 4, whose advent was whispered about by 'alternative' film-makers as though it were the panacea. Dutifully and optimistically I joined the queue with the others. Yet Channel 4, in spite of a much-vaunted alternative image, was to turn out all *beaujolais nouveau* and scrubbed Scandinavian, pot plants in place. It wasn't *our* alternative: independent cinema was to remain independent, disenfranchised by a channel for the slightly adventurous commuter.[4]

Channel 4 shelved the films until 1985, when they were finally shown in a season of twenty 'high-brow' cinema classics billed as 'Robinson's Choice' because they were curated by David Robinson, film critic of the high-brow broadsheet the *Times*. In addition to Jarman's three films and Peck's *Nighthawks*, gay filmmakers were also represented by Luchino Visconti (*Ludwig*, 1972) and Rainer Werner Fassbinder (*Fox and His Friends*, 1975). The season also included such internationally acclaimed productions as Bresson's *L'Argent* (1983), Ozu's *Tokyo Story* (1953) and Euzhan Palcy's *Sugar Cane Alley* (1983). All of them were screened late at night and Jeremy Isaacs took great pride in screening what he described as 'some of our most difficult pictures'.[5]

Jarman did eventually benefit from Channel 4's investment in the British film industry. In 1986, it partly financed *Caravaggio*, his first opportunity to direct a feature film since 1979, but seven years in the wilderness had been a long and frustrating time for Jarman. It also part-financed Stephen Frears's critically acclaimed gay romance *My Beautiful Laundrette* (1985), but for gay *television* audiences Channel 4 provided slim pickings in the drama department.

An exception was an adaptation of Michael Wilcox's stage play *Accounts* (tx 22 December 1983). Wilcox's intention was to show how gays fitted into everyday life, not make them a special case or prioritise politics, like Gay Sweatshop. Alan Sinfield described *Accounts* in *Out on Stage: Lesbian and Gay Theatre in the Twentieth Century* (1999) as the story of a mother and her two sons who are struggling to run a farm after the death of the father:

> It emerges that one of the brothers is gay, but in the understated rural Scots Border idiom through which Wilcox presents them is scarcely a matter for comment. He is also an excellent rugby player, hardly a gay stereotype; anyone may be gay … I feel that he is trying to talk his audiences into seeing homosexuality as unremarkable by depicting it like that. This too is a political project.[6]

There was also Gordon Collins (Mark Burgess) who, in the 1980s, was the middle-class gay lad in Channel 4's popular Liverpool-based soap *Brookside*. Gordon's homosexuality was mentioned briefly in 1984, but the subject was dropped with alarming haste. According to Jim Wiggins, the actor who played Gordon's father, his fictitious son's sexuality provided the scriptwriters with ample opportunity to develop the idea but, as he told *Gay Times*, 'the opportunity was completely wasted, the matter has just been abandoned with an embarrassingly brief mention … I do think it's totally unrealistic that parents just wouldn't talk to each other about something as important as that.'[7] Two years later an out and proud Gordon found himself a boy-friend, but this was after he had agonised over wearing a gay badge, and fretted when his subscription copy of *Gay Times* was delivered to a neighbour by mistake. Though Gordon remained with the series for several years, he was never as interesting or as popular as some of the outstanding, realistic working-class characters, such as the Grant family and Jimmy Corkhill.

On the other hand, lesbian and gay characters could be laughed at on Channel 4. On its opening night *Five Go Mad in Dorset* was screened as the first episode in what became their most popular comedy series: *The Comic Strip Presents. Five Go Mad in Dorset* was a laugh-a-minute parody of Enid Blyton's children's adventure books featuring the 'Famous Five'. It was set in the 1950s, with Julian enjoying a close friendship with a boy called Toby; George, the girl who desperately wants to be a boy, being called a 'dyke'; and the children's Uncle Quentin revealed as a crook *and* a homosexual (illegal in the 1950s). It *was* funny but, afterwards, gays rarely surfaced in *The Comic Strip*, though there should have been a place for them in this hilarious world of 'alternative comedy'. To add insult to injury, homophobia occasionally reared its ugly head. In *A Fistful of Travellers' Cheques*, the *Comic Strip*'s satire on Spaghetti westerns (tx 21 January 1984), a character complained about the poor facilities in his room at the Hotel Bastardos. The hotel manager responded with, 'If you want soft toilet paper, go to Hotel Gay Boy.' Four years later, Nigel Planer and Keith Allen were not funny as a couple of screaming queens who were credited in the cast list as 'Camp Actor 1 & 2' in *The Comic Strip's The Strike* (tx 20 February 1988). The writers of these two episodes were Peter Richardson and Peter Richens. What were they thinking of? Thankfully, Planer's and Allen's appearances were so brief, if you blinked you missed them.

Something had to give. It was generally agreed in the lesbian and gay community that Channel 4 was letting them down. Badly. In 1995, Colin Richardson reflected on this in *A Queer Romance: Lesbians, Gay Men and Popular Culture*:

> The fact that 'we' didn't have 'our' own show could only be construed as an insult, suggesting that unlike, say, women and black people, lesbians and gay men did not constitute a valid social group deserving of attention. So Peter Tatchell and others, through the pages of the gay press, encouraged a letter-writing campaign to put pressure on Channel 4. In May 1985, ten Labour MPs joined in, sending a letter which urged the channel to

produce a new series which 'as well as meeting the needs of the lesbian and gay community…could also potentially have a far broader appeal and educative function in relation to the heterosexual population.'[8]

It took intense lobbying on the part of the lesbian and gay community to persuade the channel to change its ways, but it took time. Meanwhile, writers and journalists continued to publish critical articles in the gay press about this situation. For example, in the May 1985 issue of *Gay Times*, Alan Brayne contributed an 'Opinion' piece called 'Gays and Television':

> In the Sixties, a stream of plays were written about unhappy queens, strident, sad and lonely. Then Gay Sweatshop created a new drama devoid of these negative stereotypes. The emphasis changed to stressing the happy, the positive, the healthy, even beyond the narrow political circle of Sweatshop itself. TV drama has followed the same trend. An early TV play by David Mercer culminated in an orgy of violence as one unhappy, tortured character murdered another. Whereas *The Groundling and the Kite*, transmitted a year ago, contained two characters as nice, affluent, respectable and generally as boring as anyone could wish for. But drama which concentrates on drawing positive gay characters eventually reaches a cul-de-sac, just as the safe, inoffensive documentaries of the last ten years. This is because they are aimed at a straight audience rather than a gay one and always have to simplify the truth.

David Mercer was considered to be one of the most outstanding television dramatists of the 1960s and 1970s. The play referred to by Alan Brayne was Mercer's *A Superstition*, made by Yorkshire TV (tx 13 August 1977). It starred a pre-*Brideshead* Anthony Andrews as a young man living with a much older man, played by Hugh Burden. They exist in a love-hate relationship in a paradise retreat in the South of France. Their lives are disturbed and disrupted by the arrival of a stranger and, as described by Brayne, 'an orgy of violence'. Some of Mercer's lines were excruciating. For example, when Hugh Burden says to Anthony Andrews: 'You emanate a reproving stench, Harry.'

So, lobbying was needed and, in 1985, a research project called *Are We Being Served?* was launched by the Gays and Broadcasting Project. There had been previous attempts at lobbying television companies. Towards the end of the 1970s there existed a Gays in Media group, founded in 1978.

Its members included the broadcaster Robin Houston and the writer Howard Schuman.[9] In 1979, they organised a meeting with television executives which led to London Weekend Television's *Gay Life* actuality series in 1980. So, a precedent had been set. Lobbying could work.

During one week (12–18 August 1985) the Gays and Broadcasting Project monitored 688 hours of television and radio. They looked at the treatment of the lesbian and gay community, but of the 268 hours of television monitored, only 9 hours and 40 minutes (3.8 per cent) had included any lesbian or gay representation. Stereotypes dominated, such as 'criminals, buffoons or fools'. The useful and informative report published by Gays and Broadcasting noted that, throughout the monitoring period, all references to gay men in news programmes were linked to AIDS. John Inman, the star of the popular BBC sitcom *Are You Being Served?*, was mentioned for his not-so-gay-friendly guest appearance in the BBC variety show *The Good Old Days* singing 'I Was Born a Bachelor' and 'Do You Believe in Fairies?'

In the report's conclusions, the monitoring group rejected nearly all of the few representations that were broadcast. Only five representations (out of forty-five in total) were judged to be 'positive'. On television, over 90 per cent of gay characters amounted to two stereotypes: the criminal and the sissy, who were, with few exceptions, white, middle-aged men. The report's final conclusion stated: 'The gay community needs to circulate information about the media, and broadcasters must become more responsive. This report is not, after all, rejecting entertainment broadcasting in total. We are merely proposing that broadcasters look at the facts and then listen to lesbians and gays offering their own proposals for change.'[10] Colin Richardson observed: 'The report didn't throw its weight behind the campaign for a series on Channel 4 so much as call for more and better representation on all the channels.'[11]

Are We Being Served? was also the title of a one-day conference organised by the Project at London's County Hall on 14 February 1986. The Project's report was presented at this event at which lesbians and gays challenged broadcasters to examine their own homophobia and that of the institutions they served. Nothing on this scale had ever been attempted before and the conference room was packed. It started badly with the Chair, Nick Ross, from BBC1's *Breakfast Time*, stating that he was a happily married heterosexual. Some members of the audience booed. Mr Ross looked uncomfortable but carried on to introduce some excellent speakers including Professor Stuart

Hall from the Open University, Mark Finch and Lorraine Trenchard, two of the Project's researchers, Paul Bonner (Channel 4), Andrew Lumsden (*New Statesman*), Femi Otitoju (*Captital Gay*) and Diane Abbott (ACTT) who offered a trade union perspective. Sue Sharples attended the conference and reported in the feminist magazine *Spare Rib* (April 1986):

> Media officials present at the conference were grudgingly forced to admit that broadcasting of lesbian and gay issues was derisory and they are now being pressed hard for an improvement. We can do our bit too: we were assured at the conference that telephone complaints are taken seriously and are effective.

Other lobbyists at this time included the lesbian and gay group of the Campaign for Press and Broadcasting Freedom, which included Colin Richardson. They had their inaugural meeting in February 1986,[12] and the following June they had a conference specifically to formulate a series of demands on Channel 4 which, said Richardson:

> We took to a meeting with the channel's then boss, Jeremy Isaacs, and most of the senior commissioning editors. Our general presentation was against a single series – largely on the grounds that it risked ghet-toisation – and in favour of more programming across the board ... in September 1986 it launched *In the Pink*, an eight week season of lesbian and/or gay films in the late night *Eleventh Hour* strand.[13]

Quentin McDermott reported in *City Limits* (20–27 November 1986) that, at the meeting, Jeremy Isaacs exclaimed that, at Channel 4, 'We're a very happy and variegated heterosexual and homosexual family. I went round the building yesterday and kissed everybody! There are a number of people who have a great time being gay in the building!' McDermott added that 'Isaacs gave the group an "unreserved" undertaking that Channel 4 "will safeguard your interests in the future by continuing to provide broader representations of lesbians and gays and their lifestyles in our actuality and in our fiction." He added: "You have more power than Mary Whitehouse because right is on your side."' An unidentified commentator in *Spare Rib* (December 1986) shared a different perspective on Isaacs: 'who was his usual rude and irritated self' but acknowledged that the meeting was 'productive and promising'. Then, shooting themselves in the foot, in 1987

Channel 4 upset everyone with their terrible 'gay' sitcom, *The Corner House*, which Colin Richardson described as 'Excruciatingly "correct", each character a "cause", it was an unfunny disaster which sank without trace.'[14]

Finally, just before 11 p.m. on Tuesday, 14 February 1989, Richardson commented:

> The sense of excitement that had been building for some time, a feeling that television would never be the same again, took on a tangible form. Channel 4's continuity announcer took a deep breath: 'And now, a lesbian and gay weekly magazine that invites you to come *Out on Tuesday*.'[15]

For drama queens, one of the highlights of *Out on Tuesday* was Richard Kwietniowski's short film *Flames of Passion* (tx 21 August 1991), a beautifully photographed, haunting gay reworking of Noël Coward's *Brief Encounter*. By lobbying, the lesbian and gay community achieved some of their goals and, in doing so, they ensured that British television would never be the same again.

Notes

1. *Gay News* (24 September 1982).
2. *Ibid.*
3. Tony Peake, *Derek Jarman* (Little, Brown, 1979), p. 305.
4. Derek Jarman, *Dancing Ledge* (Quartet Books, 1984), p. 207.
5. Jeremy Isaacs, *Storm Over Four: A Personal Account* (Weidenfeld and Nicolson, 1989), p. 120.
6. Alan Sinfield, *Out on Stage: Lesbian and Gay Theatre in the Twentieth Century* (Yale University Press, 1999), p. 349.
7. David Sefton, 'Brookside', *Gay Times*, August 1985.
8. Colin Richardson, 'TVOD: The Never-Bending Story', Paul Burston and Colin Richardson (eds.), *A Queer Romance: Lesbians, Gay Men and Popular Culture* (Routledge, 1995), p. 219.
9. *Gay News* No. 138 (1978).
10. Philip Adams, Mark Finch and Lorraine Trenchard/Gays and Broadcasting, *Are We Being Served?* (1986).
11. Richardson, p. 219.
12. Sue Sharples, 'Lifting the lid on homophobia', *Free Press* No. 34 (April 1986).
13. Richardson, p. 219.
14. *Ibid.*, p. 220.
15. *Ibid.*, p. 216.

Appendix

A list of single plays discussed in the book and their viewing status. Some of these plays are available for viewing free of charge in the British Film Institute's Mediatheques. For further information go to www.bfi.org.uk.

Rope
BBC tx 8 March 1939
Writer: Patrick Hamilton
Producer: Dallas Bower
Live transmission (no recording exists)

Rope
BBC tx 5 January 1947
Writer: Patrick Hamilton
Producer: Stephen Harrison
Live transmission (no recording exists)

Edward II
BBC tx 30 October 1947
Writer: Christopher Marlowe
Producer: Stephen Harrison
Live transmission (no recording exists)

Sunday-Night Theatre: Rope
BBC tx 8 January 1950
Writer: Patrick Hamilton
Producer: Stephen Harrison
Live transmission (no recording exists)

Rope
BBC tx 8 December 1953
Writer: Patrick Hamilton
Producer: Stephen Harrison
Live transmission (no recording exists)

Rope
Granada tx 2 October 1957
Writer: Patrick Hamilton/Adaptor: Kenneth Hoare
Director: Henry Kaplan
Live transmission (no recording exists)

Play of the Week: South
Granada tx 24 November 1959
Writer: Julien Green/Adaptor: Gerald Savory
Director: Mario Prizek
Recording exists

On Trial: Sir Roger Casement
Granada tx 8 July 1960
Producer: Peter Wildeblood
Director: Cliff Owen
Recording exists

On Trial: Oscar Wilde
Granada tx 5 August 1960
Producer: Peter Wildeblood
Director: Silvio Narizzano
Recording exists

Armchair Theatre:
Afternoon of a Nymph
ABC tx 30 September 1962
Writer: Robert Muller
Director: Philip Saville
Recording exists

Z Cars: 'Somebody … Help'
BBC1 tx 3 June 1964
Writer: John Hopkins
Producer: David E. Rose
Director: Robin Midgley
No recording exists

The Wednesday Play:
Horror of Darkness
BBC1 tx 10 March 1965
Writer: John Hopkins
Producer: James MacTaggart
Director: Anthony Page
Recording exists

The Wednesday Play:
The Interior Decorator
BBC1 tx 14 April 1965

Writer: Jack Russell
Producer: James MacTaggart
Director: James Ferman
No recording exists

The Wednesday Play:
The Connoisseur
BBC1 tx 4 May 1966
Writer: Hugo Charteris
Producer: Peter Luke
Director: Waris Hussein
Recording exists

Half-Hour Story: Friends
Associated Rediffusion tx 6
September 1967
Writer: Cecil P. Taylor
Producer: Stella Richman
Director: Michael Lindsay-Hogg
Recording exists

The Wednesday Play:
Wanted: Single Gentleman …
BBC1 tx 18 October 1967
Writer: James Broome Lynne
Producer: Irene Shubik
Director: John Gorrie
No recording exists

Playhouse:
Entertaining Mr Sloane
Associated Rediffusion
tx 15 July 1968
Writer: Joe Orton
Producer: Peter Willes
Director: Peter Moffatt
Recording exists

The Wednesday Play: Spoiled
BBC1 tx 28 August 1968
Writer: Simon Gray
Producer: Graeme McDonald
Director: Waris Hussein
No recording exists

The Wednesday Play:
The Last Train Through
the Harecastle Tunnel
BBC1 tx 1 October 1969
Writer: Peter Terson
Producer: Irene Shubik
Director: Alan Clarke
Recording exists

Edward II
BBC2 tx 6 August 1970
Writer: Christopher Marlowe
Producer: Mark Shivas
Director: Tony Robertson
Recording exists

Sunday Night Theatre:
Roll on Four O'Clock
Granada tx 20 December 1970
Writer: Colin Welland
Producer: Kenith Trodd
Director: Roy Battersby
Recording exists

Play for Today: Circle Line
BBC1 tx 14 January 1971
Writer: W. Stephen Gilbert
Producer: Graeme McDonald
Director: Claude Whatham
No recording exists

Thirty-Minute Theatre:
The Waiting Room
BBC2 tx 29 March 1971
Writer: John Bowen
Producer: Innes Lloyd
Director: Robert Knights
No recording exists

Thirty-Minute Theatre:
Under the Age
BBC2 tx 20 March 1972
Writer: E.A. Whitehead
Producer: David Rose
Director: Alan Clarke
Recording exists

Thirty-Minute Theatre:
Bermondsey
BBC2 tx 19 June 1972
Writer: John Mortimer
Producer: Anne Bead
Director: Claude Whatham
Recording exists

Total Eclipse
BBC2 tx 10 April 1973
Writer: Christopher Hampton
Producer: Mark Shivas
Director: Peter Cregeen
Recording exists

Play for Today: Penda's Fen
BBC1 tx 21 March 1974
Writer: David Rudkin
Producer: David Rose
Director: Alan Clarke
Recording exists

The Naked Civil Servant
Thames tx 17 December 1975
Writer: Philip Mackie
Producer: Barry Hanson
Director: Jack Gold
Recording exists

Play of the Month:
The Picture of Dorian Gray
BBC1 tx 19 September 1976
Writer: John Osborne, adapted
from Oscar Wilde
Producer: Cedric Messina
Director: John Gorrie
Recording exists

Laurence Olivier Presents:
The Collection
Granada tx 5 December 1976
Writer: Harold Pinter
Producers: Derek Granger and
Laurence Olivier
Director: Michael Apted
Recording exists

Crown Court:
'Beyond the Call of Duty'
Granada tx 4/5/6 February 1976
Writers: Michael O'Neill and
Jeremy Seabrook
Producer: Kerry Crabbe
Director: Stephen Butcher
Recording exists

Crown Court: 'Lola'
Granada tx 8/9/10 December 1976
Writer: David Yallop

Producer: Dennis Woolf
Director: Colin Bucksey
Recording exists

Play for Today: Scum
BBC1 1977 (tx 27 July 1991)
Writer: Roy Minton
Producer: Margaret Matheson
Director: Alan Clarke
Recording exists

Philby, Burgess and Maclean
Granada tx 31 May 1977
Writer: Ian Curteis
Director: Gordon Flemyng
Recording exists

A Superstition
Yorkshire TV tx 13 August 1977
Writer: David Mercer
Producer: Peter Willes
Director: David Cunliffe
Recording exists

Everyman:
Blasphemy at the Old Bailey
BBC1 tx 18 September 1977
Producer: Daniel Wolf
Director: Hugh David
Recording exists

Premiere: A Hymn from Jim
BBC2 tx 29 September 1977
Writer: Richard O'Brien
Producer: Graham Benson
Director: Colin Bucksey
Recording exists

Premiere: The Obelisk
BBC2 tx 13 October 1977
Writer: E M Forster/Adaptor:
Pauline Macauley
Producer: Graham Benson
Director: Giles Foster
Recording exists

The Last Romantic
Granada tx 12 March 1978
Writer: Kerry Crabbe
Producer/Director: Julian Aymes
Recording exists

Six Plays by Alan Bennett:
Me, I'm Afraid of Virginia Woolf
LWT tx 2 December 1978
Writer: Alan Bennett
Producer/Director: Stephen Frears
Recording exists

Play for Today: Coming Out
BBC1 tx 10 April 1979
Writer: James Andrew Hall
Producer: Kenith Trodd
Director: Carol Wiseman
Recording exists

The Other Side: Only Connect
BBC2 tx 18 May 1979
Writers: Noel Greig and Drew
Griffiths
Producer: W. Stephen Gilbert
Director: Richard Stroud
Recording exists

The House on the Hill:
Something for the Boys
Scottish TV tx 1 August 1981
Writer: Drew Griffiths
Producers: Robert Love and Mike
Vardy
Director: Tina Wakerell
Recording exists

Play for Today:
A Room for the Winter
BBC1 tx 3 November 1981
Writer: Rose Tremain
Producer: June Roberts
Director: Jim Goddard
Recording exists

Belles
BBC2 tx 27 May 1983
Writer: David Clough
Producer: Andrée Molyneux
Director: Paul Seed
Recording exists

An Englishman Abroad
BBC1 tx 29 November 1983
Writer: Alan Bennett
Producer: Innes Lloyd
Director: John Schlesinger
Recording exists

Accounts
Channel 4 tx 22 December 1983
Writer: Michael Wilcox
Producer: Tom Sachs
Director: Michael Darlow
Recording exists

The BBC Television
Shakespeare: Coriolanus
BBC2 tx 21 April 1984
Writer: William Shakespeare
Producer: Shaun Sutton
Director: Elijah Moshinsky
Recording exists

Play for Today:
The Groundling and the Kite
BBC1 tx 24 July 1984
Writer: Leonard Preston
Producer: Colin Rogers
Director: Peter Jefferies
Recording exists

More Lives Than One
BBC1 tx 18 December 1984
Writer: John Peacock
Producer: Alan Shallcross
Director: Michael Darlow
Recording exists

Screen Two: Blunt
BBC2 tx 11 January 1987
Writer: Robin Chapman
Producer: Martin Thompson
Director: John Glenister
Recording exists

Scene: Two of Us
BBC2 tx 25 March 1988
Writer: Leslie Stewart
Producer/Director: Roger Tonge
Recording exists

Bibliography

Aldrich, Robert and Garry Wotherspoon (eds.), *Who's Who in Gay and Lesbian History: From Antiquity to World War II* (Routledge, 2001)

Aldrich, Robert and Garry Wotherspoon (eds.), *Who's Who in Contemporary Gay and Lesbian History: From World War II to the Present Day* (Routledge, 2001)

Bailey, Paul (ed.), *The Stately Homo: A Celebration of the Life of Quentin Crisp* (Bantam Press, 2000)

Beck, Alan, 'You've Got to Hide Your Love Away: Gay Radio, Past and Present', *More Than a Music Box: Radio Cultures and Communities in a Multi-Media World*, Andrew Crisell (ed.) (Berghahn Books, 2005)

Bennett, Alan, *Me, I'm Afraid of Virginia Woolf* (Faber and Faber, 2003)

Bignell, Jonathan, Stephen Lacey and Madeleine Macmurraugh-Kavanagh (eds.), *British Television Drama: Past, Present and Future* (Palgrave, 2000)

Bourne, Stephen, *Brief Encounters: Lesbians and Gays in British Cinema 1930–71* (Cassell, 1996)

Bourne, Stephen, *Black in the British Frame: The Black Experience in British Film and Television* (Continuum, 2001)

Bourne, Stephen, *Elisabeth Welch: Soft Lights and Sweet Music* (Scarecrow Press, 2005)

Bourne, Stephen, *Fighting Proud: The Untold Story of the Gay Men who Served in Two World Wars* (I B Tauris, 2017)

Bower, Dallas, *Playback: A Life in Radio, Film and Television* (unpublished autobiography, 1995). In possession of Philip Purser/Alexandra Palace Television Society.

Brandt, George W. (ed.), *British Television Drama* (Cambridge University Press, 1981)

Brighton Ourstory Project, *Daring Hearts: Lesbian and Gay Lives of 50s and 60s Brighton* (QueenSpark Books, 1992)

Bryant, Steve, *The Television Heritage: Television Archiving Now and in an Uncertain Future* (British Film Institute, 1989)

Burston, Paul and Colin Richardson (eds.), *A Queer Romance: Lesbians, Gay Men and Popular Culture* (Routledge, 1995)

Burton, Graeme, *Talking Television: An Introduction to the Study of Television* (Arnold, 2000)

Buscombe, Edward (ed.), *British Television: A Reader* (Oxford University Press, 2000)

Byng, Douglas, *As You Were: Reminiscences by Douglas Byng* (Duckworth, 1970)

Cant, Bob and Susan Hemmings (eds.), *Radical Records: Thirty Years of Lesbian and Gay History 1957–1987* (Routledge, 1988)

Capsuto, Steven, *Alternate Channels: The Uncensored Story of Gay and Lesbian Images on Radio and Television* (Ballantine, 2000)

Carson, Bruce and Margaret Llewellyn-Jones (eds.), *Frames and Fictions on Television: The Politics of Identity Within Drama* (Intellect Books, 2000)

Caughie, John, 'Before the Golden Age – Early Television Drama', *Popular Television in Britain: Studies in Cultural History*, John Corner (ed.) (British Film Institute, 1991)

Caughie, John, *Television Drama: Realism, Modernism and British Culture* (Oxford University Press, 2000)

Clews, Colin, *Gay in the 80s: From Fighting for Our Rights to Fighting for Our Lives* (Matador, 2017)

Coldstream, John, *Dirk Bogarde: The Authorised Biography* (Weidenfeld and Nicolson, 2004)

Cook, John R., *Dennis Potter: A Life on Screen* (Manchester University Press, 1995)

Cook, Matt (ed.), *A Gay History of Britain: Love and Sex Between Men Since the Middle Ages* (Greenwood World Publishing, 2007)

Cooke, Lez, *British Television Drama: A History* (British Film Institute, 2003)

Cornell, Paul, Martin Day and Keith Topping, *Classic British TV* (Guinness, 1996)

Corner, John (ed.), *Popular Television in Britain: Studies in Cultural History* (British Film Institute, 1991)

Creeber, Glen (ed.), *The Television Genre Book* (British Film Institute, 2001)

Crisp, Quentin, *The Naked Civil Servant* (Jonathan Cape, 1968)

Croall, Jonathan, *Gielgud: A Theatrical Life 1904–2000* (Methuen, 2001)

David, Hugh, *On Queer Street: A Social History of British Homosexuality 1895–1995* (HarperCollins, 1997)

Davies, Russell (ed.), *The Kenneth Williams Diaries* (HarperCollins, 1994)

Davies, Russell T, *Queer as Folk: The Scripts* (Channel 4 Books, 1999)

Day-Lewis, Sean, *Talk of Drama: Views of the Television Dramatist Now and Then* (University of Luton Press, 1998)

de Jongh, Nicholas, *Not in Front of the Audience: Homosexuality on Stage* (Routledge, 1992)

de Jongh, Nicholas, *Politics, Prudery and Perversions: The Censoring of the English Stage 1901–1968* (Methuen, 2000)

Donovan, Paul, *The Radio Companion: The A–Z Guide to Radio from its Inception to the Present Day* (HarperCollins, 1991)

Down, Richard and Christopher Perry, *The British Television Drama Research Guide 1950–1997* (Kaleidoscope, 1997)

Elliott, Sue and Steve Humphries, *Not Guilty: Queer Stories of a Century of Discrimination* (Biteback Publishing, 2017)

Evans, Jeff, *The Penguin TV Companion* (Penguin Books, 2001)

Finch, John (ed.), *Granada Television: The First Generation* (Manchester University Press, 2003)

Flynn, Paul, *Good as You: From Prejudice to Pride – 30 Years of Gay Britain* (Ebury Press, 2017)

Galloway, Bruce (ed.), *Pride and Prejudice: Discrimination Against Gay People in Modern Britain* (Routledge and Kegan Paul, 1983)

Games, Alexander, *Backing into the Limelight: The Biography of Alan Bennett* (Headline, 2001)

Gardiner, James, *A Class Apart: The Private Pictures of Montague Glover* (Serpent's Tail, 1992)

Gardiner, James, *Who's a Pretty Boy Then? One Hundred and Fifty Years of Gay Life in Pictures* (Serpent's Tail, 1997)

Gielgud, Val, *British Radio Drama 1922–1956* (George G. Harrap, 1957)

Gray, Simon, *The Definitive Simon Gray I* (Faber and Faber, 1992)

Greig, Noel and Drew Griffiths, *As Time Goes By: Two Gay Sweatshop Plays* (Gay Men's Press, 1981)

Halliwell, Leslie and Philip Purser, *Halliwell's Television Companion* (Grafton Books, 3rd edition, 1986)

Hoffman, William M. (ed.), *Gay Plays: The First Collection* (Avon Books, 1979)

Houlbrook, Matt, *Queer London: Perils and Pleasures in the Sexual Metropolis, 1918–1957* (University of Chicago Press, 2005)

Howes, Keith and Julian Meldrum, *Declaring an Interest: A Projected Catalogue of Gay Images on Television in Britain* (The Hall Carpenter Archives, 1982)

Howes, Keith, *Broadcasting It: An Encyclopaedia of Homosexuality on Film, Radio and TV in the UK 1923–1993* (Cassell, 1993)

Howes, Keith, *Outspoken: Keith Howes' Gay News Interviews 1976–83* (Cassell, 1995)

Jacobs, Jason, *The Intimate Screen: Early British Television Drama* (Oxford University Press, 2000)

Jarman, Derek, *Dancing Ledge* (Quartet Books, 1984)

Jeffery-Poulter, Stephen, *Peers, Queers and Commons: The Struggle for Gay Law Reform from 1950 to the Present* (Routledge, 1991)

Jeffries, Stuart, *Mrs Slocombe's Pussy: Growing Up in Front of the Telly* (Flamingo, 2000)

Jivani, Alkarim, *It's Not Unusual: A History of Lesbian and Gay History in the Twentieth Century* (Michael O'Mara, 1997)

Kelly, Richard (ed.), *Alan Clarke* (Faber and Faber, 1998)

Kingsley, Hilary, *Soap Box: The Papermac Guide to Soap Opera* (Papermac, 1988)

Kingsley, Hilary and Geoff Tibballs, *Box of Delights: The Golden Years of Television* (Macmillan, 1989)

Lahr, John (ed.), *The Orton Diaries* (Methuen, 1986)

Madden, Paul (ed.), *Keeping Television Alive: The Television Work of the National Film Archive* (British Film Institute, 1981)

Magee, Bryan, *One in Twenty: A Study of Homosexuality in Men and Women* (Secker and Warburg, 1966)

Malyon, Mike, *Seems Like a Nice Boy: The Story of Larry Grayson's Rise to Stardom* (Apex Publishing, 2015)

Mann, William J., *Edge of Midnight: The Life of John Schlesinger* (Hutchinson, 2004)

Marland, Michael (ed.), *Conflicting Generations: Five Television Plays* (Longman, 1968)

Marland, Michael (ed.), *Z Cars: Four Scripts from the BBC Television Series* (Longman, 1968)

McKernan, Luke and Olwen Terris, *Walking Shadows: Shakespeare in the National Film and Television Archive* (British Film Institute, 1994)

Mercer, David, *The Parachute* (Calder and Boyars, 1967)

Miall, Leonard, *Inside the BBC: British Broadcasting Characters* (Weidenfeld and Nicolson, 1994)

Moorehead, Caroline, *Sidney Bernstein: A Biography* (Jonathan Cape, 1984)

Morley, Sheridan, *Dirk Bogarde: Rank Outsider* (Bloomsbury, 1996)

Mortimer, John, *Collected Plays Volume Two* (Oberon Books, 2004)

Murray, Raymond, *Images in the Dark: An Encyclopedia of Gay and Lesbian Film and Video* (Plume, 1996)

Newley, Patrick, *Bawdy but British! The Life of Douglas Byng* (Third Age Press, 2009)

Norden, Denis, *Coming to You Live! Behind-the-screen Memories of Forties and Fifties Television* (Methuen, 1985)

Norman, Bruce, *Here's Looking at You: The Story of British Television 1908–39* (BBC/ The Royal Television Society, 1984)

O'Connor, Alan (ed.), *Raymond Williams on Television: Selected Writings* (Routledge, 1989)

O'Connor, Sean, *Straight Acting: Popular Gay Drama from Wilde to Rattigan* (Cassell, 1998)

Pines, Jim (ed.), *Black and White in Colour: Black People in British Television Since 1936* (British Film Institute, 1992)

Porter, Kevin and Jeffrey Weeks, *Between the Acts: Lives of Homosexual Men 1885–1967* (Routledge, 1991)

Russo, Vito, *The Celluloid Closet: Homosexuality in the Movies* (Harper and Row, 1981)

Shepherd, Simon and Mick Wallis (eds.), *Coming on Strong: Gay Politics and Culture* (Unwin Hyman, 1989)

Shubik, Irene, *Play for Today: The Evolution of Television Drama* (Davis-Poynter, 1975)

Sinfield, Alan, *Out on Stage: Lesbian and Gay Theatre in the Twentieth Century* (Yale University Press, 1999)

Spoto, Donald, *Otherwise Engaged: The Life of Alan Bates* (Hutchinson, 2007)

Taylor, Don, *Days of Vision: Working with David Mercer: Television Drama Then and Now* (Methuen, 1990)

Taylor, John Russell, *Anatomy of a Television Play: An Inquiry into the Production of Two Armchair Theatre Plays* (Weidenfeld and Nicolson, 1962)

Taylor, John Russell, *Anger and After: A Guide to the New British Drama* (Methuen, 1962)

Thompson, Ben, *Ban This Filth! Mary Whitehouse and the Battle to Keep Britain Innocent* (Faber and Faber, 2012)

Vahimagi, Tise, *British Television: An Illustrated Guide* (Oxford University Press, 1994)

Various Contributors, *The Armchair Theatre* (Weidenfeld and Nicolson, 1959)

Various Contributors, *Granada: The First 25 Years* (BFI Dossier 9*)* (British Film Institute, 1981)

Various Contributors, *Face to Face with John Freeman: Interviews from the BBC TV Series* (BBC, 1989)

Weeks, Jeffrey, *Coming Out: Homosexual Politics in Britain from the Nineteenth Century to the Present* (Quartet Books, 1990)

Weight, Richard, *Patriots: National Identity in Britain 1940–2000* (Macmillan, 2002)

Wheen, Francis, *Television: A History* (Guild, 1985)

White, Leonard, *Armchair Theatre: The Lost Years* (Kelly Publications, 2003)

Whitehouse, Mary, *Cleaning-Up TV: From Protest to Participation* (Blandford Press, 1967)

Wilcox, Michael (ed.), *Gay Plays* (Methuen, 1984)

Wilcox, Michael (ed.), *Gay Plays Volume Two* (Methuen, 1985)

Wildeblood, Peter, *Against the Law* (Penguin, 1955)

Willis, Ted, *Evening All: 50 Years Over a Hot Typewriter* (Macmillan, 1991)

Woods, Gregory, *A History of Gay Literature: The Male Tradition* (Yale University Press, 1998)

Wyndham Goldie, Grace, *Facing the Nation: Television and Politics 1936–76* (The Bodley Head, 1977)

Magazines and Journals

Radio Times, 1923– . BBC Magazines. Weekly. Available at the BBC and British Film Institute.

The Listener, 1929–91. Listener Publications. Weekly. Available at the BBC and British Film Institute.

TV Times, 1955–. Independent Television Publications/IPC magazines. Weekly. Available at the British Film Institute.

Gay News, 1972–83. GN Publications Ltd. Fortnightly. Available at The Hall-Carpenter Archives at the School of Economics and in the British Library.

Gay Times, 1984–. Millivres Ltd. Monthly. Available at The Hall-Carpenter Archives at the School of Economics and in the British Library.

About the Author

Stephen Bourne is a writer, film and social historian specialising in black heritage and gay culture. As noted by the BBC among others, Stephen 'has discovered many stories that have remained untold for years.' Bonnie Greer, the acclaimed playwright and critic, says: 'Stephen brings great natural scholarship and passion to a largely hidden story. He is highly accessible, accurate and surprising. You always walk away from his work knowing something that you didn't know, that you didn't even expect.'

Stephen was born in Camberwell, south-east London, and raised in Peckham. He graduated from the London College of Printing with a bachelor's degree in film and television in 1988, and in 2006 received a MPhil. at De Montfort University on the subject of the representation of gay men in British television drama 1936–79.

After graduating in 1988, he was a research officer at the British Film Institute on a project that documented the history of black people in British television. The result was a two-part television documentary called *Black and White in Colour* (BBC 1992), directed by Isaac Julien, that is considered groundbreaking. In 1991, Stephen was a founder member of the Black and Asian Studies Association.

In 1991, Stephen co-authored *Aunt Esther's Story* with Esther Bruce (his adopted aunt), which was published by Hammersmith and Fulham's Ethnic Communities Oral History Project. Nancy Daniels in *The Voice* (8 October 1991) described the book as 'Poignantly and simply told, the story of Aunt Esther is a factual account of a black working-class woman born in turn of the century London. The book is a captivating documentation of a life rich in experiences, enhanced by good black and white photographs.' For *Aunt Esther's Story*, Stephen and Esther were shortlisted for the 1992 Raymond Williams Prize for Community Publishing.

In the 1990s, he undertook pioneering work with Southwark Council and the Metropolitan Police that resulted in the founding of one of the first locally based LGBT forums to address homophobic crime. Since 1999 he has been a voluntary independent adviser to the police. In 2002, Stephen received the Metropolitan Police Volunteer Award 'in recognition of dedicated service and commitment to supporting the Metropolitan Police in Southwark.'

In 2008, he researched *Keep Smiling Through: Black Londoners on the Home Front 1939–1945*, an exhibition for the Cuming Museum in the London Borough of Southwark, and that same year he worked as a historical consultant on the Imperial War Museum's *From War to Windrush* exhibition.

In 2014, Stephen's book *Black Poppies: Britain's Black Community and the Great War* was published by The History Press to coincide with the centenary of Britain's entry into the Fisrst World War. Reviewing it in *The Independent* (11 September 2014), Bernadine Evaristo said: 'Until historians and cultural map-makers stop ignoring the historical presence of people of colour, books such as this provide a powerful, revelatory counterbalance to the whitewashing of British history.' For *Black Poppies* Stephen received the 2015 Southwark Arts Forum Literature Award at Southwark's Unicorn Theatre.

In 2017, Stephen's acclaimed *Fighting Proud: The Untold Story of the Gay Men who Served in Two World Wars* was published by I B Tauris. *Attitude* magazine described it as 'Touching, often funny and inspiring' and *BBC History Magazine* called it 'Engaging and heartfelt … highly readable.'

In 2017, Stephen was given a special award from Screen Nation and an Honorary Fellowship from London South Bank University for his contribution to diversity.

For further information go to www.stephenbourne.co.uk.

Selected Publications

Aunt Esther's Story (ECOHP, 1991)
Brief Encounters: Lesbians and Gays in British Cinema 1930–1971 (Cassell, 1996/ Bloomsbury, 2016)
Black in the British Frame: The Black Experience in British Film and Television (Cassell, 1998/Continuum, 2001)
Sophisticated Lady: A Celebration of Adelaide Hall (ECOHP, 2001)

Elisabeth Welch: Soft Lights and Sweet Music (Scarecrow Press, 2005)

Speak of Me as I Am: The Black Presence in Southwark Since 1600 (Southwark Council, 2005)

Ethel Waters: Stormy Weather (Scarecrow Press, 2007)

Dr Harold Moody (Southwark Council, 2008)

Butterfly McQueen Remembered (Scarecrow Press, 2008)

Mother Country: Britain's Black Community on the Home Front 1939–45 (The History Press, 2010)

The Motherland Calls: Britain's Black Servicemen and Women 1939–45 (The History Press, 2012)

Black Poppies: Britain's Black Community and the Great War (The History Press, 2014)

Evelyn Dove: Britain's Black Cabaret Queen (Jacaranda Books, 2016)

Fighting Proud: The Untold Story of the Gay Men who Served in Two World Wars (I B Tauris, 2017)

War to Windrush: Black Women in Britain 1939–1948 (Jacaranda Books, 2018)

Black Poppies: Britain's Black Community and the Great War (2nd edition) (The History Press, 2019)

Index

People

Index

Television Programmes

Films